ASA STUDIES

General Editor: Edwin Ardener

3

The Interpretation of Symbolism

ASA STUDIES

First titles

The Interpretation of Symbolism

Edited by
Roy Willis

A HALSTED PRESS BOOK

John Wiley & Sons
New York

First published in 1975
by Malaby Press Limited
Aldine House, 26 Albemarle Street, London W1X 4QY

This book has been set in 11 on 12 point Times New Roman
PRINTED IN GREAT BRITAIN

© Association of Social Anthropologists of the
Commonwealth, 1975

Published in the U.S.A.
by Halsted Press, a Division
of John Wiley & Sons, Inc.,
New York

Library of Congress Cataloging in Publication Data
Main entry under title:

The interpretation of symbolism.

(ASA studies; 2)
"A Halsted Press book."
Based on papers originally presented at the
decennial conference of the Association of Social
Anthropologists of the Commonwealth, entitled
"New directions in social anthropology," held at
St. John's College, Oxford, 4–11 July 1973.
Includes index.
1. Ethnology—Congresses. 2. Symbolism—
Congresses. I. Willis, Roy. II. Association of
Social Anthropologists of the Commonwealth.
III. Series: Association of Social Anthropologists
of the Commonwealth. ASA studies: 3.
GN320.I57 1975   301:2'1   75-4111
ISBN 0-470-94920-1

Contents

75565

General Editor's Note

ASA Studies is a new series largely based upon selected sessions of the special Decennial Conference of the Association of Social Anthropologists of the Commonwealth, entitled, 'New Directions in Social Anthropology', and held at St John's College, Oxford, 4–11 July 1973.

The last special conference had taken place at Jesus College, Cambridge, in 1963, and a preliminary word should be said about it, to provide a suitable perspective. Those who convened it had, as they later wrote, two main purposes in mind: to provide a 'joint, organized stock-taking' between British and American social anthropologists, and to reflect 'the problems and views of a younger generation of anthropologists'. It was pointed out that between 1946 and 1962 the Association of Social Anthropologists had increased its membership from under a score to over one hundred and fifty. In retrospect, the 1963 Cambridge Conference can be seen to represent on the one hand a kind of coming-of-age of the ASA as an organization (in its rather awkward seventeenth year) and, on the other, an awareness of changes to come in the aims, interests, and personnel of the formerly close-knit British branch of the subject. The four volumes that emerged from that Conference were entitled *The Relevance of Models for Social Anthropology, Political Systems and the Distribution of Power, Anthropological Approaches to the Study of Religion*, and *The Social Anthropology of Complex Societies* (published by Tavistock, 1964–6) each with a general Introduction by Max Gluckman and Fred Eggan, from which my quotations here and later come.

It was that occasion which provided the base-line for the 1973 Decennial Conference. The ASA committee, under the Chairmanship of Professor Meyer Fortes, wished the 1973 Conference to play the same kind of role in its period as the previous one had done in its own time. The task was, however, quite complicated. The membership of one hundred and fifty or so of ten years before had now risen to several hundreds, while the Conference was this time to be international, not merely Anglo-American. Furthermore, although 'new directions' were to be emphasized as far as possible, subjects which had in recent years been covered by the regular annual ASA conferences (and thus published) or were already scheduled for the future, were to be excluded.

Eventually the Committee chose eleven topics, each to be covered in a half-day session, and invited a convener to organize each of them. Finally, the Conference was placed by the Committee under my general convenership. This, I should emphasize, was seen as largely an organizational task, which I have been invited to continue here as General Editor of these volumes. The session-conveners had a free hand in the choice of contributors on their topics, within certain limits of numbers and finance, and each session-convener decided the structure of his own half-day session.

An immediate difference between this conference and the 1963 one lies in this much looser 'federal' structure. The Committee were of the opinion that all sessions should be consecutive, so that all could be attended by the participants despite the wide range of topics covered. These were: Social Anthropology and Ethology (Robin Fox), Social Anthropology and Psychology (Esther Goody), Social Anthropology and Development (Peter Lloyd), Social Anthropology and Oral and Literary Sources (Ravindra Jain), Structuralism (Nur Yalman), Marxist Analysis (Maurice Bloch), Mathematical Analysis (Clyde Mitchell), Transactions (Bruce Kapferer), Systems of Thought (Edwin Ardener), The Analysis of Symbolism (Roy Willis), and Problems of Fieldwork (Julian Pitt-Rivers). The Conference ended with general statements from the Chairman (Professor Meyer Fortes), Professor Raymond Firth, Professor R. F. Salisbury, and Dr Ralph Grillo. There were daily attendances of two hundred and fifty or more, including a large international group of guests and observers from, for example, France, Germany, the United States, Sweden, South America, Denmark, Holland, Israel, and Japan, as well as very many from the countries of Commonwealth tradition from which the Association draws its main membership. Most senior members in the British profession were able to attend part, at least, of the sessions, and many made contributions from the floor. In addition, it was frequently pointed out that there were present on this occasion more generations of British social anthropologists than at any Association meeting in the past: from recent graduates to founding members of the modern subject. The uniqueness of this occasion was underlined by the fact that this turned out, sadly, to be the last public appearance before his colleagues of the Life President, Professor Sir Edward Evans-Pritchard, who opened the sessions of the second day.

No one can make an easy assessment of the intellectual impact of this conference. A look back on the 1963 gathering may offer us some lessons. While that ASA conference does in retrospect seem to mark the close of one period of social anthropology, its 'new approaches' turned out to hint only remotely at the kinds of controversies that were actually to fill the next decade. All that can be safely said without adding fresh controversy is that controversy did become commonplace, while France, hardly mentioned by the 1963 conveners, frequently supplanted

Britain or the United States as a source of new or fashionable theory. On the whole, the topics and styles of the 1963 contributors did not necessarily or entirely prefigure the immediate future, although a number of them were important in it. The joint conveners wrote 'that the essays . . . reflect the feeling of their younger colleagues', and that they favoured 'clarification, the breaking down, and the refinement, of standard concepts, together with the closer specification of narrower social contexts . . .' That remained in part true, but the very process of clarification was changing the view that social anthropologists had of their subject, in ways that 1963 did not directly express. Things in fact moved more quickly, some thought more interestingly, others thought more hastily (many thought less surely) than they had been doing.

It is certainly doubtful then whether the 1973 Conference will turn out to be more predictive of 'new directions' than the last was of 'new approaches'. It should best be regarded as the record of a particular moment, with no exaggerated aims. In this respect the Conference was of its age. Its structure and its topics were approached perhaps with a little more reserve, even scepticism, than greeted 1963. For some the range of topics and their 'interdisciplinary' appearance seemed to represent a dispersal of academic energy. For some the balance appeared to have moved in the direction of various 'ideological' or 'transactional' analyses, and away from more tried methods. For others, on the contrary, the chosen topics were already ageing or old and did not reflect the most promising lines for the future. For still others the occasion appeared merely as a useful tribal rite of little intellectual significance. A women's session met amicably outside the official programme. Some radical leaflets were circulated. The third world now figured as a political as well as an academic subject. The historical period at least (it may well be thought in 1983) was unmistakable.

But, taking as neutral a view as possible, it is quite reasonable to say that, by contingency as well as by design, the volumes published in this series, which are based on a selection of the sessions, represent a number of subjects developed in social anthropology either relatively newly, or in greater depth, or with greater insight, over the last decade. This is certainly true of the first three titles: *Biosocial Anthropology, Marxist Analyses and Social Anthropology*, and *The Interpretation of Symbolism*; which will be followed shortly by *Text and Context, Transaction and Meaning, Numerical Techniques*, and *Structuralism*. All these titles represent recognized and authoritative developments in the current repertoire of social anthropology, which have grown from deep roots in the subject over more than one generation. Although not every social anthropologist in this more specialized age will be competent in or even sympathetic to all of them (they incidentally straddle several theoretical divides), they reflect a number of characteristic concerns in the subject today which, taken together with the regular annual series of ASA publications, suggest that social anthropology still retains its traditional

General Editor's Note

curiosity and adventurousness—a feature emphasized by the number of younger contributors represented. Even a 'Decennial Conference' can do no more than that.

The present volume is based on a session convened on 10 July 1973. Editors have been free to seek amendments or additions to the papers in the sessions they convened, and to shape their volumes as they saw fit.

The ASA would like to thank warmly the President and Fellows of St John's College, Oxford, and the Warden of Rhodes House, Oxford, for providing the home for the Conference, and the staff of both for their willing assistance. It records its deep gratitude to the Wenner-Gren and H. F. Guggenheim Foundations for their welcome financial help. The major convening task was shared with me by Shirley Ardener, who found smooth solutions to many problems. In addition, the practical arrangements would have been impossibly complicated without the help of Nigel Barley, Martin Cantor, Christine Cooper, Robert Heath, Joy Hendry, John Mathias, David Price, Matt Schaffer, and Drid Williams, all then mostly graduate students of the Oxford University Institute of Social Anthropology.

As General Editor, I should like to acknowledge the role of the present chairman of the ASA, Dr Jean La Fontaine, and her Committee, in establishing this series.

Roy Willis

Introduction

Suppose a world in which every object is unique. Besides being totally incomprehensible, such a world would be entirely devoid of symbols, and symbolism.

Contrast this wholly notional construct with the classical world of social anthropology, so often damned of late, even while yet inhabited by such distinguished figures as Sir Raymond Firth, where the anthropologist–observer proves his ingenuity, and establishes his claim to scientific objectivity, by uncovering the hidden connections between disparate social phenomena, demonstrating the mystical participation of gold and jaundice, or of self and sacrificial ox. The sum of these revealed correspondences constitutes the specificity of each particular culture, while between their unique specificities the abstract and value-free language of social anthropology constitutes an ultimately unifying matrix, the firm ground of scientific reality. In this world there are certainly symbols and symbolism, but they and it remain quarantined, as it were, within the bounds of each socio-cultural system.

What is interesting about the present collection of papers, all but one of which (that by J. J. Fox) [1] were presented to the Decennial Conference of the ASA in Oxford in July 1973, is how symbolic significance is breaking through the classical constraints and implicating the ideas and values of the observer–analyst. The current upsurge of anthropological concern with symbolism and its interpretation reflects a tendency, which is more or less explicit in all the papers, to shift from the fixed and unitary perspective of classical anthropology to a dual and dialectical perspective which addresses itself as much to the subjectivity of the anthropologist–observer, and of his cultural stance, as to the observed society and culture. The archetypal hero of this new and precarious self-awareness in social anthropology is of course Carlos Castaneda, who out of his perilous confrontation with the 'separate reality' of the world of a Yaqui Indian sorcerer comes to recognize the cultural specificity of what he had taken to be the safe and solid ground of fact.

The dual perspective epitomized in Castaneda's extraordinary dialogue with don Juan necessarily entails the abandonment of the comforting assumption implicit in classical anthropology that all non-Western cultures can be accounted for within the conceptual resources of Western natural and social science. Early in the first paper in this volume, Renato Rosaldo considers the question of whether the Ilongot term *be:rtan* is 'a better or worse approximation' of the anthropological concept of cognatic ('nonunilineal') descent. He would perhaps have done more justice to the scope of his inquiry if he had put it the other way round: How far does the anthropological concept of nonunilineal descent correspond to the Ilongot concept of *be:rtan*? For he finds that the anthropological concept is, when compared with the native one, deficient in historical significance. Having made this discovery, Rosaldo is then able to 'decode' the symbolic meaning of the origin conventionally ascribed by Ilongots to all their descent names, which is the most specific meaning of *be:rtan*, to reconstitute an important part of their history. The point of the exercise, as I take it, is to demonstrate that an analysis which contented itself with identifying Ilongot ideas and practices in the field of kinship with the established anthropological notion of 'nonunilineal descent' would have failed to perceive the symbolic component in *be:rtan* and so deprived our understanding of Ilongot society of a historical dimension.

Where Renato Rosaldo reads off the symbolic meaning of an existing concept of the Ilongots to reconstruct their history, Anthony Jackson takes a historical text and convincingly argues that much of the complex symbolism contained in it refers to a submerged social structure. Jackson's meticulous analysis of a key Na-khi myth and of its constituent symbols reveals a contradiction between the patent meaning of the text and the latent meaning contained in the constellation of symbols; the contradiction between the two meanings of the text is shown to correspond with a structural conflict in Na-khi society between an underlying social organization based on matrilineality and patrilateral cross-cousin marriage and an overt system of patrilineality imposed on the Na-khi by Imperial China. The Na-khi accomodated themselves to the situation by developing a new religion in which symbolic expression was given, in a remarkable efflorescence of ritual texts, to the deep but hidden conflict in their society. Jackson's elegant resolution of the problems posed by his text raises some interesting further questions bearing on the analysis and interpretation of 'mythological charters', in particular how far such myths can be understood historically as reflecting the development of structural contradictions between groups and strata in different societies.

With Michelle Rosaldo's and Jane Atkinson's 'Man the Hunter and Woman' we enter the field of comparative cosmologies. Again we are among the Ilongots, and the analysis seeks to determine the symbolic significance of 'man' and 'woman' and their relationship in Ilongot culture and then to propose cross-cultural parallels. The authors suggest that the sexual division of humankind everywhere provides a metaphorical basis for the elaboration of cosmological systems. They argue, in words which inevitably implicate Western cultural concepts and exemplify the explosion of symbolism under way in anthropology, that 'the celebration of motherhood and female sexuality implies a definition of womankind in terms of nature and biology; it traps women in their physical being, and thereby in the very general logic which declares them less capable of transcendence and of cultural achievement than men' (p. 63). The structural determinants which in many, perhaps all, cultures do so relegate important features of female identity to the realm of wild nature have been defined by Edwin Ardener in an important article (Ardener 1972). He shows, through an examination of material from the Bakweri of Cameroon, how the dominant indigenous model of any society, defining its bounds against nature (and other societies) is inevitably a male model. His generalization would appear to hold for the Ilongots. Yet it would also seem that, whereas Bakweri men and women alike envisage the world as structured by an opposition between nature and culture, albeit drawing the line differently between these two realms, Ilongots appear, in a significant area of their symbolic thought and action, to postulate a transcendence of the nature/culture division altogether: Rosaldo and Atkinson correlate this symbolic affirmation with the excellent Ilongot tenet that, in contradistinction to the inequality of symbolic 'man' and 'woman', real-life men and women are equal partners in the social process. Rosaldo and Atkinson develop this interesting argument through a detailed discussion of magical spells, which in Ilongot culture consist of recitations of conventional formulae combined with manipulation of specific plants. Some of these plant-linked spells are associated with success in the male activity of hunting, others with the female activity of gardening. But there is also an important third category of spells which are valid for both male and female activities. The names of the plants appropriate for use in this latter kind of spell mostly evoke productive social labour: 'come together', 'hoard, pack', 'addition'. Moreover, the plants concerned in these sexually undifferentiated spells are all taken from the forest, the wild, and, as it were, 'domesticated' by their symbolic role as generators of economic production. Clearly there is matter here for cross-cultural comparison.

Social interaction has, for individuals, both positive and negative aspects. The individual may gain or lose from each transaction. For Ilongots the negative potential of cooperation is symbolized in the plant *Athyrium cordifolium* which, in the context of economic spells, has the meaning 'evil, curse', a representation of the jealousy of competitors; this emotion taints food distribution with the possibility of supernatural contagion. Such ideas, often translated as 'witchcraft' or 'sorcery', are frequently found in unstratified societies and usually have the effect of constraining individuals to adhere to the norms governing economic production and exchange. Here the Wik-mungkan concept of *ngaintja* affords an interesting contrast. As David McKnight describes the operation of this fundamental concept of the Wik-mungkan in his richly documented 'Men, Women, and Other Animals', the effect of *ngaintja* seems to be to define the limits of the acting autonomous individual in relation to others. The essentially active and intentional character of *ngaintja* is evident from the fact that objects may be appropriated by the physical act of 'stepping over' them, thus making them *ngaintja* (forbidden) to others, and an individual can even constrain the acts of others by 'swearing' parts of their bodies, which then appear to be, as I interpret McKnight's account, brought in some sense within the self of the swearer. Such committal of the self is not without risk, because an individual's self-extension may be challenged by another who may, for example, if he believes he can get away with it, help himself to goods which he knows have already been 'stepped over'. Individuals in Wik-mungkan society must therefore weigh the situation carefully before extending their self-limits through *ngaintja*. In the latter part of his paper, McKnight shows how Wik-mungkan culture works out the *ngaintja* principles of inclusion and exclusion (or 'container and contained', as McKnight expresses it) by analogical argument about the relation of men, women, and certain wild animals to one another, basing their conclusions on a comparison of the physiological characteristics of these various examples of animate being. McKnight's distinctive material suggests that 'actor-oriented' cosmologies may occur as well in the primitive world as in the world of industrialized democracies.

James J. Fox's paper 'On Binary Categories and Primary Symbols' approaches the analysis of a cosmological system on a level which is distinct from, but also importantly complementary to, that followed in the first four papers in this volume. Where these four contributors describe the interrelation of symbolic domains through opposition and formal parellelism, concentrating as it were on the grand design, Fox looks at the ideational linkages between the primary symbolic divisions of the Rotinese world and plots them as a configuration of semantic pathways. I see his paper as both a valuable empirical complement to the intuitively-derived insights of such 'structuralists' as Lévi-Strauss and Victor Turner and as containing important theoretical refinements of both the 'binary' and the 'dominant symbol' models of cosmological analysis.

The last paper in this volume, by Sherry Ortner, is a fascinating synthesis of separate analyses of cosmological symbolism, the diachronic structure of a Sherpa ritual and of the meaning of personal interaction in the context of hospitality. In 'Gods' Bodies, Gods' Food' she thus brings together the symbolism of convivial eating and drinking, underlining the essentiality ambiguity of both the host and guest roles, the significance for a Sherpa community of the dualistic Buddhist pantheon of opposed gods and demons, and the relevance of the internal division of the former into peaceful and warlike aspects to both the local perception of the relation of monks to lay priests and to the psychological dynamics of party-giving. The focus of the whole multifaceted analysis is a single Sherpa ritual in which pieces of dough, the *torma*, are physically and mentally conjured into the forms of god–guests. The purpose of the ritual, Ortner argues, is morally to coerce the gods into assuming the angry aspect in which they can repay their hosts by fighting the demons which menace the human community. Dr Ortner seeks to show, in conformity with the avowedly Geertzian framework of her analysis, that the significance of the ritual she describes is both to pose a complex of cosmological, sociological, and psychological problems arising from the conjunction of Buddhist theology and Sherpa social norms and to propose a satisfactory solution to all these problems. She achieves this theoretical objective in an analysis of consummate elegance and considerable aesthetic appeal (although one could have wished for more reference to indigenous notions at several points in the complicated argument). Her paper is a model of what a holistic interpretation of social symbolism should be, addressing simultaneously the structure of society, the individual psyche, and the collective worldview.

The various papers in this volume bring together a rich diversity of ethnographic experience and theoretical interest. What they have in common is a concern to reveal the meaning of symbolic ideas and symbolic (or 'ritual') behaviour, what, in terms comprehensible to us, observers from an alien culture, they 'stand for'. The next major step, demanded by the unfolding logic of the subject, will surely be the formal incorporation of the problem presented by the enigmatic presence of that uninvited guest, the anthropologist.

Note

1. In a letter to the Editor, Professor Fox said he had intended to submit his paper *in absentia* for consideration at the Oxford Conference, but postal delays between Indonesia and Britain had prevented it reaching Oxford in time.

References

ARDENER, E. 1972. Belief and the Problem of Women. In J. S. La Fontaine (ed.), *The Interpretation of Ritual: Essays in Honour of A. I. Richards*. London: Tavistock.

CASTANEDA, C. 1971. *A Separate Reality*. New York: Simon and Schuster; Harmondsworth: Penguin.

FIRTH, R. 1973. *Symbols Public and Private*. London: Allen and Unwin.

Renato Rosaldo

Where Precision Lies

'The hill people once lived on a hill.'

Arguably three central conceptions guide and inform the conduct of anthropological research. One finds images of a 'bathtub', an 'archive', and a 'conversation'. A 'bathtub' implies a sense of total immersion and complete absorption in one's immediate surroundings. It may also convey optimistic intimations of warmth and comfort before confronting the brute fact of fieldwork, perhaps swayed by the persuasive spell Malinowski's incorrigibly confident magician casts from a distant coral garden. An 'archive' is a more restrospective view of anthropology: we travel to Bugabuga, transcribe texts from the natives, perhaps venture into an actual archive, and collect additional manuscripts. Afterwards we peruse and begin to interpret the texts, texts for which we have been both scribe and collector. A 'conversation' takes place throughout the period of field research. Like Castaneda with don Juan, we ask smart people dumb questions, and learn through surprises and bafflement. The conversations are themselves variously situated; some take place in the marketplace and some in the plaza. And the plaza may manifest itself in myriad ways—it may seem dark, mysterious, and intimate, as it did to Lorca, or the bright, garrulous, and eminently social place that Unamuno described. Alternatively, there may be neither marketplaces nor plazas: thus we found ourselves in the hills of Northern Luzon, Philippines.[1]

My point is this: just as we have guided our conduct in terms of such central notions as 'bathtubs', 'archives', or 'conversations', so should we recognize that this is true of the people we study as well. Though we may stutter, mispronounce, and ask stupid questions, eventually we come to speak in other tongues and gain some measure of insight into other people's social lives. Indeed, one of our jobs is to attempt to grasp the central concepts that shape and reflect the conduct of those we study. This particular kind of conceptual analysis should be directed toward learning to specify just precisely what people mean by their guiding concepts in the full range of senses in which they are employed. We should discover empirically those instances where we and the so-called natives use cultural categories in an 'open-textured' way.[2] I believe that all people's cultural categories (and especially those most

1

central) often encompass a wide range of meanings and this fact of usage has certain implications for the anthropological interpretation of culture.

In the anthropological literature one need not look for concepts that have a broad range of applications and permit various degrees of approximation; one cannot avoid them. Is this not the actual subject of the debate that has grown out of the Trobriand category *tabu* (Malinowski 1929: 101–102, 502; Leach 1958; Lounsbury 1965)? Or consider Evans-Pritchard's lengthy and subtle expositions of basic Nuer cultural constructs such as *cieng* and *kwoth* (1940: 135–136; 1956: 1–143). Such fundamental anthropological concepts as 'marriage', 'family', and 'descent' are used in similar ways and have provoked comparable and equally acrimonious debate (e.g. Murdock 1949; Gough 1959; Leach 1961; Goodenough 1970; Needham 1971). Central concepts often are polysemous: that is, their centrality derives in large part from the fact that they encompass a number of distinguishable senses, from broad to narrow and from metaphoric to literal. My solution to this fact of social life and cultural categories is not to give stipulative and narrow definitions to words normally used in a wide range of senses, but rather to inquire into the nature and degree of similarity and of differences among various phenomena that intuitively appear to have deep resemblances.[3] In my view symbolic analysis should proceed in two phases. Initially, the full range of meanings of a native category are the focus of inquiry. Then the investigation becomes one of the determination and specification of the criteria and reasons for saying that a native term is a better or worse approximation of an anthropological concept. To call any two things the same is, after all, to say that their similarities are more salient than their differences.

In this paper kinship is my subject. Among other things, I shall ask to what degree there is a point-by-point correspondence between an indigenous cultural category (*be:rtan*) and the anthropological concept of nonunilineal descent. The case I shall discuss is distinctive in that it demonstrates the general applicability of the tools of symbolic analysis, emphasizing that they should not be strictly confined to the interpretation of such phenomena as religious ritual and belief. I do not claim originality in stating that symbolic analysis applies beyond the realm of formalized religion; I trust that the work of Geertz, Leach, Needham, Schneider, and others has already made this clear. Indeed one might speculate that a 'latent function' of Leach's broad definition of 'ritual' (as the communicative aspect of all behaviour, rather than as a kind of behaviour, 1964: 10–14) was to liberate him from the overly delimited Durkheimian domain of religion, hedged about as it is with prohibitions. By using ritual in its widest sense, Leach was able to interpret cultural categories in relation to Kachin social structure.

Having mentioned the seminal work of Leach I want to exorcize the phantom verbal categories of the Kachin hills to be certain they do not

2

follow me to Northern Luzon. Neo-Zandian applications of 'witch-craft' and 'sorcery' as well as the abortive proliferation of 'African models in the highlands of New Guinea' highlight the dangers inherent in daring to borrow models tailormade for particular ethnographic cases. However much can be learned from studying the Tikopia, the Nuer, or the Kachin hills, each new case must be viewed with eyes at once informed and fresh. In my particular case-study, I should beware of the largely illusory *as if* fictional models spoken of so winningly by the Kachin Platonists. What I found instead was that native cultural categories bear a close and even insightful relation to the workings of their social structure. Though my route must perforce be circuitous and laboured I shall in the end conclude, as Kenneth Burke has said, that

> Charts of meaning are not 'right' or 'wrong'—they are relative *approximations* to the truth. And only insofar as they contain real ingredients of the truth can the men who hold them perpetuate their progeny (Burke 1957: 92).

While those Kachin who speak of *gumsa* and *gumlao* appear to have immersed themselves in Plato, the people I know best speak of *be:rtan* and seem familiar with Burke.

In what follows, then, I proceed to define the native cultural category in all its senses. Then I ask to what extent the native category corre-sponds with the anthropological concept of nonunilineal descent. Finally, I attempt to explicate the truth embodied in the indigenous conception for I find it an informed, if imperfect, vision of social life, as most native categories probably are.

THE ILONGOTS

The case I consider is based on two years of field research (1967–1969) among the Ilongots (M. Rosaldo 1971; 1972; 1973; R. Rosaldo 1970a; 1970b). The Ilongots, close to 2500 in number, inhabit the hill country at the headwaters of the Cagayan River in Northern Luzon, Philippines. Like other hill peoples of the area they are predominantly non-Christian and they are viewed by the national government as a cultural minority group. Their subsistence is based on dry rice cultivation (swidden) and the hunting of venison and wild boar; correspondingly, women do most of the continuous agricultural labour while men tend to devote their energies to the hunt. One of their focal cultural practices is headhunting, and on this basis they have achieved considerable notoriety among Christian Filipinos of the neighbouring lowlands (cf. R. Rosaldo n.d.). Ilongots occupy an area of some 1536 square kilometres with an average population density of less than 1.6 persons per square kilometre. Widely scattered and dispersed, Ilongot settle-ments are fluid in their composition as households move, divide, and merge, often to seek new swiddens or to flee from the law.

3

Renato Rosaldo

The primary units of social organization are four: (1) the conjugal family, (2) the household, (3) the settlement, and (4) the district. The *conjugal family* is the focal unit from which ties of bilateral kinship are reckoned (R. Rosaldo 1970a; 1970b); marriage bonds appear solidary in day-to-day interaction and the divorce rate is relatively low. Single-room *households*, on stilts and with thatched roofs, are easily isolable domestic units and may contain from one to three conjugal families; their composition is based on a strictly-adhered-to uxorilocal rule of post-marital residence in combination with the phases of the domestic cycle. *Settlements* are composed of about ten dispersed households (range 2–19), or about 65 persons; they are discrete social units (that is, mutually exclusive and nonoverlapping). The first three units, then, are hierarchically organized; like nested Chinese boxes, each lower-order unit is contained within a higher-order unit. Thus, settlements are made up of households and households in turn are made up of conjugal families.

The fourth and highest-order unit, the *district*, is the most problematic in its definition. As a localized group the unit is made up of about three settlements (range 1–6) with a mean population of about 180 (range 64–307); since Ilongots generally marry close relatives the district tends to be endogamous (though this is a culturally recognized empirical regularity, rather than the outcome of a normative role). More than any other unit I am familiar with from the anthropological literature, the district resembles the 'deme' (cf. Murdock 1949: 62–64; Good-enough 1970: 51–52). For one thing, everyone 'born into' the district is considered a relative by the other members; even if someone moves out upon marriage, his or her district membership remains constant. The problem is as vexing as it is familiar: the social unit appears to vacillate between Maine's opposition of kinship and territory—or, as we would say today, descent groups and local groups. As is probably apparent, the term district is an inadequate translation for this social unit. But I move too hastily for, in one of its senses, the cultural category I shall be concerned with refers to this social unit. Hence I now turn directly to the native category itself.

BE:RTAN: CLASSIFIER AND CATEGORY OF AFFILIATION

The native term I shall explicate is *be:rtan*. In its most general sense the word might be glossed as 'class, kind, type, or taxon', referring to any number of things ranging from house types to species of plants and animals, and from kinds of basketry to kinds of men. The division into 'kinds' may be based on any of a number of principles of classification. Baskets, for instance, may be classified in accordance with the way they are woven, or the materials used in their fabrication, or the uses to which they are put, or all the preceding in combination; people may be so classified as tall/short, fat/thin, dark/light, curly-haired/straight-

4

haired, mild-mannered/hot-tempered. In its widest sense, then, the term *be:rtan* is the Ilongot classifier *par excellence* and may be used to make verbal discriminations in virtually any domain.

However, the term may be used in a more restricted sense as a category of affiliation. Using the term in this narrower sense a person may speak of 'his' or 'her' *be:rtan*. The term so employed refers to a particular 'kind' or group of people and it is used in a marked sense as contrasted with its wider, unmarked sense (cf. Jakobson 1957; Greenberg 1966; Scheffler and Lounsbury 1971: 11–12, 42–48). This semantic relation is shown in *Figure 1*. It should be noted that the Ilongot semantic relation between a classifier and a term associated with

Figure 1   Relations between the senses of *be:rtan*

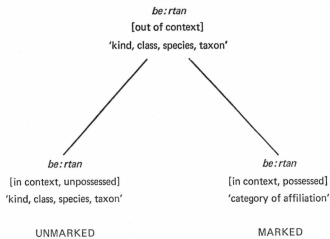

be:rtan
[out of context]
'kind, class, species, taxon'

be:rtan
[in context, unpossessed]
'kind, class, species, taxon'

be:rtan
[in context, possessed]
'category of affiliation'

UNMARKED

MARKED

genealogical connection is consistent with the etymology of English usage. The OED, for instance, gives the following among archaic senses of 'kind': (a) 'Birth, origin, descent –1649', (b) 'The station, place, or property belonging to one by birth –ME', (c) 'A race; a natural group of animals or plants having a common origin –OE', (d) 'of persons: rightful (heir, etc.) –ME; natural –1589; related to kinship –1509'. An English-speaking person, then, has little reason to be surprised by the association of senses contained in the Ilongot term *be:rtan*.

CATEGORY NAMES: NON-LOCALIZED GROUPS AND DISTRICTS

Used as a category of affiliation *be:rtan* refers to a named group of persons. Much as the term *be:rtan* suggests, these names appear to be associated with natural classes or kinds of people. For instance, food taboos and such shared personal characteristics as fierceness and hunting ability are often associated with membership in groups so named. I have collected a total of 67 such names which I am certain is a virtually complete list of those now current in the Ilongot region. Of these names,

5

45 in their folk etymologies are place names (usually names of rivers), nine are words for prominent geographical features, nine are plant names, and the other four are: 'game, edible wild animal', 'pot', 'white', 'black'. The meaning of these names suggests a strong association between the groups so designated and a particular locality. Furthermore, such names may be modified by the prefix *qi-* 'from' which otherwise is used only with names designating inhabited places. Hence with place names people from the settlement of Kakidugen are *qikakidugen*; with category names the Biaw people are *qibiaw*.

However, in the present day such names may be used in more than one sense: some may be used to speak of current residential or localized groups (districts) and others may not. Hence some (but not all) names could be substituted in the sentence, 'I am going to Xplace'. For instance, using such a name a person might say, *quNkitaqak di rumyad*, 'I am going to Rumyad'. However, other names may not be used in such a sentence, e.g. **quNkitaqak di biaw*, 'I am going to Biaw', is never said. To put this another way, the above frame is a heuristic for determining whether or not a particular category name may be used to refer to those who now inhabit a certain district. It should be noted that whether or not a name may refer to a present-day district bears little relation to its meaning, as is seen in *Table 1*.

Table 1 Meanings of category names designating (a) non-localized groups and (b) districts

Meaning	Non-localized No.	%	District No.	%	Total No.	%
Place name	38	(70)	7	(54)	45	(67)
Geographical feature	6	(11)	3	(23)	9	(13)
Plant name	6	(11)	3	(23)	9	(13)
Other	4	(7)	n.a.		4	(6)

To further complicate matters, some category names refer to both districts and non-localized groups. This notion might be represented in the following fashion, where each letter of the alphabet stands for a distinct name:

DISTRICT   A B C D E F

NON-LOCALIZED   d e f g h i j k l m n

When category names may be used in both senses (as with 'D/d', 'E/e', and 'F/f', above), Ilongots identify the members of the non-localized group as the 'real' or 'true' members of that category of affiliation (e.g. *pipiyan qirumyad* 'true people from Rumyad'). In such cases, then, category names may be used in the following four senses: (a) to designate an area, as in the phrase, 'I am going to Rumyad',

(b) speaking loosely, to designate all the people who inhabit that area, (c) to designate members of the district, as claimed by ties of filiation and thereby excluding those who have 'married in', and (d) strictly speaking, to designate some but not all members of the district, as in the phrase 'true people from Rumyad'. The narrow and focal sense of such category names appears to be based on the historical priority of ancestral claims to membership in that particular named district.

Thus far I have shown that *be:rtan* may be used in a wide sense to mean 'kind' and in a narrower sense to refer to categories of affiliation. These categories of affiliation are all named and the names in turn may be used in a wide sense to designate districts (aggregations of settlements) and in a narrower sense to designate non-localized groups of persons. In all cases the meaning of the names appears to indicate local associations. In what follows I inquire into indigenous theories, however cryptic, about the meaning of these names; at the same time I explore the relative degree to which the groups are based on location and ancestry.

MEANING: WHY ARE THEY CALLED HILL PEOPLE?

In theory, names should present the simplest case of meaning. Just as Fido names a particular dog, so a category name designates a particular group of people—and that is that. In fact, when Ilongots are asked about the 'meaning' or 'origin' of their category names they have a readily available elliptical cultural cliché that is consistently given in response. Ilongots say that primal co-residence is the 'reason' for present-day sharing of such a name. For instance, when asked about the category name *besilid*, 'hill', saying: 'Why are they called the hill people?' I was told: 'The hill people once lived on a hill.' I was as annoyed by the fact that everybody gave the same response as by the impossibility of gaining further clarification. However persistent my efforts to clarify the meaning of this pithy reply I found it to be self-contained, almost proverbial and apparently self-evident; none of my questions uncovered any further evidence—mythical, historical, or other.

My initial interpretation was that the cultural cliché applied only to names for present districts; I thought it might be a 'what is' statement referring to the *status quo*. This was quickly proven wrong as I discovered that all 67 category names were explained in the same manner. Even in the least plausible cases the cliché remained the same. For instance, the people who claim the category name of 'Biaw' were said to have descended from a group that once lived together near a large stand of *biaw*, 'runo grass' (Miscanthus). Even the 'Bude:k' people (*bude:k* 'white') were said to have derived their name from a once, and long-past, co-residential group of light-skinned ('white') people. It became clear that such statements should be taken to apply to putative origins, rather than as a rationalization of present circumstances.

7

While verbal descriptions from the Kachin hills may grow out of a present-day situation and be construed as 'a simplified description of what is' (Leach 1964: 286), Ilongot statements refer to the past and should be taken as a simplified vision of what was, as I shall argue below. Ignoring the time dimension for the moment, however, the putative ancestral group has certain characteristics that make it an appropriate model to apply in the present, to both 'districts' and 'non-localized groups'. First, as a residential group its membership is in principle unambiguous in that there is a clear-cut criterion for determining who is in (those who reside there) and who is out (those who do not). Second, localized groups are associated with particular named places, hence they comprise groups that are both named and clearly bounded (at any given point in time). A partial interpretation of the Ilongot cultural cliché, then, is that it comprises an indigenous model of a social group with two characteristics: (1) it is named and (2) it is unambiguously bounded in its membership. Indeed, all 67 category names designate bounded aggregates of persons.

TRANSMISSION: CATEGORY NAMES HAVE BEEN HANDED DOWN

When asked how they acquired their category names Ilongots said they were handed down through the generations from their ancestors; the names themselves were described variously as 'names', 'remembrances', or 'keepsakes'. Persons who shared a named category (whether or not their kin relations were specifiable) were said to be related because they *kaqwit*, 'hook into, intertwine, interlace', with one another. The Ilongot term *kaqwit* in its focal sense refers to the 'hooks' on a woman's belt, which is made of quarter-inch bits of curved brass wire that interlock with one another, something like links on a chain. In response to my query about the reckoning of ancestry and how category names were handed down, an Ilongot drew the diagram below (*Figure 2*), explaining this as a representation of *kaqwit*:

Figure 2   An Ilongot representation of *kaqwit*

Here, the horizontal arrays were sets of siblings (or classificatory siblings), and the (implied) vertical connections were parent–child ties. While the drawing shows only three generations, I was told that the above pattern hypothetically could be extended through infinite generations. What I have discussed here is an indigenous model; it is a diagrammatic representation of an Ilongot verbal metaphor for the kind of connectedness that follows from sharing the same named category of affiliation.

TRANSMISSION: IN WHAT SENSE DESCENT?

In this section I explore the problem of the degree to which indigenous cultural categories correspond with anthropological concepts in kinship studies. I shall specify certain criteria to apply in deciding whether or not, or to what extent, these categories should be regarded as non-unilineal descent constructs. Initially the question is: in what sense is the indigenous model of the transmission of category names a descent construct? Do Ilongots conceive of themselves as having descended in a continuum of parent–child links from the putative ancestral group (cf. Schneider 1967: 66)? A further and perhaps more penetrating question is this: given knowledge of Ilongot social life, how strong and clearly defined should one expect their conception of descent to be? Maintaining that cultural categories may not be a perfect mirror-image of social structure should not lead to the opposite extreme of saying that they are randomly or accidentally related. While few would deny that most cultural categories are closely linked with on-going processes of social life, the questions are how, in what way, and for what reasons?

A continuum of parent–child links?

Ilongots speak of their category names as having been handed down from their ancestors and infer that the known chain of parent–child links extends into the unknown past (as in the *kaqwit* diagram above). I should stress that they do not devote their time and energy to meticulous calculations and recitations of their ancestry. In fact, the entire matter of their ancestry—at least beyond the third ascending generation—is left relatively undefined, and is hardly even a topic of speculation; indeed, the names of the dead are never mentioned and soon forgotten. My queries about the deceased usually met with this reply: 'I did not see the person—how could I know his name?' Ilongots find it difficult even to recollect the names of those dead people whom they did know personally. In indigenous terms, the dead simply are not named: the omission constitutes a cultural practice in contrast to an explicit 'prohibition'. The tracing and specification of ancestry, then, rarely extends beyond the grandparental generation, and beyond that point the continuum linking descendants to their ancestors is ill-defined and quite hypothetical. The Ilongots have what H. and C. Geertz (1964) so vividly called 'genealogical amnesia'.

Certainly there are better examples of descent constructs in most introductory anthropology textbooks: in a case of descent *par excellence* every link of the continuous parent–child chain between descendants and their ancestors would be specified and part of public knowledge. However, such definitional problems are by no means unique to Ilongot society. The Lakalai, for instance, are reported to be

9

'generally uninterested in origins', in fact so little so that Goodenough is led to conclude that

> In this case it is hard to say whether we are dealing with matrilineal or with what should be called matrifilial divisions of society (1970: 47).

Goodenough's mistake lies in having asked whether or not the Lakalai have a concept of descent, as though there were only two possibilities. Even with the most precise concepts there will be borderline cases. I maintain that in such cases the issue is not an 'either/or' question of kind, but rather a matter of determining degrees of approximation. Rather than debate about whether such a cultural category is (or is not) descent, I prefer to recognize that the anthropological concept of descent may be employed in a strict sense (descent *par excellence*) and a looser sense (something very like descent), and that the concept has boundaries (not really descent at all).[4] The goal of this kind of inquiry, then, is to determine the criteria and reasons for saying that a native term is more or less like a descent label (or any other anthropological concept).

Consider further three brief examples showing that cultural constructs may approximate the notion of descent to differing degrees. First, if I trace and specify my ancestry in a unilineal manner I clearly am employing a descent construct (descent *par excellence*). Second, if I say that we are all children of God (meaning that each of us was created by God), it is equally clear that I am not talking about descent (filiation; not really descent at all). Finally, however, if I say that Jews are descendants of Abraham (supposing a hypothetical linkage between known ancestry and Old Testament genealogies), then I am using something that is not strictly a descent construct but resembles one (something very like descent). It is the last example which resembles the Ilongot conception of the transmission of category names, a recognizable case of a descent construct (though not the best example). To say that Ilongots definitely have a concept of descent would be to convey a false sense of certainty, leading to ethnographic inaccuracy. Ethnographic precision should mean the ability to specify the reasons for making discriminations of degree (more and less) as well as differences in kind (either/or).

Why are the ancestors anonymous?

The Ilongots' short-term ancestral memory seems consistent with its functional load. In terms of social action the major entailment of category names is related to feuding and constitutes a strong reason not to specify ancestry in great depth. In those instances where category names designate districts, and when Xman beheads a member of another named district, all the members of his own district are equally vulnerable to be killed in vengeance. The risk of incurring such retalia-tion for the action of an individual member is a matter of group liability, rather than what either party to the feud would consider group guilt, blame, or responsibility. Virtually all members of a named district may gather together to make a covenant in which both sides 'pay' for past beheadings and take an oath to desist from further killing. Short-term memory of past headhunting grievances, then, benefits those living in the present time, providing them with a relatively greater degree of manœuvrability and increasing their range of political options. It simply would be too much of a burden to carry on all the grudges accumulated by one's ancestors.

In addition there is no positive reason to specify ancestry in great depth. To mention only what seems most conspicuously absent in this regard, there is neither land nor property to inherit and there are no offices for which to reckon succession. As Ilongots themselves put it, a category name is just that, a 'name'.

In the light of the preceding discussion, the anonymous and putative co-residential group posited by the Ilongot cultural cliché emerges as the apical reference point for the members of named categories of affiliation. Much as the units of descent groups may be composed of groups as well as individuals (cf. Goodenough 1970: 65–67), so apical ancestors may be individuals, married couples, families, or groups of one kind or another. The notion of category names should be examined with respect to a number of possible criteria available for their construction. For instance, such inquiry might proceed along the lines of asking the following of apical ancestors: one, two, or more? male or female? and so on. From a comparative perspective the relation between descent constructs with, among other things, a single apical ancestor and an ancestral group would become clearer. Based on this strategy for com-parative research, I have drawn the following representation, designed to show the affinities of Ilongot named categories with other possible descent constructs:

Figure 3   Descent: Ilongot conception in solid lines with apical reference point 'A'; another possible conception derived by adding broken lines with apical reference point 'a'

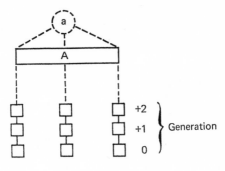

In addition to asking about the presence or absence of criteria, I ask whether a particular criterion is strongly or weakly manifest—whether it is more or less present, as with the Ilongot sense of the continuity between descendants and their ancestors.

NAMED GROUPS: ONE WORD AND TWO OBJECTS?

Establishing that category names may be interpreted as descent constructs leads to a discussion of the nature of the groups so designated. My discussion is phrased largely in terms of criteria developed in the anthropological literature on nonunilineal descent.[5] I shall concentrate on the elementary organizing principles that underlie the formation and delimitation of these groups. My focus, then, will be twofold: (a) from the viewpoint of the individual, what is the mode of transmission in making legitimate claims to a category name? and (b) from the viewpoint of the aggregate, are the groups so formed discrete or overlapping in their membership?

In terms of these two criteria an initial definition of the groups designated by the two senses of category names is as follows:

District:
(a) a person has one and only one such name; where the parents are from different named districts transmission is utrolateral (through either the mother or the father, but not both).
(b) groups so formed are discrete, that is mutually exclusive and non-overlapping in their membership.

Non-localized:
(a) a person may have as many as five such names; transmission is ambilateral (through either the mother or the father, or both).
(b) groups so formed are overlapping in their membership.

Most anthropological typologies of nonunilineal descent groups would classify Ilongot districts and non-localized groups as the polar opposites of one another. Fox, for instance, would call the non-localized groups 'unrestricted' and the districts 'restricted'; he would go on to point out that districts are similar to unilineal descent groups in that they both divide members of the society into discrete groups (1967: 146–174). In this section I distinguish districts from non-localized groups in accord with the synchronic criteria of anthropological literature.

District

In the Ilongot area at present there are at least thirteen distinct districts, and these divide the entire Ilongot population into the following mutually exclusive and non-overlapping groups (with population figures indicated in square brackets): (1) Abe:ka [251], (2) Aymuyu

[68], (3) Belansi [?], (4) Beqnad [216], (5) Be:nabe: [?], (6) Dekran [212], (7) KebinaNan [64], (8) Payupay [?], (9) Pugu [103], (10) Rumyad [307], (11) Sinebran [104], (12) TaaN [257], (13) Tamsi [225]. Members of a particular named district become visible socially and gather together as a group when they confront a similar unit; as action groups, they exist above all in relation with and in opposition to other groups.

With the transmission of district-name affiliation often both parents are from the same district, hence choice usually is not at issue and the affiliation of their children is recognized to have been inherited through both the mother and the father. In these cases, then, transmission is ambilateral. This situation is due to the fact that about four marriages of every five are within the same district, reflecting the cultural practice of marrying relatives more often than non-kin. What this implies, then, is that the category name is at issue in only about one marriage in five, that is, with those marriages between districts. In the case of such a marriage the husband follows the rule of uxorilocal residence and becomes a member of his wife's settlement, participating in social life and subsistence routines there, but this does not alter his own category name: he retains the name of the district where he was raised. At issue here is the category name, not of the parents, but of their children, who may claim the district name transmitted either through the mother or through the father, but not through both.

What, in indigenous terms, determines the named district membership of the offspring in the case of marriage between members of different districts is whether or not bridewealth payments have been completed, thereby permitting the married couple to reside with the people of the husband's district. The decision as to when bridewealth payments have been completed involves reaching a consensus among the close kin on both the mother's and the father's side of the family, and normally it does not involve the children. The completion of bridewealth does coincide roughly with a change in residence (from uxorilocal to virilocal) yet in Ilongot ideology it is the completion of bridewealth payments, rather than the residence change, that is decisive in the determination of the children's membership in a named district. Here it is significant that Ilongots say the children have no category of affiliation because they are children and not yet full adult members of the society. The effect of not giving social recognition to a child's category of affiliation is to allow a span of time for the completion (or non-completion) of bridewealth payments. As a consequence, children may not have two successive named district affiliations (first the mother's, then the father's).

While in certain cases district-name affiliation is utrolaterally transmitted and as a result there are some degrees of freedom in the overall system, this flexibility in the system should be distinguished from the notion of choice on the part of the person whose affiliation is being determined (contrast Firth 1957; Fox 1967: 150–153; but cf. Goodenough 1970: 57–65). That is, a choice may be made in only about one

13

marriage of every five and the decisive question concerning the completion of bridewealth payments resides with the parents and their close kin, rather than with the children whose district-name membership is being determined (hence the system is not 'optative' in the sense in which Firth (1957) employs the term). Furthermore, each Ilongot has one, and only one, named district affiliation over the course of his or her lifetime (rather than having a succession—first one, then another, and so on—of such affiliations) and this affiliation is known and socially recognized (rather than being private). In contrast with some discussions of nonunilineal descent groups, there is limited flexibility and no ambiguity in the Ilongot system of named district affiliation (contrast Leach 1962; but cf. Schneider 1965: 61–63). A district name, then, is never altered and lasts a lifetime; it is like a fact of nature.

Non-localized groups

Names designating non-localized groups are ambilaterally claimed and relatively unrestricted. Each Ilongot individual may claim simultaneous and multiple category names of this sort as traced through either or both their parents and any of their four grandparents. However, in practice people rarely have recognized claims to more than five such names. While in a particular context it may be politic to prefer one category name over another, these preferences fluctuate and they are fickle and transitory (cf. Sankoff 1972). In a given situation Ilongots may legitimate their claim to a particular category name by citing variously any of the following rules of transmission: (1) completion or non-completion of bridewealth payments as with district names, (2) a man inherits from his father and a woman inherits from her mother, as in an ambilineal system and as Tugby (1966) reported, and (3) a person receives these names through either the mother or the father, or both, as with ambilateral transmission. These socially recognized possibilities encompass the following modes of transmission: (a) parent–child, (b) father–child, (c) mother–child, (d) father–son, (e) mother–daughter. There is no general sense, obtaining across situations, in which any one of the above rules is preferred and, for the moment, I shall characterize the rule of category-name transmission as ambilateral because this is the most general and encompasses the others.

It would be misleading to view the role of the individual in such transmission as being simply passive. In the first place, children have no socially recognized category-name affiliation; second, adults frequently come to use more and more categories of affiliation as they grow older and enter into more widespread relations, exchanging pots and raiding together. Over time as people enter into a wider net of social relations with more diverse groups of people from different districts, they 'activate' more category names. No one ever loses a category name and, because of alterations and vicissitudes of residence or social situation, one may invoke previously held, but never publicly asserted, category names. In principle, then, all known category names available through either or both parents may be claimed.

To say that a person is a member of a particular non-localized named category means, above all, that his or her claim to the name is legitimate and recognized socially (cf. Firth 1957: 6). Ilongots say that membership in these named categories is often associated with the knowledge of certain magical spells and that it may entail the observance of distinctive dietary 'prohibitions'. Whether or not they are able to specify their exact genealogical relationship, persons can claim to be kin solely by virtue of the fact that they share a category name. In so justifying claims to be unspecifiable kin relations the indigenous supposition is that the ultimate origin of a particular category name lies with its putative co-residential ancestral group, all the members of which surely were related and all the descendants of which thereby must be related. Though the past may lie beyond memory and recollection, what matters here is not so much the ability to specify the intervening links as the socially recognized fact that people share a category name (cf. Gluckman 1950: 173).

HOW THE SYSTEM WORKS: USAGE

In this section I examine on-going usage of category names. While the primary goal of my account is ethnographic, it also illuminates two problems that have thus far remained obscure. First, an ambilateral rule provides the most general and parsimonious account of the Ilongot system: yet Ilongots themselves have gone on to develop explicit rules of utrolateral and ambilineal transmission. In effect, the system appears redundant and one wonders whence and why the 'extra' rules. Second, if in fact there are so few restrictions on category-name transmission why in practice does nobody claim more than five? A fuller sense of native categories and their meaning can come only by looking closely at usage.

In actual discourse category names are invoked by persons making a statement of their connectedness—to claim a category name is to affirm an allegiance—especially in the contexts of oratory and public discussions, ranging from redress for past beheadings to the regulation of minor disputes (cf. M. Rosaldo 1973). These category names may be employed to assert strong opposition, e.g. to speak of 'us' rather than 'them' in the context of raiding and headtaking. Or they may be employed to assert closeness, as when a gifted orator from a distant place is invited to speak at a public meeting and invokes a category name which is shared by those who have invited him. A statement of category affiliation is an assertion of solidarity with members of a bounded aggregate seen as excluding members of other like units.

The association of category name affiliation with feuding requires further comment. As I mentioned above, the members of a named

15

district constitute the maximal unit which may be considered liable for retaliatory killings to avenge past beheadings. Even if only a few members of a district participated in the raiding party, all its members are appropriately susceptible, to an equal degree, as potential victims. In feuds between units, then, the retributive infliction of death is not directed towards particular persons, households, or settlements, but rather towards a person (or persons) by virtue of his or her membership in a named category of affiliation. Furthermore, opposing districts may gather together to seek redress for bygone killings and swear on oath not to kill in the future, establishing a covenant between the groups.

What I have said does not imply, however, that feuding involves only groups with rigid boundaries and that the determination of who is a friend and who is an enemy is always strictly defined. In one case, for instance, members of two districts met on their way to a fishing trip. The Xpeople immediately mentioned an earlier killing of one of their members by a Yperson. The Ypeople rose to the occasion and proved ingenious in their use of the multiple rules of category-name transmission. One man said he had only one category name and that was from his father (ambilineal rule), thereby denying any connection with the killers; another invoked his mother's name in order to affirm his kinship with the Xpeople (bridewealth was never paid; utrolateral rule). With tacit and mutual acknowledgement of their liability to be killed in retaliation for prior beheadings, then, Ilongots may speak in the idiom of non-localized category names and engage in dialogue with their enemies, perhaps eventually leading to a tenuous and uneasy covenant between the two groups.

When people feud and draw boundaries between groups it may be a matter of life and death to retain 'furry edges' which can potentially muddle things, can claim to be a little on this side and a little on that, somwhat attached to both parties but not necessarily and unambiguously involved. The upper limit on the number of category names actually claimed (five) is probably set by the range of social obligations to which any one person may potentially be committed; in such circumstances to have too many allies may be to place oneself in the midst of a cross-fire. At the same time people who are enemies on one basis may claim to be friends on another. Cultural recognition of multiple rules of transmission provides a ready-made means to contract or expand the category names claimed in any given situation. Hence conflicting loyalties and potential shifting category names both permit and promote multiple, cross-cutting claims of affiliation and provide a viable degree of flexibility in social intercourse.

HOW THE SYSTEM WORKS: HISTORY

In what follows I return to my initial observations about the native categories and pose two problems. First, why is it that such polar groups (restricted/unrestricted) are designated by a single native category (*be:rtan*)? Second, why does a common cultural cliché concerning putative origins apply to all 67 category names, regardless of their present-day status? I shall argue that a synchronic view of Ilongot category names leaves the system obscure: instead I shall follow the lead provided by the native model and base my account on the historical formation of such named groups.

To introduce a time dimension in the apprehension of Ilongot social structure I shall rely on what Hocart has so aptly called 'circumstantial evidence' (1970: 11–27). Lest there be any confusion, I am quite familiar with Radcliffe-Brown's long-heeded (and I think debilitating) strictures upon 'conjectural history' and I have read that even seemingly reliable genealogists remake and fabricate their ancestral past (e.g. Bohannan 1952; but contrast Fox 1971). Indeed, I have hesitated before embarking for the shadowy terrain that Ilongots themselves warn is inhabited only by their forgotten ancestors. My choice at this point seems to lie between: (a) a synchronic view, where my evidence is virtually complete but the system remains unintelligible, and (b) a diachronic view, where my evidence is relatively less complete but the system becomes much more plausible. I find the latter course of inquiry to be the more productive of the two.

In ethnohistorical research I am now carrying out I have found evidence indicating that Ilongot category names first come into being as names for a settlement or aggregate of settlements: that is, initially they were names for districts. Later, with loss of population or owing to external pressures, the members of a named district may have dispersed and affiliated with one or more of the remaining named districts. At this point they retained their former category name, but it ceased to designate a district and referred instead to a non-localized group. From my examination of eighteenth-century documents I infer that in the long run non-localized category names tend to disappear from the system altogether. The historical formation and dissolution of such groups, then, is an irreversible process and not cyclical or oscillatory.

My evidence for the above diachronic process is based on the following four kinds of category-name case histories:

1 *Initial creation:* In 1900–1910 a splinter group left district A. Initially they called themselves by a place name from their former district. By 1967–1969 they were named after a river in the district where they then resided (Sinebran).

2 *From district to non-localized group:* In 1906 a settlement name was reported (UmpataN). By 1967–1969 it had become a non-localized category name with members in more than one district.

3 *Wide and narrow senses, both district and non-localized group:* In 1900–1910 two districts were reported (X and Y). During the

17

Second World War the Y people were reduced in numbers and affiliated with district X; by 1967–1969 their former district name had become a non-localized group name at the same time as they became known as the people of district X. However, the former members of district X and their descendants became the 'true' X people in the narrow sense of the term (Tamsi).

4 *Loss of name:* In the eighteenth century Spanish missionaries reported a number of category names. Most of these names were unknown by 1900–1910 and 1967–1969.

Other case histories I have collected would only provide further illustrations of these four kinds (cf. Barrows 1909; Jones 1907–1909; Norbeck 1956). While my documentary evidence does not allow me to follow any single category name through all its possible phases, I have inferred that the case histories are but moments in a larger historical process. The cumulation of short-run illustrations points to a highly plausible long-run pattern.

Ilongot category names should be interpreted, then, not as labels for two kinds of nonunilineal descent groups, but rather as a means of identifying bounded groups at differing phases in a single historical process. Further evidence for this inference emerges from the anthropological literature. In elaborating Murdock's views, Goodenough provides the following account of the historical origins of the 'deme':

> In an endogamous community, the course of time will produce an increasing overlap of membership in such groups, until eventually everyone is descended from all the founding ancestors and the several descent groups have become congruent in membership and coterminous with the community itself (1970: 51).

This account is consistent both with the documentary evidence and with the Ilongot sense that persons who share a category name must be related.[6] Indeed the historical origins of the deme correspond with the native supposition that 'the hill people once lived on a hill', hence their name. Whatever evidence Ilongots may have used for arriving at their cultural cliché, there is wisdom in lengthening one's time perspective to comprehend better this aspect of their social structure.

PRECISION: THE PARTICULAR AND THE COMPARATIVE

I have attempted to convey a sense of how to transform a generally accepted theory into a mode of understanding a specific ethnographic case. In so doing one cannot rely on general recipes, for no two 'cases' are ever precisely 'the same'. This position implies that central concepts, both of the anthropologist and of the native, should be construed as having a number of senses and as permitting a number of degrees of approximation. Anthropological investigation, then, may be more productively directed toward the specification of evidence and reasons for deciding that over a range of cases resemblances are more salient than differences.

Some anthropologists may counter that the experience of living a particular social life is so idiosyncratic as to push the translation of culture beyond our limited grasp. I simply take it as an article of faith that, however imperfect, such translation is possible and I believe that I have so demonstrated with yet one more case in point. A more serious objection, I find, is that raised by those who perceive an inherent contradiction between ethnographic precision and comparative studies. Defining marriage in terms of legal paternity, Gough, for instance, has taken a position diametrically opposed to my own, saying that

> I would argue that for purposes of cross-cultural comparison, we do need a single, parsimonious definition, simply in order to isolate the phenomenon we wish to study (1959: 23).

More recently and with comparable theoretical justification, Gough's definition has been revised and brought up to date by Goodenough (1970: 6–17). The issue is still alive and thus obviously worth considering. In general I believe that it is inaccurate to strive for precision in determining whether or not a phenomenon meets strict criteria for membership in a category or class. I feel that those who have embarked on the quest for the unifying and universal criterion in the definition of marriage have been misguided from the start. Even if they were to discover what they seek, it would do little more than identify those cases to be counted in as opposed to those counted out.

I find that we inhibit ourselves from asking the most compelling questions when we draw strict boundaries around what may be included in our investigations. A minimal definition of marriage, after all, says virtually nothing about the significant human content of such relations; nor does it lead to such potentially rich comparative juxtapositions as marriage, sex out of wedlock, friendship. Or one might so reason by analogy with the concept of 'friendship': 'true friend', 'bosom friend', 'old friend', 'buddy', 'acquaintance', 'fair-weather friend', 'no friend of mine'. This implies a continuum of friendship: authentic, probable, possible, and false. At what point and for what reason do we draw the line? If a social phenomenon is many-layered, multifaceted, and richly textured, parsimony is a poor criterion by which to judge the best analysis, regardless of whether the goal is to grasp a particular case or engage in a broader comparative study. My strategy for comparative investigations, then, is to use central concepts in as full a range of senses as possible and strive to map and apprehend the contours of complexity in human relations as they are found in a plurality of cultures. What is needed is not the spurious precision of minimal definitions, but rather the capacity to use cultural categories so as to capture the complexity of actual social perceptions and relations.

19

Notes

1. The research on which this paper is based was financed by a National Science Foundation pre-doctoral fellowship and by National Science Foundation research grant GS-1509. My wife, Michelle, and I lived among the Ilongots of Northern Luzon for some twenty-one months, from October 1967 through June 1969. An earlier and briefer version of this paper was read at the 1970 meetings of the American Anthropological Association in San Diego and as lectures in Anthropology 133 at Stanford (spring 1973). While I alone am responsible for the final version of this paper, I have benefited from the comments of Harold Conklin, Roberto Da Matta, Steven Fjellman, James Fox, Charles Frake, Steven Harrell, Bridget O'Laughlin, Sherry Ortner, Yosal Rogat, Michelle Rosaldo, Harold Scheffler, and Katherine Verdery.
2. The term 'open-textured' is from Waismann (1965) whose work in linguistic philosophy, deeply influenced by Wittgenstein, has shaped my sense of the nature of certain critical concepts, both those of the natives and those of the anthropologist.
3. My sense of inquiry has been inspired by Wittgenstein and his notion of 'family resemblances' (compare Geertz 1959; Needham 1971). Wittgenstein explains that a single concept may have a number of senses and that no single criterion is the common denominator of all these senses. Instead, the multiple senses of the concept are related in different ways, much as the members of a family are related to one another in different ways. In the following central passage Wittgenstein clarifies his notion of 'family resemblances' by using the image of a thread and its numerous fibres: 'And we extend our concept of number as in spinning a thread we twist fibre on fibre. And the strength of the thread does not reside in the fact that some one fibre runs through its whole length, but in the overlapping of many fibres (1958: 32e).'
4. My phrasing of this problem has been influenced by a recent paper in linguistic theory by Lakoff (1972). When I use terms such as 'approximates' and 'more or less' I intend that they be understood in accord with Lakoff's investigations of more colloquial terms such as 'sort of' and 'kind of'—those which he generally terms 'hedges'.
5. Some representative and I think particularly crucial works on the topic of nonunilineal descent are the following: Davenport (1959), Firth (1957; 1963), Fox (1967: 146–174), Goodenough (1955; 1970: 39–67), Keesing (1970), Peranio (1961), Scheffler (1966).
6. In a more speculative vein, the congruence of meanings between the English 'kind' and the Ilongot be:rtan may have grown out of comparable social systems. English villages in the Middle Ages and Kentucky mountain communities are characterized as demes and appear similar to Ilongot districts (cf. Goodenough 1970: 52).

Bibliography

BARROWS, DAVID P. 1909. Trip to Iloilo and Antiki, Notebook No. 13 From Carton No. 25, pp. 65–108. Unpublished field notes, Berkeley, Bancroft Library.
BOHANNAN, LAURA 1952. A Genealogical Charter. *Africa* 22: 301–315.
BURKE, KENNETH 1957. *The Philosophy of Literary Form.* New York: Vintage.
DAVENPORT, WILLIAM H. 1959. Nonunilinear Descent and Descent Groups. *American Anthropologist* 61: 557–572.
EVANS-PRITCHARD, E. E. 1940. *The Nuer.* Oxford: Clarendon Press.
— 1956. *Nuer Religion.* Oxford: Clarendon Press.

FIRTH, RAYMOND 1957. A Note on Descent Groups in Polynesia. *Man* 57: 4–8.
— 1963. Bilateral Descent Groups, An Operational Viewpoint. In I. Schapera (ed.), *Studies in Kinship and Marriage*. Royal Anthropological Institute Occasional Paper No. 16. London: Royal Anthropological Institute.

FOX, JAMES J. 1971. A Rotinese Dynastic Genealogy: Structure and Event. In T. O. Beidelman (ed.), *The Translation of Culture*. London: Tavistock.

FOX, ROBIN 1967. *Kinship and Marriage*. Harmondsworth and Baltimore: Penguin.

GEERTZ, CLIFFORD 1959. Form and Variation in Balinese Village Structure. *American Anthropologist* 61: 991–1012.

GEERTZ, HILDRED, and GEERTZ, CLIFFORD 1964. Teknonymy in Bali: Parenthood, Age-Grading, and Genealogical Amnesia. *Journal of the Royal Anthropological Institute* 94 (part 2): 94–108.

GLUCKMAN, MAX 1950. Kinship and Marriage Among the Lozi of Northern Rhodesia and The Zulu of Natal. In A. R. Radcliffe-Brown and Daryll Forde (eds.), *African Systems of Kinship and Marriage*. London: Oxford University Press.

GOODENOUGH, WARD H. 1955. A Problem in Malayo-Polynesian Social Organization. *American Anthropologist* 57: 71–83.
— 1970. *Description and Comparison in Cultural Anthropology*. Chicago: Aldine.

GOUGH, E. KATHLEEN 1959. The Nayars and the Definition of Marriage. *Journal of the Royal Anthropological Institute* 89: 23–34.

GREENBERG, JOSEPH 1966. Language Universals. In T. E. Sebeok (ed.), *Current Trends in Linguistics*, Vol. 3. The Hague: Mouton.

HOCART, A. M. 1970. *Kings and Councillors*. Chicago: University of Chicago Press.

JAKOBSON, ROMAN 1957. *Shifters, Verbal Categories, and the Russian Verb*. Harvard University: Russian Language Project.

JONES, WILLIAM 1907–1909. The Diary of William Jones. Unpublished Manuscript, Chicago Natural History Museum.

KEESING, ROGER M. 1970. Shrines, Ancestors, and Nonunilineal Descent: The Kwaio and Tallensi. *American Anthropologist* 72: 755–775.

LAKOFF, GEORGE 1972. Hedges: A Study in Meaning Criteria and the Logic of Fuzzy Concepts. Papers from the 8th Regional Meeting, Chicago Linguistic Society, Chicago.

LEACH, EDMUND 1958. Concerning Trobriand Clans and the Kinship Category Tabu. In Jack Goody (ed.), *The Developmental Cycle in Domestic Groups*. Cambridge: Cambridge University Press.
— 1961. *Rethinking Anthropology*. London: Athlone Press.
— 1962. On Certain Unconsidered Aspects of Double Descent Systems. *Man* 62: 130–134.
— 1964. *Political Systems of Highland Burma*. London: Bell; Boston: Beacon.

LOUNSBURY, FLOYD 1965. Another View of the Trobriand Kinship Categories. In E. A. Hammel (ed.), *Formal Semantic Analysis*. American Anthropologist, Special Issue.

MALINOWSKI, BRONISLAW 1929. *The Sexual Life of Savages in Northwestern Melanesia*. London: George Routledge & Sons.

MURDOCK, GEORGE PETER 1949. *Social Structure*. New York: Macmillan.

NEEDHAM, RODNEY 1971. Remarks on the Analysis of Kinship and Marriage. In Rodney Needham (ed.), *Rethinking Kinship and Marriage*. London: Tavistock.

NORBECK, EDWARD 1956. David P. Barrow's Notes on Philippine Ethnology. *Journal of East Asiatic Studies* 5: 229–254.

PERANIO, ROGER D. 1961. Descent, Descent Line, and Descent Group in Cognatic Social Systems. *Proceedings* of the 1961 Annual Spring Meeting of the American Ethnological Society, pp. 93–113.

ROSALDO, MICHELLE Z. 1971. Context and Metaphor in Ilongot Oral Tradition. Unpublished Ph.D. Dissertation, Harvard.

21

Renato Rosaldo

ROSALDO, MICHELLE Z. 1972. Metaphor and Folk Classification. *Southwestern Journal of Anthropoogyl* **28**: 83–99.
— 1973. I have Nothing to Hide: The Language of Ilongot Oratory. *Language in Society* **2**: 193–223.
ROSALDO, RENATO I., JR. 1970a. Ilongot Kin Terms: A Bilateral System of Northern Luzon, Philippines. *Proceedings* of VIIIth International Congress of Anthropological and Ethnological Sciences, 1968, vol. 2 pp. 81–84.
— 1970b. Ilongot Society: The Social Organization of a Non-Christian Group in Northern Luzon, Philippines. Unpublished Ph.D. Dissertation, Harvard.
— n.d. The Rhetoric of Control: Ilongots Viewed as Natural Bandits and Wild Indians. MS.
SANKOFF, GILLIAN 1972. Cognitive Variability and New Guinea Social Organization: The Buang Dgwa. *American Anthropologist* **74**: 555–566.
SCHEFFLER, HAROLD W. 1966. Ancestor Worship in Anthropology: or Observations on Descent and Descent Groups. *Current Anthropology* **7**: 541–551.
SCHEFFLER, HAROLD W. and LOUNSBURY, FLOYD G. 1971. *A Study in Structural Semantics*. Englewood Cliffs, New Jersey: Prentice-Hall.
SCHNEIDER, DAVID M. 1965. Some Muddles in the Models or How the System Really Works. In Michael Banton (ed.), *The Relevance of Models for Social Anthropology*. London: Tavistock Publications.
— 1967. Descent and Filiation as Cultural Constructs. *Southwestern Journal of Anthropology* **23**: 65–73.
TUGBY, DONALD J. 1966. A Model of the Social Organization of the Ilongot of Northeast Luzon. *Journal of Asian and African Studies* **1**: 253–260.
WAISMANN, FRIEDRICH 1965. Verifiability. In Anthony Flew (ed.), *Logic and Language*. New York: Doubleday, Anchor Edition.
WITTGENSTEIN, LUDWIG 1958. *Philosophical Investigations*. Translated by G. E. M. Anscombe. Oxford: Basil Blackwell.

Anthony Jackson

The Descent of Man, Incest, and the Naming of Sons
Manifest and Latent Meanings in a Na-khi Text

THE PROBLEM

Kinship, as the title indicates, is the real problem underlying this analysis of symbolism. Certain puzzling features in the Na-khi myth about the descent of man are examined in order to throw light upon two peculiar features of Na-khi society, viz. their phenomenally high suicide rate and the production of thousands of pictographic manuscripts from the eighteenth century onwards.[1] These texts exclusively concern their religion, a syncretic form of Tibetan Bön, which contains a high proportion of Bön symbolism. It is the very consistency with which this symbolism has been used in the Na-khi texts that reveals certain ambiguities when, for example, an indigenous myth is grafted into the new ritual repertoire. It is just such a myth that will be discussed here.

ETHNOGRAPHIC BACKGROUND

The Na-khi are one of the many ethnic minorities (e.g. Lo-lo, Min-chia, Lisu) who settled in south-west China a millennium ago and managed to preserve their own language and customs because of their remoteness from the Han Chinese. At present there are some 150,000 Na-khi living along the upper reaches of the Mekong and Yangtze Kiang in Yün-nan province near the border with Tibet. The people are agriculturalists and live in small settlements wherever there is level ground and an adequate water supply. The mountainous terrain confines the dispersed villages to the valleys of these major rivers which cut vast gorges in the landscape and thus provide natural trading trails. Hence the Na-khi villages are strung out along the caravan routes from Tibet, which follow the rivers down to the Na-khi capital, Li-chiang, which is the entrepôt town for the area and around which some 50,000 people live. Despite a general elevation of some 10,000 feet the climate is equable and both wheat and rice are grown besides other grains, fruits, and vegetables. The Na-khi rear cattle, sheep, and pigs while deer are hunted on the hills. Until recently there was no wheeled transport and communications were difficult.

THE CHINESE INFLUENCE

It was its strategic importance, from both the economic and military viewpoints, that caused the Chinese to become interested in this area. At first the Chinese were content to let the Na-khi kings defend the Imperial frontier against the unruly Tibetans in return for titles and tribute. However, at the beginning of the eighteenth century the internal dissensions within Tibet looked too dangerous to be left to the old principle of 'barbarians fighting barbarians' so the Chinese took control and set about civilizing the Na-khi.

Up until A.D. 1723, the year of nationalization, the Na-khi tribe consisted of a number of clans ruled over by a petty king who was recognized by the Chinese Emperor. Both the Na-khi and the Hli-khin, a neighbouring tribe living on the other side of the Yangtze, were referred to collectively by the Chinese as the Mo-so tribe. There was in fact little difference between these two tribes as far as clan organization, kinship terminology, language, and ritual practices were concerned. Their history was very similar up to the eighteenth century. Then in 1700 the Hli-khin were converted *en masse* to the Yellow hat sect of Tibetan Buddhism and the indigenous Black Bön monks were driven out. Although the Na-khi rulers were converts to the Red hat sect, then in favour at the Chinese court, this was not enough to stay fears of further Tibetan encroachment from the militant Yellow hats. The Chinese moved in, sacked the king, and set up a Chinese magistracy to enforce national laws among the Na-khi. The marriage customs were changed to fall into line with Chinese arranged betrothals, cremation was banned and replaced by inhumation, while the inheritance laws must have been altered to allow the sons to inherit from fathers—all to encourage filial obedience, the mainstay of proper authority in Chinese eyes.

The result of these Chinese innovations among the Na-khi was twofold: a sudden and phenomenal increase in female suicide and an equally sudden appearance of thousands of pictographic texts. This curious reaction prompts the reflection that something drastic had happened to the Na-khi, for nothing of this nature occurred among the Hli-khin. But then the Hli-khin were not taken over by the Chinese and no changes were made to the social order by the Tibetan monks. Today the Hli-khin are reported as being a matrilineal people practising patrilateral cross-cousin marriage whereas the Na-khi are now patri-lineally inclined and not given to asymmetrical marriage arrangements. It would seem that the Chinese indoctrination was successful but it implies that Na-khi society must have been very different before 1723. The obvious conclusion is that the Na-khi had a similar kinship system to the Hli-khin when the Chinese arrived.

RITUAL

The new Na-khi ritual and the suicide rate were definitely related.[2] The reasons why young girls committed suicide were that they objected to the parent-arranged marriages, the new low status of wives, and the diminution of women's rights, but besides these they believed that lovers would live together in paradise if they died together. This belief was promulgated by the new ritual specialists, the *dto-mbas*, who performed expensive ceremonies for the families of suicides. These dto-mbas were proscribed Black Bön monks, who not only invented a new pictographic script but elaborated their Tibetan-inspired rites under the Chinese administration. Significantly enough the traditional ritual specialist was a female shaman, but after 1723 she was replaced by a male shaman. The new shamans were both recruited and initiated by the dto-mbas but their ritual sphere was drastically reduced by the dto-mbas. It should be noted that the dto-mbas did not constitute a church nor were they organized in any way. Thus they presented no threat to the Chinese but rather served to funnel discontent away from the administration and its laws.

Many traditional Na-khi myths were incorporated into the dto-mbas' texts and blended with Bön ideas to produce a new form of religion for the people. As these new rites had to be adapted to Chinese-imposed standards there is a superficial acknowledgement of the *status quo*. However, Bön symbolism has precise meanings and hence it was difficult for the dto-mbas to reconcile Na-khi myths with Chinese legislation, especially in the field of kinship. It is this crucial point which is at the focus of this analysis.

The aim of this paper is to show that the manifest content of a ritual text may be belied by the latent symbolism of the myth contained within it. The particular myth to be examined is the Na-khi myth of origin, *Tso mber ssaw* or *The Descent of Man*, which is widely known and hence was never completely susceptible to a satisfactory reworking by the dto-mbas. What will be shown is that beneath the apparently patrilineal bias of the myth are traces of matrilinearity which contradict the overt sense of the text and lend substance to the case that the Na-khi and Hli-khin had identical kinship systems before 1723.

MYTHS

The myths concerning the Na-khi culture hero, Ts'o-zä-llü-ghügh, were incorporated into the dto-mbas' texts in order to legitimize particular ceremonies. The primal myth, *Tso mber ssaw*, is to be found in most major rites, but it is suitably modified in each case to aptly encharter the ceremony. The following version concerns one of the principal Na-khi rites, *The Sacrifice to Heaven*. A distinction must be drawn between traditional Na-khi rites and the newer dto-mba written ceremonies which subsume the indigenous rites. The difference is found in this particular ceremony because dto-mbas were not strictly necessary, since it was conducted by the head of the household. Nevertheless, without the dto-mbas' text there would have been no record left at all for both the oral traditions and the dto-mbas' rituals were swept away when the Red Army marched into the area in 1949.

SUMMARY OF THE MYTH

Before analysing selected passages of the myth a brief summary of *Tso mber ssaw*[3] is given:

The myth tells of the physical descent to Earth of the first post-flood ancestor, Ts'o-zä-llü-ghügh, besides giving his genealogical descent from Heaven. Ts'o is stated to be nine generations removed from the Egg of Creation. After the flood (which is omitted here) he seeks for a wife in Heaven to accompany him down to Earth. He is successful straight away and so the ancestral couple proceed to unlock the gates of Heaven to obtain the livestock, grain, and fertility which they need for life on Earth. They prepare to descend with the requisite items: clothing, riches, horses, cattle, grain, diviners, and slaves. However, because of faulty divination their departure is delayed for seven months, in any case they had not got fertility. They open some more gates in Heaven and eventually find fertility. They start their descent and by performing seven rituals they find the seven stages down to Earth, where they settle down as rulers. Unluckily they obtain no children, so they send seven messengers to Heaven in order to discover why this is so. Their emissaries find out that Ts'o and his wife, Ts'ä, have not performed the *Sacrifice to Heaven and Earth* which is necessary for fertility. The ancestral couple duly repair this omission and are rewarded with sons. Unfortunately the sons are born dumb and so the messengers are sent again to discover the proper ritual. After this rite has been performed the sons are indeed able to speak but the eldest son speaks Tibetan, the middle son speaks Na-khi, and the youngest son speaks Min-chia (the tribe directly south). Each son in his turn tries to perform the *Sacrifice to Heaven* but it is only the Na-khi-speaking son that can do it correctly. The benefits that flow from Heaven after this rite has been performed are then discussed and another genealogy is given showing the unbroken chain of custom from the time of the ancestors until today. The four clans of the Na-khi who perform this rite are mentioned and the myth concludes by stressing the importance of following tradition.

ANALYSIS OF THE MYTH

(a) 'On the day the heavens are full of stars and the land is covered with grass, on that day, in the beginning, Heaven laid an egg. The Earth hatched it. Ts'o-zä's egg was as white as the conch.

The white-as-conch egg became hot and from the hot egg came forth vapour. From the hot vapour came forth hot dew, from the hot dew came forth three drops. One drop fell on a high cliff, whereupon the Juniper with the white root was born: this tree is the mother's brother of Heaven. One drop fell on the oak tree: this is the mother's mother of Earth. One drop fell into a lake and from the golden lake was born Khü-zä (the first human being). From Khü-zä came forth La-zä, from La-zä was born Muan-zä. The next generation was Muan-zä Ts'u-ts'u, then followed Ts'u-ts'u Ts'u-yü, Ts'u-yü Ts'u-dgyu, Ts'u-dgyu Dgyu-zä, Dgyu-zä Dzi-zä, Dzi-zä Ts'o-zä and the next generation was Ts'o-zä Llü-ghügh.'

The opening phrase is a standard formula to denote a propitious time, for it is held that unless the beginning is lucky the outcome of any activity cannot be successful. Hence the importance of divination to determine the most advantageous time to begin any activity played a significant role in Na-khi life and ritual.

Creation from an egg is a common Chinese and Tibetan belief but the kinship-forming action of the three drops is not. To the Na-khi a mother's brother meant a protector and it was considered essential that everyone have one, while here even things like trees act this role. This symbolism becomes clearer when it is noted that in the rite of the Sacrifice to Heaven there are three trees placed upon the altar: a juniper flanked by two oak trees. One oak tree stands for Heaven, the other for Earth while the juniper stands for the gods. Another text tells how Heaven is the mother's brother of the Na-khi and the juniper with the black root. In the Na-khi tongue *na* means black and *p'er* means white. They refer to themselves as *Na*-khi (people of the black) and call the Tibetans *P'er*, whom they regard as their elder brothers.

In the genealogy Ts'o, the culture hero, comes ninth in line after the first human being, which is in accordance with the symbolic use of numbers whereby nine stands for male and celestial but seven for female and terrestrial. Male descent is often reckoned back nine generations while female descent is only counted back seven; however, in practice they seldom remember more than three generations. The myth makes this point inasmuch as three sets of generations are distinguished, but here again the number three is symbolic of completeness. Other versions of this myth only credit the Na-khi with seven antediluvian ancestors. Finally it may be remarked that the naming of sons follows a pattern whereby the son acquires the latter half of his father's name as the first half of his own. This nomenclature will be examined later but it should be pointed out that it is a curious feature to have in a putative patrilineal system. So far, the myth superficially supports the male line of descent but attention has been drawn to certain incongruities which cast doubt on the purity of this account.

(b) 'He had no wife so he went to Heaven to search for one. They met at P'er-na-nddü-gkan chung where a white, blossoming plum tree grew. They both liked one another and became united as man and wife. They leaned against the tree and became one tree. She changed herself into a crane, took him under her wing and flew to Heaven. They arrived in Dzi-la-ä-p'u's Heaven.'

The story of the Flood is omitted in this myth but the immediate cause of this disaster was the fact that Ts'o and his siblings committed incest. As will be seen, the theme of incest runs throughout the accounts of the ancestors of the Na-khi, if one accepts the versions of the myths given by the dto-mbas. Disregarding the first three ancestors in the genealogy who appear to be self-reproducing, Ts'o's male forbears had the practice of choosing wives in Heaven. Thus there are seven pairs of ancestors who married in Heaven before the descent to Earth and the cessation of this practice. The genealogy will be discussed in detail later.

It is worth noting the meaning of some of the names used in the myth since they carry certain interesting connotations. In the culture hero's name *Ts'o* means people and *zä* means demon. His wife is called Ts'ä-khü-bu-bu-mi, in which *khü* means lake and *bu-mi* means to think of a wife. This allusion could refer to the primordial lake or the flood. The pair meet where the black and white lands adjoin—the lands of the *Na* and the *P'er*. There is a double meaning here for it refers to the border between the demons and the gods but also to the centre where east and west meet. Colour symbolism is employed throughout the texts and in this case black is synonymous with the west and demons, while white stands for the east and celestial things. Incidentially, Ts'ä is elsewhere described as being the mother of two tribes, the P'er and the Na, who are always associated with the centre of the Na-khi universe.

Dzi-la-ä-p'u is the personification of the Second Heaven and his name means the grandfather of all the people—*dzi* means people, *la* is everyone, and *ä-p'u* is the kin term for grandfather. There are three heavens (*muan*) in Na-khi belief. The First Heaven is *Ssa-bbu-mber yu* (paternal guest ancestor) and the Third is *Gkyi-gkv ddu-mä* (great mother above the clouds) which refers to the actual sky. There are also three corresponding Earths. The Second Earth is personified by *Ts'ä-khü-ä-dzi*, consort of Dzi-la-ä-p'u and mother of Ts'ä-khü-bu-bu-mi; the kin term *ä-dzi* means grandmother. The First Earth, *Mä-mä-khi-zaw-du-ggo* (elder sister upbringer of descendants on land) refers to the maternal ancestors, while the Third Earth, *Llu-dtv-ddu-mä* (great mother of a thousand grandchildren), is the actual earth. These three sets of heavens and earths are not conceived spatially as forming any sort of hierarchy but are simply part of a basic threefold classification which is common in Na-khi thought. The paternal and maternal ancestors are considered to reside somewhere to the north while the grandparents of the people (the Second Heaven and Earth) are believed to be not far away and are the source of all good things.

(c) The myth then relates how they open three sets of nine gates in Heaven: the gates of the domestic animals, grain and fertility. Ts'o demands Ts'ä as his wife and receives her. Their descent is delayed for nine months and then they come down bearing all the necessities of life: clothing, riches, horses, cattle, diviners, and slaves.

The number nine, besides meaning celestial, refers to all the known varieties of animals and plants used by man in this case. The nine gates of fertility are described in symbolic terms that have sexual reference.

Seven pairs of objects are taken down to Earth, nine of each item for Ts'o and seven for Ts'ä.[4]

(d) At this point the myth seems to backtrack and continues: 'Nyi-lä who casts the star horoscopes well, cast them badly. Ssu-t'o who casts the planet horoscopes well, cast them badly. They waited for the Na-dtv (the 30th of the month, a lucky day) for seven months. When the father divides his property with his son it is not the custom for the father to follow the son to his new home. A girl is given in marriage when the bu-dto and bu-ma stars are in harmony with her; when the daughter has been sent off it is not the custom for the mother to follow. *Na-gkv-ssu-lv-mä*, she opened the three golden gates from right to left. *Shou-lä-bu-yu-mä* opened the three silver gates from left to right. There they opened a gate where the father sat and the son stood, they opened a gate where the mother sat and the daughter stood. They opened an upper gate which was the heavenly gate where a man sat and the *nnü* (the spirit of male semen) stood. They were desirous of nnü and *o* (female fertility), they lighted a juniper torch before the father of nnü and the mother of o and descended with a brilliant torch.'

A slight discrepancy seems to have crept into the myth for now the ancestral pair wait for only seven months and not nine months as mentioned previously. The residence rules indicating neolocality appear almost as an intrusion at this point. Again we find nine more gates being opened and these deserve close scrutiny.

Table 1

Gates opened by:	Gates
Na-gkv-ssu-lv-mä	3 golden gates from right to left
Shou-lä-bu-yu-mä	3 silver gates from left to right
Ts'o and Ts'ä	(1 gate: Father and son
	(1 gate: Mother and daughter
	(1 gate: Man and the spirit of semen

The last three gates are similar to those already mentioned before but what is the significance of the first two sets of three gates? The obscure people who are the gatekeepers are never mentioned elsewhere and why are the gates opened in a particular direction? What is the relevance of all this to the theme of marriage, the subject of this passage?

Although a few of the symbolic statements have been examined in the preceding extracts they give little idea of the nature of this symbolism. Essentially Bön symbolism is dualistic and there are many forms in which these complementary oppositions are to be found. In the present case the articulating opposition is a sexual one in which position, colour, and number differentiate the pair. This is commonplace in the ethnographic literature but one significant variation here is the association of the male with the left-hand side and not the right.

With the above points in mind and considering the pervasiveness of symbolic referents in the texts, the problematical gatekeepers will be carefully investigated. A literal translation of the names and of the gates is:

Na-gvk-ssu-lv-mä	*opens*	3 golden gates from right to left
Maternal relative first *Ssu* granddaughter	links	3 female generations from female to male
Shou-lä-bu-yu-mä	*opens*	*3 silver gates from left to right*
Say wish wife mother-in-law	links	3 male generations from male to female

While this interpretation sounds equally cryptic as it stands, one must remember the context is marriage. If, as suggested earlier, the Na-khi were originally like the Hli-khin and practised patrilateral cross-cousin marriage in a matrilineal kinship system, then the symbolism takes on meaning. Consider the following diagram (*Figure 1*).

Figure 1

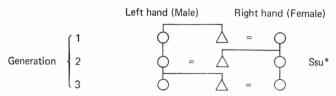

* N.B. The names of all the celestial wives end in *ssu* in the following genealogy.

In the case of two lineages practising patrilateral cross-cousin marriage, the (Ssu) granddaughter on the right-hand side completes the exchange cycle by accepting her MBS, a man from the left-hand lineage, thus linking three female generations from female (wife-givers) to male. Correspondingly, her mother-in-law on the left-hand side links three male generations (father, son, and grandson) by accepting her MBS, a man from the right-hand lineage, thus linking these generations from male to female. In this way the granddaughter and mother-in-law play complementary roles in the formation of these two sets of three generations.

Should this form of marriage exchange continue over a period of time the complementary roles of granddaughter and mother-in-law alternate as the direction of bride-giving alternates.

Figure 2

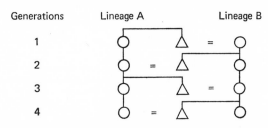

Hence when the son of granddaughter B3 marries the girl A4, B3 becomes the mother-in-law of A4, but A4 herself is the granddaughter of A2, who is the mother-in-law of B3. Thus the relations between lineages A and B are maintained, and only maintained in accordance with these prescriptive rules, by the reciprocal and alternating roles of these two key women, which is why they are given prominence as the openers of the gates of the three generations. This interpretation makes sense of this curious passage and is consistent with what we suspect about Na-khi traditional kinship. No alternative kinship pattern would fit this case and this strengthens the above analysis.

(e) Next the pair seek for and find fertility. Then they descend onto a mountain and find their way to the land, performing seven rituals as they do so—one ritual for each stage of the journey. When they eventually settle down as rulers they get no children and so they send seven messengers to Heaven in order to discover why this is so. Their emissaries overhear the divinities discussing why Ts'o and Ts'ä are infertile—they have not performed the proper rituals, the very rites which this myth encharters. The ancestral couple duly repair this omission and perform the Sacrifice to Heaven and Earth for fertility. They are duly rewarded with sons but unfortunately they are born dumb. The messengers are again sent and the correct ritual is discovered. After this rite has been performed the sons are able to speak but the eldest son speaks Tibetan, the middle son speaks Na-khi, while the youngest son speaks Min-chia. Each son in turn tries to perform the Sacrifice to Heaven but it is only the Na-khi son who can do it correctly. 'The family who are descendants of Ts'o and are of his image do not prevent any good things from descending from on high. His six generations of grandfathers bought six generations of grandmothers. Six of them resided in Heaven, three generations resided on Earth.'

A genealogy then follows, but instead of giving this verbatim it is compiled in the form of a table. The names of the ancestors and their wives are given in two parts so that the construction of these names can be more clearly seen.

Table 2   The genealogy of the Na-khi ancestors

Generations	Ts'o-zä : the Egg of Creation				
1	Khu-zä : the first Human Being				
2	La-zä				
3	Muan-zä				

	MALE NAMES			FEMALE NAMES		
	1st half	2nd half		1st half	2nd half	
4	Muan-zä	Ts'u-ts'u		K'ö-ddv	Mun-ssu	
5	Ts'u-ts'u	Ts'u-yü		Dta-ts'ä	Ts'ä-ssu	
6	Ts'u-yü	Ts'u-dgyu		Dzi-llü	Dzi-ssu	Celestial Women
7	Ts'u-dgyu	Dgyu-zä		Ä-dzi	Ä-ssu	
8	Dgyu-zä	Dzi-zä		K'wua-dtv	Mber-ssu	
9	Dzi-zä	Ts'o-zä		Ghügh-khü	Lä-ssu	
1	Ts'o-zä	Llü-ghügh		Ts'ä-khü	bu-bu-mi	FLOOD
2	Ghügh-khü	Non		Ssu-t'a	La-lv	
3	Non	Bä-p'ö		Ä-dzi	Ssu-lv	
4	Bä-p'ö	O		K'wua-dtv	Mber-lv	Terrestrial Women
5	O	Gkaw-lä		Gyi-ssu	Mun-lv	
6	Gkaw-lä	Ts'u		(Gyi-mi	Gyi-dsu)	
7	Ts'u	(zo lu szi)		—	—	

(four sons)
a) Ts'u-gkyi-dtv-lv-gv   (Ssu clan)
b) Muan-zä-khi-ho-gv   (Ho clan)
c) Ts'ü-gkv-mbbue-d'a-ssu(Mä clan)
d) Ndü-t'khi-ngv-yu-gv   (Yu clan)

The binary system of naming sons can be readily seen from the table whereby the second half of the father's name becomes the first half of the son's name. This system did not apply to women although they too had four-word names, some of which were repeated. The first nine generations of male ancestors, who come before the flood, may be divided into three groups of three: the first group have names ending in zä, the second group contain ts'u, and the last group end in zä. It will be recalled that both zä and ts'u mean demon. After the flood the male names have only three elements to them.

Before the flood the wives' names end with ssu but afterwards they end with lv. Ssu means serpent and lv means dragon; they are regarded as accompanying one another and as being very powerful. According to another myth it is related that Ts'o's father was also the father of Ssu, a serpent spirit who shared the Earth with Ts'o. The six (demon?) grandfathers took six celestial women as wives and so did Ts'o himself but thereafter the post-flood ancestors took earthly women. If the flood destroyed the Earth and its inhabitants, where did Ts'o's sons get their wives from? This myth wisely omits the flood and makes no comment: the answer would be embarrassingly clear. Other myths, however, face up to this problem (Rock 1952: n 95, n 862; 1955: 166). For example, Ts'o is alleged to have committed incest with his sister and this was partly responsible for the flood. The third post-flood ancestor commits incest with his mother. The fifth post-flood ancestor has incestuous relations with both his mother and his sister, while his son marries a woman whose name is suspiciously like his mother's. At this point the genealogy breaks down and we are given the names of the latter's sons who are the founders of the four Na-khi clans. Why is it that the first, third, and fifth post-flood ancestors allegedly commit incest and not the others?

THE CENTRAL DISCUSSION

It is this part of the myth which brings to a focus the title of the paper: The descent of man, incest, and the naming of sons. Can all these things be resolved? It is suggested that they can be *if* this genealogy records patrilateral cross-cousin marriage within a matrilineal kinship system, not otherwise. The rest of this paper is devoted to showing that this assumption not only makes sense of the myths but explains something about the nature of traditional Na-khi kinship patterns. Consider first the binary naming system. It is an unusual practice for naming sons even though it was adopted by the royal house of the Nan-chao (Southern Kingdom) prior to Kublai Khan's conquest of south China. What could have been its function? It seems too clumsy a method for tracing descent but if it is considered in terms of patrilateral cross-cousin marriage then the system becomes an elegant device for telling a girl whom she ought to marry, viz. that man who has the same name as her 'protector'—her mother's brother. Thus this naming system enables one to avoid 'incorrect' matches despite the complication that bride-givers and bride-receivers alternate every generation. The bias of this system favours a matrilineal kinship network and until recently the Na-khi had no patronymics but only named clans.

In matrilineal societies ZS inherits from MB but, given the practice of patrilateral cross-cousin marriage whereby a man marries his FZD and a women marries her MBS, it is highly likely that residence after marriage will be avunculocal. On this assumption the Na-khi ancestral genealogy begins to show some structure which has certain societal consequences.

Taking the seven post-flood ancestors and their wives (indicated by their initials) and assigning them to four avunculocal residences (M, Y, S, H) which correspond to the four clan ancestors: Mä, Yu, Ssu, Ho, the following diagram (*Table 3*) results:

Table 3

Avunculocal residences

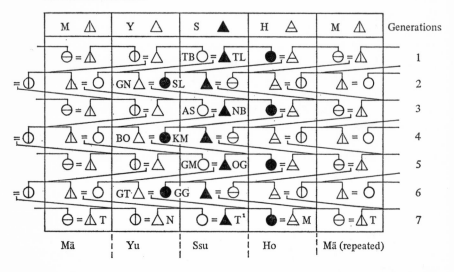

| Mä | Yu | Ssu | Ho | Mä (repeated) |

While only two avunculocal groups (Y & S) are involved in the Na-khi genealogy it is necessary to have four such groups in order to generate symmetry with regard to residence after marriage. To show these interrelationships more clearly group M has been repeated. At this stage no necessary relationship is assumed between the avunculocal groups and the clans of the Na-khi for this will be discussed later. In the diagram, therefore, the avunculocal groups are identified by a letter and a kinship symbol: the clan names are placed there for later reference.

The Na-khi binary naming system begins, in the above diagram, with group S and then goes to group Y and back again to S—as far as the sons are concerned. Although a grandson succeeds to his grandfather's house this will not be indicated in the naming system. However, this would not be surprising in a matrilineal society since the purpose of naming is to indicate not descent but marriage partners.

From a woman's point of view she should marry someone with the same name as her guardian (MB) and she will go to live where her maternal grandmother (MM) went to live. Since a man inherits from his MB he will go to live there but he will also marry a woman from the same group as his MB did. Such a symmetrical arrangement only follows if there are four avunculocal groups that intermarry.

As an example of how this arrangement works out, consider the fourth generation. K'wua-dtv Mber-lv marries Bä-p'ö O who has the same name component as *her* mother's brother, Non Bä-p'ö. She comes from group H and goes to live in group Y after marriage—just like her grandmother, Ssu-t'a La-lv. Her husband, Bä-p'ö O, inherits from his mother's brother in group Y but marries a woman from group H— which is precisely where *his* mother's brother's wife also came from. This residential symmetry is not of course matched by lineage symmetry since this only repeats itself in alternate generations. This is shown in the diagram. Such a symmetrical arrangement as postulated here is congruent with the earlier discussion about the two women, the granddaughter and the mother-in-law, who opened the gates of the three generations of males and females (p. 30). The granddaughter goes to live where her grandmother went to live, while her mother-in-law is not only her mother's brother's wife but also the sister of her husband's mother's brother. As can be seen, the linkage through mother's brothers is both important and tightly arranged in such a system. This accords well with the stress placed upon the role of mother's brother in Na-khi society and hence lends support to the notion of avunculocal residence. The conclusion regarding the Na-khi naming of sons is that it indicates patrilateral cross-cousin marriage and avunculocal residence patterns in a matrilineal society. Not surprisingly this rigid system eventually broke down after seven hypothetical generations but before this is considered there is still the question of incest.

THE PROBLEM OF INCEST

If one examines the complete genealogy of the Na-khi it will be seen that there are certain patterns in the naming of women apart from the *ssu/lv* distinction already mentioned. Thus the name *Ts'ä* occurs in the 5th pre-flood and the 1st post-flood generation, *A-dzi* occurs in the 7th pre-flood and the 3rd post-flood generation, *K'wua-dtv* occurs in the 8th pre-flood and the 4th post-flood generation. The common feature in each case is the fact that the pre-flood women are the great-great-great-grandmothers (MMMMM) of the husbands of the post-flood women. How is this connected with the alleged incest of the 1st, 3rd, and 5th post-flood ancestors with their sisters or mothers?

A solution to this problem is given if the Na-khi genealogy is taken to be a record of patrilateral cross-cousin marriage in a matrilineal system. If one begins with a pair of ancestors then one finds that the woman's daughter's daughter marries the man's son's son and this pattern repeats itself in alternate generations. Hence the first and third generations are lineally related, so are the fifth, seventh, ninth, and so on. It is suggested that the accusation of incest is really a misdescription of the true state of affairs and arises from the assumption that the genealogy is one of patrilineal descent.

35

What the texts actually say is that the male ancestor *lived* with his sister or his mother, not that he married them, nor that he slept with them. It suggests that a man was unwilling to leave his father's home and take up his inheritance with his mother's brother. The remarks may be construed more as injunctions to follow custom regarding residence for they indicate where the man was before his marriage. They are applied only to the lineal descendants of Ts'o, it will be noticed. The fault seems to lie with group Y for not maintaining its obligations to Group S. The genealogy ends in confusion after the seventh generation with the appearance of the four sons of Gkaw-lä Ts'ü. It may be noted that there was no hint of incest in this particular myth but that the number seven, the female number, was very prominent throughout. Again, this suggests that the genealogy was matrilineal and that only by trying to interpret it as tracing male descent, which the dto-mbas tried to do, does the question of incest arise. Indeed, the genealogy could be read as dispensing with males altogether, for are not the husbands called *ts'u* and *zä*—demon? Even the First Heaven is called 'paternal *guest* ancestor' as if the male ancestry was not all that important. Nevertheless, descent is important in this myth since the Na-khi trace their clan membership back to this genealogy.

NA-KHI CLANS

With regard to the four Na-khi clans it is useful to look again at the last diagram where a hypothetical derivation of them is given. The *Ssu* clan founder is a direct descendant of Ts'o (his SSSSSS) while the *Yu* clan founder is a direct descendant of Ts'ä (her DDDDDS) and both these clans (groups S & Y) are said to live together. Correspondingly, the *Ho* clan founder is a direct descendant of Ts'o's sister (her SSSSSS) and the *Mä* clan founder is a direct descendant of Ts'ä's brother (his DDDDDS) and these two clans are said to live together (groups H & M). It is of interest to note that *ho* refers to male and to son while *mä* means female or daughter. It seems more than coincidence that the four clan founders should display such a symmetrical descent pattern and that the pairing of clans just happens to fit the kinship diagram given. The myth confirms this interpretation.

(f) 'The Ssu and Yu did not separate, they wanted to be rich and ride horseback so they went to Yi-gv-dü (Li-chiang, the capital) to dwell. The Ho and Mä did not separate, they liked the hot sun, so they went to Zher-dü (north of Li-chiang) to dwell.'

Although different texts give differing names to the four sons of Gkaw-lä Ts'ü they all agree that they are the originators of the four Na-khi clans: Ssu, Yu, Ho, and Mä (op. cit.: 116, 123, n 61–63). If one summarizes the various information given about the four clans, the following details emerge (*Table 4*):

Table 4

Clans	SSU	YU	MÄ	HO
Founder	*Ts'u*-gkyi-dtv-lv-gv	Ndu-t'khi-ngv-*yu*-gv	Ts'ä-gkv-*mbbue*-d'a-ssu	Muan-zä-khi-*ho*-gv
Eponym	Goral deer	Yak	Tiger	Bear
Protecting emblem	Hawk	Eagle	Unicorn	Yak
Clan colour	Black	Blue	White	Yellow
Reside (near to)	(yellow) elephant	Deer	Yak	Tiger
Land: covered by	Grass	Felt	Tiger skins	Tibetan cloth

Put into diagrammatic form, this becomes (*Figure 3*):

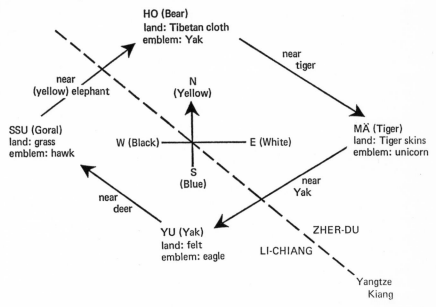

The interesting feature about this information is how the symbolism locates the various clans around the compass so that the Yangtze Kiang divides the two sets of clans into a northern and southern moiety. Another point of interest is the reference to the nearby clan— indicated by arrows in the diagram. If one reduces this diagram to its essentials, it becomes:

Figure 4

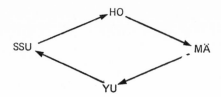

When this basic relationship is converted into kinship terms it becomes:

Figure 5

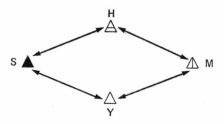

This pattern of kinship relations is, of course, identical with the type of relations found between avunculocal residences (p. 34). It is exactly the pattern to be expected when there is an exchange of spouses between four avunculocal residences and between lineages. Thus several myths about the Na-khi clans support the underlying hypothesis of this paper.

From the above diagrams it is seen that certain clans do not exchange spouses, viz. Ssu & Mä, Ho & Yu, and this strengthens the possibility that the Na-khi had two moieties. This non-exchange of spouses is also true of avunculocal residences but here there is an alternation every generation.

At this point one can return to the question of the relationship between the Hli-khin and the Na-khi. Is there a possibility that the two present tribes are, or were, the two moieties referred to above? Obviously, the changed historical circumstances have made a present difference but there are striking similarities, The Hli-khin (see Reshetov 1964) have four exogamous clans: Ssi, Ya, Ä, Hu, which sound just like the Na-khi: Ssu, Yu, Mä, Ho clans, allowing for dialect and transcription differences. The two tribes have similar kinship terms and both use eponyms. However, the Hli-khin economic unit is a household consisting of several members of the matrilineage; husbands do not reside with their wives but merely visit them at night. The Na-khi live in patrilineally organized households today but this is an understandable difference after two centuries of Chinese rule. It should be noted that the rulers of the Na-khi and the Hli-khin have practised patrilineal succession since the time of Kublai Khan. This is because the rulers are descendants of Kublai's officers who were left to govern the area. The commoners, however, continued in their own way and it is the traditional kinship that has been under discussion. There is little difficulty in understanding why the Na-khi might have changed their kinship and marriage customs; the question is whether they did. The evidence suggests that this is the case, for this analysis of the Na-khi myth of origin rests on that assumption. Unless an alternative explanation can be given of the curious features of this myth *and* can account for the suicide rate and proliferation of ritual among the Na-khi, the conclusion must be that the Na-khi did practise patrilateral cross-cousin marriage and that they had a matrilineal kinship system, besides residing avunculocally after marriage. It is difficult to envisage any alternative solution that could account for all these facts so economically and thus the contention is that the above conclusion is the only correct one.

CONCLUSIONS

This analysis of some of the symbolic features of a myth has illuminated many aspects of Na-khi society which have been puzzling, besides explaining some of the curious points in the myth of descent. One consequence of their kinship system is that they needed just four clans to operate it and these clans formed a moiety. This explains who the *Na* and the *P'er* really are. The two tribes lived in the centre and were descended from Ts'ä, the first post-flood ancestress, according to the myths. The *Na* are the Na-khi living in the west (symbolized as black, *na*) and the *P'er* are the Hli-khin living to the east (symbolized as white, *p'er*). They are the two moieties, illustrated in the diagram (*Figure 3*), separated by the Yangtze. One also notes that the northern clan (Ho) is in contact with the Tibetans while the southern one (Yu) is in contact with the Min-chia people, hence the story about the three sons of Ts'o. It is not surprising that the Hli-khin have the same clan names and kin terms since they had the same system and, despite their physical separation, they needed all four clans to operate the marriage exchange and residence rules even though there were moieties.

In establishing the identity of social structure between the Na-khi and Hli-khin—the common kinship systems of the rulers (patrilineal) and ordinary people (matrilineal) being an important element in this, common social stratification, common economy, and common belief and ritual are other features—the question arises why the Na-khi moiety became susceptible to a high female suicide rate and a new religion. The answer has been given in terms of the Chinese intervention. Only if the Na-khi were forced to give up their traditional ways is such a violent reaction possible. From the Chinese point of view it was only sensible to break the power of the matrilineages and in this they were partly aided by the fact that the Hli-khin had been converted to the Yellow sect of Buddhism; a partial breakdown had occurred. Furthermore, the Chinese wished to instil filial obedience if the Na-khi were to become citizens. Their new regulations turned the society on its head and the increasing suicides began to take their toll. In these circumstances the rites of the dto-mbas were a palliative and were not discouraged. Thus the new religion gained ground, texts were compiled and, in the process, left us a record of the myths and rituals of the Na-khi. The Bön bias of the dto-mbas caused them to make the most of their symbolism, which they tried to adapt to the traditional myths of the Na-khi. It is the discrepancies in these accounts that enable us to unravel the story of the decline and fall of the Na-khi moiety, long after it occurred. Without the symbolism this task might have proved impossible.

This analysis of symbolism has concentrated on elucidating a problem of kinship but there are other aspects which could have been examined, e.g. the structure and use of Bön symbolism. Even the myth is structured along a ninefold sequence which is the ritual paradigm for all Na-khi rites (cf. Jackson, forthcoming). The paper demonstrates that the obduracy of symbols to change can reveal latent meanings in myth.

FINAL REMARKS AND SUMMARY

My concern here has been to show how a myth may be understood, and my starting-point has been certain obscurities in this myth of descent, viz. the odd relationship between the two openers of the heavenly gates, the binary naming system for sons, the accusations of incest among certain ancestors, the existence of four named clans and their particular interrelationships. I suggest there is only one possible solution to this problem and that is to postulate a mythical norm of patrilateral cross-cousin marriage, avunculocal residence in a matrilineal kinship system. As such a precise formulation resolves these obscurities, there cannot be an alternative or simpler solution.

Having demonstrated this point, I do not therefore suppose that the Na-khi actually practised this custom *because the myth says so*. I turn to what we know about the Na-khi people and to the other problem: suicide and the ritual texts. Elsewhere, I mention that the Na-khi did, at one time, have the norm of patrilateral cross-cousin marriage and a matrilineal kinship organization. Thus, if the societal norms and the mythical norms do coincide we have a *prima facie* case of homology. Having established this and noting the scruplulous consistency of the *symbolism* throughout the Na-khi texts, it follows that any verbal discrepancies in the myth are likely to be later emendations.

Now, the object of this paper was to show that the symbolism could reveal the latent structure of the myth, and the reason why any latent meaning should exist at all arises from the fact that the Na-khi people were turned from matrilinearity to patrilinearity by the Chinese in 1723. This forced change led to the suicides and ritual texts, as was explained at the beginning of the paper. In such circumstances it would be surprising if the myths (which are chanted at the rituals) did not pay some nominal attention to this fact and we could expect some emphasis being laid upon the new role of the male. This is seen in section (d) about inheritance, (e) about buying wives, and elsewhere. In other words, if the symbolic meanings are disregarded, we could *almost* take this myth as being compatible with patrilineal descent. The noticeable feature about the patrilineal emphasis is that it generally consists of non-symbolic phrases about the superiority of the father. However, given the correctness of the kinship norms in the myth which explain the symbolism, the importance attributed to the male line becomes incomprehensible. Either the explanation offered here is false and/or the inverse of reality or it is correct and the patrilineal overtones are later emendations. The former suggestion seems too far-fetched in view of what we know about the historical development of the Na-khi.

The conclusion is that the myth shows a dual parallelism with the social structure: it reflects the changes in the kinship system but also reveals the traditional norms. Thus should the myth and the social structure be homologous, in this case, it seems worth pursuing this further to see if it matches the relations between the Hli-khin and Na-khi tribes as well. It is suggested that the myth again bears out the historical evidence.

Notes

1. The location of Na-khi manuscripts is given in Jackson (1965). An analytical account of the texts is found in Rock (1965). For an analysis of Na-khi rites and symbolism, see Jackson (1970). Tibetan Bön religion is treated by Hoffman (1950; 1961; 1967). See also Snellgrove (1967).
2. The relationship between suicide and Na-khi ritual is more fully discussed in Jackson (1971; 1973).
3. A full translations of this myth is given in Rock (1948).
4. Other myths do not allow Ts'o such an easy success. In one case he has to perform nine difficult tasks to win his bride, cf. Rock (1952: 675–687).

References

HOFFMAN, H. 1950. *Quellen zur Geschichte der tibetischen Bon-religion.* Wiesbaden: Franz Steiner.
— 1961. *The Religions of Tibet.* London; Allen & Unwin.
— 1967. *Symbolik der tibetischen Religionen und des Shamanismus.* Stuttgart: Hiersemann.
JACKSON, A. 1965. Mo-so Magical Texts. *Bulletin of the John Rylands Library* **48** (1): 141–174.
— 1970. *Elementary Structures of Na-khi Ritual.* Göteborg University.
— 1971. Kinship, Suicide, and Pictographs among the Na-khi (S.W. China). *Ethnos* **36**: 52–93.
— 1973. A Na-khi Folk-tale. *Folklore* **84**: 27–37.
— (forthcoming). *Tibetan Bön Rites in China.* The Hague: Mouton.

Anthony Jackson

RESHETOV, A. M. 1964. Matrilineal Organization among the Na-khi (Mo-so) 7th International Congress of Anthropological and Ethnological Sciences, Moscow.

ROCK, J. F. 1948. The Muan Bpö Ceremony or Sacrifice to Heaven as practised by the Na-khi. *Monumenta Serica* **8**: 71–88.

— 1952. *The Na-khi Naga Cult and Related Ceremonies*. Rome; Is. M.E.O.

— 1955. *The Zhi ma Funeral Ceremony of the Na-khi of Southwest China*. Vienna:

— 1965. *Na-khi Manuscripts*. Wiesbaden: Franz Steiner.

SNELLGROVE, D. 1967. *The Nine Ways of Bön*, London: Oxford University Press.

Michelle Zimbalist Rosaldo and Jane Monnig Atkinson

Man the Hunter and Woman
Metaphors for the Sexes in Ilongot[1] Magical Spells

*The ensemble of a people's customs always has its particular style;
they form into systems. I am convinced that the number of these
systems is not unlimited and that human societies, like individual
human beings . . . never create absolutely: all they can do is to choose
combinations from a repertory of ideas which it should be possible to
reconstitute . . . Lévi-Strauss (1970: 160)*

For the Kayans of Borneo, as for the Aztecs of ancient Mexico, a
special place in heaven was shared by women who died in childbed and
men who died in wat (Hastings, Vol. II: 683, 685). For certain African
groups, like the Ndembu, male hunting cults have counterparts in cults
which guarantee female fertility and encourage childbirth. Childbirth
and killing, life-giving and life-taking, constitute opposed and complementary terms which provide a framework for symbolic conceptualiza-
tions of men's and women's roles quite generally, and perhaps,
universally. If, as Lévi-Strauss suggests, 'societies . . . never create
absolutely' (1970: 160), if, by virtue of similarities in human experience
everywhere, certain symbolic idioms are available to people around the
world, then it is, perhaps, not surprising that an idiom which opposes
men and women is among them. Since issues of sex-role definition
appear to be inevitable both socially and psychologically, since man—in
very different social systems—conceives himself as opposed and generally superior to woman, the symbolism of the sexes is a likely ground for
discovering abstract and universal symbolic themes. Even the anthropologist's myth of Man the Hunter—of males, autonomous and
agentic, creating the first forms of culture, cooperation, and technology
—is only one culture's articulation of a very general pattern. Man the
Hunter is a form of man the killer, the life-taker, opposed implicitly or
explicitly to Woman the Childbearer, the *giver* of life through birth.
    Our purpose in this paper is to show how the framework of an
abstract opposition, between life-giving and life-taking, illuminates
symbolic definitions of the sexes in one particular culture. By posing the
problem in this way, we hope to suggest that culture-specific configura-
tions of symbolic materials reflect a variety of constraining factors:

43

universal themes and oppositions; symbolic materials available to historically or locally related cultures; the shaping of culture by particular social systems; and, finally, the need for human actors in specific situations to organize their experienced worlds. Although our programme, in its general outlines, resembles the one which Lévi-Strauss proposes in *Mythologiques* and elsewhere, our interest lies less in universal generalizations than in the place of general considerations in the analysis of particulars. We assume that men and women are defined everywhere in relation to one another, and that an opposition between life-givers and life-takers is often the form in which this relation is cast. Still, it is necessary to examine the realization of this opposition in any given instance, to ask how the myths, metaphors, and symbols which express it are related to their social and cultural context, and to show how these work for actors to orient, interpret, transform, or legitimize their everyday concerns.

In the interpretation of a particular culture, general assumptions of the sort we are discussing govern one's choice and, ultimately, one's ordering of data. At the same time, however, any interpretation or analysis of symbols must emerge from their actual contexts of use. The symbols and metaphors used in conventional cultural performances may be seen to exemplify or articulate themes of a general nature; through them, abstract and even universal considerations may be cast in a particular culture's mould. Yet metaphors are also produced, and experienced as meaningful, by socially situated actors. They provide an interpretation of individual needs and desires, a vehicle which orients actors towards the distinctive, intelligible, and orderly views of experience which their culture, in fact, provides.

Analysis must, then, begin with the complexities of actual cultural practice. Methodologically, we can think of two approaches from which such analysis might proceed. The first, illustrated by Turner's (1964b; 1967) discussions of 'dominant symbols' or Pepper's (1942) 'root metaphors', is given systematic treatment in a recent paper by Ortner (1974a). 'Key' or dominant symbols are selected out of the webs of interrelated cultural expressions because they are felt to provide a focus for crucial activities, like rituals, and again, because they supply a metaphorical framework which relates a variety of cultural concerns. They may be 'life' symbols (Langer 1942) which build upon associations salient universally and address existential preoccupations important to people around the world. So, the *mudyi* or 'milk tree' dominates the girl's initiation for the Ndembu, and by virtue of its associations with maternity, matriliny, women, the girl, her mother, and so on, it acquires importance as a focal expression of Ndembu feeling and thought (Turner 1964b). In the case of our own data, such a key symbol would be headhunting, which is at once a kind of male initiation, a focus of group identity, and an image of grace, masculinity, health, and violence, all of which are (in some sense) cultural ideals. The key symbol, in other words, is laden with a variety of deeply salient meanings; its successful analysis depends on a careful explication of the ways in which its multiple metaphorical associations are realized in a wide range of activities, and the ways in which these articulate with one another in a particular focal event.

The second approach, less common in anthropological writings, begins with those cultural performances which pile image on image, in the manner of a Lévi-Straussian *bricoleur*. By combining what once was separate, by saying the 'same thing' in a variety of symbolic forms, the *bricoleur* creates a context in which new meanings are realized, and the experienced world is re-ordered in terms of unique orientation or goal. In magical spells, for example, practitioners typically call on a wide range of objects (cf. Strathern and Strathern 1968; Tambiah 1968; Munn n.d.). Health is like a plant which glistens, like sunrise, like loose flying feathers, like a tree whose thorny trunk keeps predators from reaching its fruit. Taken together, all of these images suggest something clean, pure, and invulnerable; the various metaphors combine to establish a particular idea of health as a principle which orders and humanizes an uncontrollable natural world.

A systematic study of such essentially redundant metaphorical expressions can isolate the principles in terms of which they are selected, the particular ideas of order, the emotional orientations and cultural themes which they are intended to express. Such ideas, in turn, can be systematically related. From an analysis of actual metaphors one can begin to isolate the structural associations which underlie a multiplicity of cultural expressions. Each metaphor, taken by itself, may seem arbitrary, yet combined with others it can be shown to signify and re-flect an underlying system of meanings, and to serve as a vehicle through which that system is constituted and reaffirmed.

The magical spells of the Ilongots, a group of hunters and swidden agriculturalists in Northern Luzon, Philippines, provide a rich field for the exploration of this second approach to metaphor. The spells are about things like hunting and headhunting, agriculture, accidents, and disease. They are a part of every adult Ilongot's knowledge, and, among those Ilongots who have not yet become Christians, hardly a day goes by without someone's calling on plants, birds, clouds, sweet things, or poisons, to guarantee success in the hunt or the harvest, safety and glory to the warrior, or comfort and personal good health. Our approach in this paper will, then, involve a detailed exploration of Ilongot magical metaphors. We begin by discussing spells for agri-culture and hunting, which, through their relation to the life-giving/ life-taking opposition, lead to a number of suggestions as to the conceptualization of men and women in the Ilongot cultural order. In a final section, comparative evidence is introduced to suggest that the Ilongot system represents one variant of what we take to be a universal or 'natural' structure of male and female associations, and we discuss the importance of postulating such universal schemata in the interpretation of any particular case.

THE ILONGOTS

There are some 2500 Ilongots living in scattered settlements in the rugged and fertile hill country just south of the Mountain Province in Northern Luzon, Philippines. Their household, community, and larger political ties are organized by relations of bilateral kinship (R. Rosaldo 1970b). Residence on marriage tends to be uxorilocal, but when closely related men marry into a community, they provide the focus of its political identity. Relations between women and men are cooperative and relatively egalitarian; husband and wife participate equally in most family decisions, both care for young children, and both provide food for the home. Ilongot women are gardeners, producing the rice which is the staple of the family diet. Ilongot men are hunters, deft and at home in the forest, and aside from their activity in clearing the woodlands for planting, they have little to do with the production of the staple food, rice.

Power, in Ilongot society, is not the prerogative of individuals of any particular status, nor do criteria like age, esoteric wisdom, success in hunting or even in headhunting, provide grounds on which men establish fixed rankings among themselves. Young men should take heads and marry, and those who have not done so are unlikely to be influential in later community life; but the boy who has killed no one has a perfect right to resist his father's decisions; some men never take heads; some never marry; and the successful hunter and killer will be powerful only if he has the verbal precocity and human intelligence which enable him to persuade, rather than command. Formal norms dictate that everyone is his fellow's equal, and while some people have more influence than others, none has permanent authority, nor can anyone take for granted that his recommendations will be followed. This stress on individual autonomy and equality is reflected in the fact that men, women, and children all receive equal and individual portions whenever food is being distributed, and it is implicitly recognized in the artful, prolonged, and careful oratorical confrontations (cf. M. Rosaldo 1973), where, again, what is desired is not the grudging compliance of subordinates, but a meeting of minds and of hearts.

Magical spells are, like oratory, a method of metaphorical persuasion. The spirits cannot be coerced, but they can be influenced, to comply with human desires. They may be frightened or threatened, coaxed or coddled, but no one can be sure they will obey. There is no single fixed form for a magical performance, no correct or certain set of expressions, images, or commands. The spells of even a single practitioner are always different. Ilongots describe their magic, like their oratory, as an attempt to find the 'right words', which will win the spirits' compliance. At the same time, examination of a number of spells of any single type reveals that they are all alternative realizations of a shared and constraining sense of order, that each draws on a common repertory of possible expressions, which, in turn, reflect a small set of culturally significant themes.

The metaphors of magical spells [2] are, for the most part, familiar to all adult members of the community. Men and women alike know that plants with red sap make a tea which cures bloody diarrhoea, that a good harvester is like a 'spinning bug' in her infinitely productive garden, that spirits are apt to be frightened when a plant known as 'toothless' is invoked in the course of a spell. They know that betel spit, which changes from green to red, suggests a change towards good fortune, and that splashing water on a patient may wash away a disease. Metaphors, in word and in gesture, are realized in a variety of forms in any particular performance. They may be associated with a particular object or action, they may be announced in a simile, or again, they may be suggested by the name or physical characteristics of a plant which is used in the spell.

Thus, when an Ilongot woman prepares for a harvest, or a man, having fed his hunt dogs, is about to set off after game, each gathers a collection of herbs which are, typically, charred with pitch or steamed over a preheated hearthstone. An object like steam is said to 'quicken' the pulse of the performer, producing the feeling of excitement which foretells a successful endeavour. The hearthstone itself is a symbol of closeness and stability, of rice so thick that the harvester stays in a single spot throughout an entire day's reaping, of game which meets the hunter near to his home. The plants have names which resemble the Ilongot words for 'meet', 'hasten', 'near', and 'encounter' (cf. M. Rosaldo 1972; n.d.); they too suggest that success is available close by. Finally, the spoken spell is rich in images of plenty; it asks that the practitioner be dizzied and overwhelmed with the rice or the game he desires, that quantities—like stars in the night or leaves which fall in a windstorm—will appear before his eyes.

Hunting and agricultural spells both belong to the subset of magical performances called 'preparations'. 'Preparations' or *qaimet* include spells for agriculture, hunting, and headhunting; *qaimet* can also mean 'an ornament' or 'to ornament oneself, to dress up'. The variety of *qaimet* used for headhunting is called *kuiri*; relatively fixed in form and limited in its occasion, *kuiri* will not concern us here. *Qaimet* used for hunting and gardening have, on the other hand, a number of variations. Agricultural spells can be performed shortly after planting, when the gardener 'washes' the young shoots which are described as her 'children', and again, at several points during and after the harvest (when the rice is dried, put in the granary, and first removed to eat). Similarly, hunting spells may be recited over dogs before a collective hunt; by the lone hunter who has encountered an animal's footprint; or, in the home,

47

when preparing one's gun or one's bow. These spells differ in their typical 'action metaphors'; varieties of hunting and agricultural spells may be distinguished as to whether they involve things like washing, steaming or beating the herbs, building a fence which will ward off bad spirits, tying plants around a rice stalk, or turning dirt in a footprint to signify the death of the game. On the other hand, all varieties of agricultural spells, and all spells used for hunting, tend to be relatively constant in their repertory of plants, their characteristic verbal expressions and metaphors, and these are what will concern us here.

Whether he steams his herbs on a hearthstone, or lights pitch in the footprints of game, the hunter's words are apt to be something like the following (plant names in the two following texts are asterisked*):

> You, spirits who walk by the rivers, come join my steaming here!
> Here I do steam magic on my hand on the hearthstone
> Don't fail me, let me shoot, you spirits, my grandfathers!
> They like you, hand
> Hand that is steamed on the hearthstone, hand
> At your finishing place, hand
> May they be full* hand, the wild game, hand
> They like you, hand
> Make it a hoard* of wild game, hand
> Make them meet* you hand, the wild game, hand
> Make the eyes of the deer bulge, hand, in a clear place, hand
> They like you, hand
> May they be like stars to you, hand, the wild animals, hand
> Don't, please, hand, go too far away, hand
> Make your hunting place near,* hand
> Be, hand, like the sure hand of a Negrito hunter, hand
> They like you, hand . . .

Similarly, a gardener, at the beginning or end of her harvest, when she wonders how healthy her plants are, or later, when she puts the harvested bundles in her granary for use through the rest of the year, will use much the same language and images, asking again and again that her rice supply be unending, that its 'fruitfulness' remain in her field:

> Here, I steam you, rice, with your fruitfulness,* rice
> Rice, you have a spell performed, now, rice
> Make it pile high, rice, your fruitfulness, rice
> They like you, rice
> Beckon* your fruitfulness,* rice
> Here is the plant called beckoning,* rice
> Don't act childish, rice, don't be troublesome, rice
> They like you, rice
> Be like the rice of the lowlanders, rice

Make it so people everywhere speak of you, rice
They like you, rice
And may I be, please, rice, like a spinning bug in the centre of
  the field, rice
They like you, rice
This is the plant called hoards,* rice
Let there be hoards* of you, rice
And be full,* rice
May your fruitfulness* flourish,* rice. . . .

Such spells may be as short as the fragments recorded here, or they
may go on for as much as five or ten minutes, the rhythmic tones of the
practitioner rising to call on the spirits or falling to mutter a wish.
Whatever their length, they seem to be produced by a process through
which the performer repeats stereotyped lines ('they like you, hand')
and inserts appropriate images and metaphors into a small set of
relatively fixed grammatical forms or 'frames'. Possible frames include,
for example, the simile:

simaqeNkan	X	nuy	Y	X
be-you	X	like	Y	X

where the first blank term ('X') may be the hunt dog, the rice, or the
'hand' of the hunter or harvester, and the second ('Y') an image like
'stars', 'the hand of a Negrito', 'the rice of lowlanders', and so on. A
second frame permits the practitioner to cast the name of one of the
plants he has collected into the form of a verb which describes the
desired result. So, a plant called *nemu* may become:

say	nemuwenmu	ma	qitaruna	deyeka
now	meet-you	the	wild game	hand

Or again, *mabetuwan*, whose root, *betu*, means 'to fill', appear as:

pabtuma	pagi	ma	tekarmun	pagi
fill-you	rice	the	fruitfulness—yours	rice

The line glossed 'they like you . . .' appears in most Ilongot spells as a
refrain, and is said to be meaningless. Like the 'weird' utterances
discussed by Malinowski (1966: 211–250), it probably serves as a
relational element, asserting a tie between the practitioner and intangible
magical powers. Other frames, too, could be isolated (like the negative
command form 'don't . . .'), but similes and plant verbs are by far the
most common, not only in *qaimet*, but in the vast majority of Ilongot
spells. Such frames serve, minimally, as a heuristic device which
permits a variety of magical spells to be generated. As will be seen in
the discussion which follows, they also provide a framework through
which aspects of an underlying system of meanings are articulated in
actual spells.

49

In the analysis that follows, we borrow the structural linguist's intuition that all terms which can appear in a single frame or grammatical context are likely to share certain features of meaning. Much as ethno-scientists have used frames to isolate domains for semantic analysis, so Ilongots use the stereotyped forms of their magic to construct new and significant fields of meaning; by naming very different kinds of things in a single formulaic context, they bring them into parallel alignment, highlighting those features they share. Thus, through an examination of all of the kinds of plants which can be burned or steamed in a single magical context, or all of the plant verbs or similes which may be used in any one kind of spell, it becomes clear that the choice of plants, similes, and so on reflects a shared and relatively constant system of meaningful constraints. The principles which govern the choice of plants and similes are 'signified' by their selection; and so, by examining all possible choices, we can begin to understand how any one spell may be experienced as meaningful, and what it is trying to say.

CALLING ON PLANTS

All but the simplest Ilongot spells require the use of plants and botanical metaphors (M. Rosaldo 1971; 1972). Plants with flowing red sap are used to cure bloody diarrhoea; a grass which has thorns 'pierces' shooting pains in the chest; the sweet pungent odour of a wild variety of ginger is said to bring game which 'has flavour'; the sharp prongs on a rattan vine 'cling' like rice in a harvester's hands. In some spells, it appears that plants are selected because they are odd or peculiar in appearance. In others, plants seem to be chosen because they grow in or near a particular spirit's home. Finally, of the 400 plants we know to be used in magic, the majority have names like 'thigh', 'finger', 'twist', 'evil', 'encounter'; most of these plants have no physical characteristics which suggest that their names are appropriate, yet Ilongots say they are chosen because of their names, which make sense in the spell.

This use of plant-naming presents a number of problems for analysis. Metaphorical uses of plants have, of course, been noted elsewhere in the anthropological literature (Fox 1972; Turner 1964a). But why should plants have names like 'twist' or 'finger'? Is naming completely arbitrary? And what can be said of the significance of plants which are chosen for any particular spell? The problem has two aspects: first, what sets of names are used in what categories of magic and, second, why are these names assigned to particular kinds of plants?

To begin, an equation between plants and people is common in Ilongot metaphor (as it may be universally). Plants, especially wild species, are associated with intangible forces which give life. So, in oratory, plants are used to speak of humans; 'shoots' can mean 'children', and 'young leaf' describes a child's growing up. In spells, on the other hand, human characteristics are used to name botanical species, which are called after body parts or feelings, emotions, or characteristic modes of action. What is more, these names are ordered. Examination of lists of all plants which can be used in any category of magic reveals that the plants used in any one kind of spell tend to have names which reflect a single semantic conception. Thus, the plants used for the spirit *lampuN* can represent the spirit's body; and they are identified as its 'fingers', 'thighs', and 'thumbs'. Or again, plants which chase the threatening ancestors have names like 'twisted', 'toothless', 'dizzy'—names which suggest physical defects which a trouble-some spirit might avoid. Furthermore, most if not all plants used in a particular spell and having names of related semantic value appear to grow in a particular part of the physical environment. Body-part plants, for example, are almost exclusively arboreal orchids; the equa-tion is hardly surprising, since the *lampuN* are said to inhabit high places, like trees. Similarly, ancestor plants tend to be found in the thicket, an area which spirits of the dead are particularly likely to haunt. In other words, all plants which can be used in a single spell may be said to signify, and participate in, two underlying systems of meaning: one having to do with the human characteristics of super-natural objects and aspirations; and the second relating to the environ-ment in which the spirits are often found. Through the use of real plants from particular environments, aspects of the natural and spirit worlds are subordinated to human manipulation; and by naming these plants in his magic, the Ilongot connects his own sense of his body, its needs and aspirations, to external and tangible symbols from a 'humanized' (and so controllable) physical world.

Semantic conceptions and environmental categories operate in a similar way in the selection of plants for agriculture and hunting. This can be seen through an examination of all plants which are used in their respective 'preparations'. Any combination of plants from Lists A and C, or B and C, may be used in most instances of agricultural and hunting spells, respectively. A list of all plants used in the two kinds of magic is given in *Table 1*.

Perusal of these lists suggests an initial distinction, between the plants used in either agriculture or hunting (lists A and B), and those which are used in both kinds of spells (list C). Plants of the first kind are a mixed collection. Some, like 'she-boar', and 'teeth of the rats' (which eat rice plants), have names which are uniquely appropriate to one kind of spell or the other. Others, like the rattans used for garden-ing, the plant whose lobed leaves look like rice bundles, or those whose smell suggests 'flavour', have physical characteristics which explain their use in the spells. These tend to be named in similes ('be rice, like a rattan vine which clings to me, rice') and not in the plant–verb frame. In general, the plants in both of these lists seems to be used to *describe* properties of the practitioners' desired outcomes, to characterize

51

Table 1 Plants used in agricultural and hunting spells

A. PLANTS USED EXCLUSIVELY IN AGRICULTURAL SPELLS

Plant Name	Botanical Identification	Interpretation [3]	Environment
maNri	Calamus	all are rattans	secondary forest
ligen	Calamus	which 'cling'	secondary forest
teNpat	Calamus	to passers-by,	secondary forest
ritukur	Calamus	like rice in a harvester's hand	secondary forest
tekar	Drymaria cordifolia (Linn.) Willd.	'fruitfulness', thick shoots	garden
takdeN	Belamcanda chinensis (DC) Stapg.	'ladder' (?)	garden
taday	Cymbopogon citratus (DC) Stapg.	thick, healthy shoots, like healthy rice	garden
ginisigetan	Pothoideum lobbianum Schott	lobed leaves suggest rice bundles	forest, epiphyte (?)
rapurap	Pogonatherum paniceum (Lam.) Hack.	?generally, powerful plants, used in many kinds of spells	forest
kage:sikat	Drynaria quercifolia Sm.	,, ,,	forest
parked	?	strong roots stick to rocks, like rice in a harvester's hand	river banks
qensip	?	leaves blow in grassland, as a 'curse' will blow away from rice	grassland
beNar nu be:ki	Ophiorrhiz acuminata DC	'teeth of the rats'	thicket

B. PLANTS USED EXCLUSIVELY IN HUNTING SPELLS

Plant Name	Botanical Identification	Interpretation	Environment
mabe:Nru	Zingiber	(smell or taste presages flavour from game) forest relative of ginger	forest
de:giwaN	Marattia pellucida Presl. Angiopteris palmiformis (Cav.) C. Chr.	has a pepsin-like smell	forest
buayaqen	Piper	appears to be a plant used as a condiment elsewhere in the Philippines	forest
qubuwan	Piper aurilimbum DC	'she-boar'	forest
ramuttu	Oxymitra sp.	'his (the forest spirit's) root'	forest
mabe:tad	?	'straightening'	forest
pasir nu gipnan	Poikilospermum oblongifolium (Berg.-Petr.) Merr.	'tusk of the male boar'	forest
quduN nu makbet	?	'thigh of the male deer'	forest

Plant Name	Botanical Identification	Interpretation	Environment
takumbaN	?	'encircling', leaves grow in verticilate cluster from base	forest
puri	?	'return'	forest
patukur	*Globba sp.*	? the red underside of leaf suggests, for some informants, blood on dead game	forest
gelaqyeN	(*Araceae*)	? a forest relative of taro	forest
sinepruNan	*Aglaonema oblongifolium* (Roxb.) Kunth.	a medicine for backache, said to stiffen the back of the game	forest

C. PLANTS USED IN BOTH AGRICULTURAL AND HUNTING SPELLS

	Botanical Identification	Interpretation	Environment
	At least one variety of these is of family *Aspidiaceae*:[4]		
gidu	*Cyclosorus sp.*	'evil, curse'	forest
	Athyrium cordifolium (Blume) (*Polypodiaceae*)		
teNed	*Cephalomanes oblongifolium* Presl.	'base'	forest
	Athyrium cordifolium (Blume)		
qayapNed	*Microsorium heterolobum* (C.Chr.) Copel.	'near'	forest
	Callistopteris aplifolia (Presl.) Copel. *Ardisia*		
kinagiyan	*Lindsaea gracilis* Bl.	'beckon'	forest
	Cyclosorus matutumensis Copel.		
kuaqmet	*Teratophyllum aculeatum* (Blume) Mett.	'intensify, hasten'	forest
	All varieties are of genus *Chloranthus*:		
nemu	*Chloranthus oldhamii* Solms.	'come together, meet'	forest
	Chloranthus officinalis Blume		
padupaduN	*Chloranthus oldhamii* Solms.	'meet, encounter'	forest
	Chloranthus monander R.Br.		

Plant Name	Botanical Identification	Interpretation	Environment
de:qet	Asplenium phyllitidis Don	'meet, come up against'	forest
mabetuwan	?	'filling'	forest
de:uyunen	Rhododendron sp. Vaccinium	'hoard, pack'	forest
de:qpir	Scindapsus pictus Hassk. Pothoideum ovatifolium Engl.	'addition'	forest
sinaqlaN	Aglaomorphia brooksii Copel	'quickening'	forest
dinukuge:n	Drynaria quercifolia Sm.	'pushing'	forest
qaimbe:Nun	Coleus igolotorum Brig.	'awakening'	forest, garden
be:qriw	Elephantopus mollis HBK Elephantopus mollis	'change'	thicket
qamumur	(Gramineae)	'equal'	river bank
rinmuwan	?	'feeling'	river bank

healthy rice and productive harvests, or to name varieties of sought-for game.

Plants of the third group, by contrast, address the active and affective orientations of the hunter or gardener. They provide the practitioner with images of the meaning of activities he or she is involved in, of the feelings and social implications which Ilongot men and women associate with productive labour and the distribution of food. These plants are by far the most common in actual instances of both hunting and agricultural magic. All have names, used as verbs, which do not correspond to their actual morphological characteristics. Most of them have small and numerous leaves, which may suggest plenty, and most grow close to the ground, in the damper parts of the forest. The names for these plants speak of: (a) evil, a curse (or 'feeling') cast by an envious competitor; (b) meeting, joining, coming together; (c) quantity, plenty, producing the most (by 'equalling' past performances, or even by 'adding' on more) that one can.

Many of the names in this group refer, then, to fears, aspirations, and actions associated with productive successes. They orient the practitioner to the social implications of his work: greeting or cursing, coming together or avoiding an unhappy fate. While no Ilongot has said as much, we imagine that this association itself is related to the fact that distributing food is a requirement of most social encounters, and can also be a source of supernatural contagion. The names of plants used for both agriculture and hunting can, then, be said to highlight what both have in common: both are concerned with a sociable outcome, both with the production of food.

The fact that so many of the same plants are used in two kinds of magic makes spells for agriculture and hunting unique in the Ilongot

54

repertory. Ilongots explain this by saying that 'the plants are the same because it is the same food that we eat'. We would like to go further, in suggesting that these plants signify the symmetry and complementarity of female and male activities, of garden and forest, of rice and of game. Only when this is established can we begin to see why the plants come from the forest, rather than some other environment.

As we noted earlier in this essay, Ilongot women are gardeners and Ilongot men like to hunt. The products of the two—rice and game—should complement one another in the ideal diet; men and women are felt to contribute their comparable, but separate, kinds of foods. Though men may, in practice, help with hoeing and harvesting, and women occasionally hunt, this sexual division of labour extends ideally through all aspects of food production, preparation, and distribution. Aside from clearing the woodlands for planting—which pollarders describe as raping or beheading the forest—men are never obliged to assist in the cultivation or preparation of rice. We found, for example, that even though women plant between 10 and 25 varieties of rice in a single garden, their husbands did not know the variety names. And again, where men of neighbouring swidden groups may help to pound rice, or sow the seed while women dibble, Ilongots see all of these as female chores. An Ilongot woman, when she feels angry, goes to sit beneath her granary; a man runs off to the woods to think. Men hunt, butcher, and prepare meat dishes; the forest is their domain.

On another level, this opposition is mirrored in a dualistic classification of things which grow in garden and forest, and in a pair of deities, who dominate each of the two domains. The forest lord, *qagimeN*, is usually called *qiruNut*, 'from the forest', and his wife, *made:kit*, the Maiden, is also known as *qiquma*, 'from the fields'; they are patrons, respectively, of hunting and agricultural pursuits. In magical and mundane contexts alike, Ilongots indicate that there is a forest world equal to, and opposing the garden, which is associated with the domestic one. Several plants and animals of the forest are classified according to a domestic model: we find, for instance, 'his banana', 'his piper betel', 'his areca nut', and 'his root'. A wild chicken is distinguished by its name, *qikaratan*, 'of nature, of the forest', from its unmarked opposite, *manuk*, 'bird' or 'chicken', which belongs to the house. And the forest spirit himself is pictured in myths as both the wild boar and its keeper. In prayers addressed to *qagimeN*, people speak of the wild boar as *be:buymu*, 'your—domestic—pig'.

Spells for hunting and agriculture can both be called *qaimet*, or preparations. And spells, in both cases, can bring pain as well as success; both *qagimeN* and *made:kit* are sensitive to greed, carelessness, or other abuse by their followers, and people who make themselves vulnerable by performing *qaimet* must, at the risk of severe illness, avoid laughing and shouting, and observe a number of taboos. In both cases, also, it is not the edge, or *gelibgib* which is dangerous, but the

55

beNri, or 'centre' of the garden or forest, where play is restricted and productive activities are the only legitimate tasks. (It is equally true in houses, that while 'centres' are used for distributing and serving food, the 'edges' are where people will eat, talk, and relax.) Angering either patron in its magical 'centre' may bring on a sudden illness, called *beut*.

There is, then, both a sex-linked economic opposition, and a marked symbolic parallelism, between the male and female domains. This is illustrated in *Figure 1*.

Figure 1   The opposition of garden and forest

forest	garden
qagimeN	*made:kit*
men	women
game	rice
wild boar	domestic pig
wild chicken	domestic chicken
his banana, his piper betel, etc.	cultivated banana, piper betel, etc.
qaimet	*qaimet*
magical centre	magical centre
beut	*beut*

This parallelism, and the implied symmetrical conception of male and female activities, are signified in spells by the use of the same plants and plant verbs in both agricultural and hunting magic. The use of the same plants in both contexts corresponds to the fact that, in most situations, Ilongot men and women are seen as one another's equals, and, in terms of the production of foodstuffs, they operate in complementary spheres.

Why, then, do the plants come almost exclusively from the forest? If the sharing of plants in hunting and gardening magic suggests the symmetrical statuses and shared orientations of the sexes, why should the site of men's productive activity furnish the magical plants necessary for both men's and women's subsistence work? Certainly this imbalance hints at sexual asymmetry. But the association of the plants in list C with the forest takes on an additional interpretation in the context of Ilongot magic as a whole. To begin, with only a few exceptions, all of the 400 plants used in Ilongot spells are wild species, and these can be collected by both women and men. The forest, associated on one level with maleness, holds no sacred powers from which women are kept apart.[5] Furthermore, Ilongot see in the forest, as in all things wild, the free and auspicious power of nature called *karatan. Karatan*, equated with nature, with sunshine, and the capacity for life in general, is sexless. It is a force which both men and women can bring to the service of life. We imagine that wild plants constitute the bulk of the Ilongot's magical repertory because of their association, not with maleness specifically, but with the all-embracing forces of a natural world which surrounds, constrains, and ultimately sustains the life

56

enterprises of both sexes. While men surpass women in their knowledge of the forest and wild things generally, the idea of *karatan*—of power in nature, and so, in wild botanical species—suggests that the plants in list C have a spiritual efficacy which transcends the distinction of sex.

In formal terms, we can say that wild and technologically unimportant plants—plants associated with *karatan* or untrammelled nature—are 'unmarked' for all forms of Ilongot magic. The only contexts in which cultivated or economically important plants are used are specifically those in which sexually marked contrasts are relevant, as for agricultural spells. Thus, of those plants used only in gardening (list A), several are cultivated (*taday, takdeN, tekar*) or of real economic value (the rattans); and these can be seen as opposed to the forest equivalents of garden plants ('his root', which seems to suggest a wild tuber; *gelaqyeN*, a forest plant related to taro; *mabe:Nru*, a wild variety of ginger) which are used exclusively for the hunt. In contrast to these opposed sets are the plants used in both kinds of magic. These are wild, and come from the forest, rather than, say, the thicket (which yields plants for the ancestors) because only forest plants are relevant to the dichotomous organization of labour which underlies Ilongot conceptions of both agriculture and the hunt.

The cultural choice of forest over garden as the source of plants suitable for both hunting and gardening magic may be compared to the linguistic observation that male, as against female, categories are 'unmarked' in most languages. The fact that forest rather than garden plants are suitable for both kinds of magic is paralleled, for example, by pronominal usage in English, which favours 'he' over 'she' when referring to a generalized third person. By analogy, the forest is opposed to the garden, but it also has an 'unmarked' status which permits it to signify both wild and domestic spheres. 'Unmarked' terms,[6] in linguistic parlance, tend to be valued more positively than their 'marked' counterparts; perhaps here we see an expression of the asymmetry, as well as the complementarity, of Ilongot conceptions of male and female, a point to be developed in the discussion below.

SIMILES

The selection of plants and plant verbs highlights the complementarity of men and women in Ilongot cultural conceptions; the sexes are thought of as equal in emotional and spiritual orientations in so far as both are producers of food. It would be misleading, however, to assume that rice and game have equal value as foodstuffs. The asymmetry in their evaluations, suggested in our earlier observations, is reflected, perhaps, in the fact that while individual women produce rice, which is the staple of the individual family's diet, game is usually hunted by the men of the community collectively, and it is either sold for prestige goods (cloth, brass wire, and other products, which are used in the payment of brideprices and the resolution of feuds), or distributed through the community as a whole. On a cultural level, game is the most desirable part of the diet, and while Ilongots minimize expressions of sexual asymmetry, an examination of the similes used in magic suggests that hunting is equated with headhunting, that killing of animals is like killing of men, which is a focal cultural theme (cf. R. Rosaldo 1970a).

Using the methods described earlier, we drew up a complete list of the similes used in all hunting and agricultural spells respectively. Out of a list of some 40 (cf. M. Rosaldo n.d.) only one, which compares hunt dogs and rice to a sweet potato plant—which has many and closely spaced roots—is found in both kinds of spells. Beyond this, most of the similes used for hunting have violent connotations. Hunt dogs are compared to songs which celebrate the headhunter, to duelling, and to the loud call of a bird whose beak is a headhunter's ornament. They are equated with violent natural images, like whirlpools, rapids, lightning, rushing wind and water; with the crash of pollarded branches and overgrowth that falls in the forest; with destructive, inedible animals, like roaches, bees, crocodiles, and pythons; with exchanging betel, which suggests a gift to any enemy; with fish which jump; with boiling water; with harpoon arrows; and with large-scale destructive fires. The bow is said to kill like the bows of Negritoes, who are known to use poison on their arrows. The gun claps like drums which celebrate the return of successful killers. And game is compared to flowing water, to ants, and to stars in the sky. Most of these images suggest violence, destruction, and quantity. While one might imagine equations of hunt dogs, bows, or whatever, with pacific images of closeness, a good harvest, success, the Ilongots have chosen to use similes to signify those features which hunting shares with killing. Taken together, most of these similes can be seen to be saying the same thing; and spells, by aligning these diverse images of violence, equate hunting, a mere productive activity, with a 'key symbol', an idea of great cultural significance: the headhunter's taking of life.

It is more difficult to isolate a single theme which underlies the similes in spells for agriculture. Some can be interpreted in juxtaposition with complementary images for hunting. Thus, while game is like stars, rice is like clouds, and where hunt dogs are equated with destructive fires, the rice is said to be warm like the fires one lights in the hearth. Hunting similes suggest wildness, action, and quantity, while those used in agriculture indicate domesticity, passivity, and mass. This becomes clear in a number of additional examples. Rice is to 'cling' like rattan vines (and rattans have domestic uses), to be anchored like a banana, and to flourish like a few other cultivated plants; it is compared to solid rock formations, to deep pools, to sand which cannot be counted, to a plant which clings to a rock. And the harvester, too, is anchored, like a bug which burrows in the ground, or another which spins in the water. Agriculture, in these similes, is pictured as domestic, passive, and certain, none of which are virtues that are celebrated in the hunt.

Thus, where the metaphorical uses of plants suggest an equation between hunting and agriculture, the images used in similes suggest crucial differences in the emotional orientations and cultural themes associated with women and men. Hunting is violent; gardening passive. Hunting involves killing; agriculture, a kind of sympathy between the gardener and her desired object, the rice. Since headhunting is an activity which both men and women admire, the importance of hunting and, we would argue, of male activities in general, is communicated in these spells through the simile frame which transforms a complementary conception into an asymmetrical one. If hunting is like headhunting, it is also an act of will and of discipline, an activity of utmost cultural value.

ADDITIONAL EVIDENCE

By examining sets of metaphors used in spells for agriculture and hunting, we have seen that they are concerned with two opposed cultural conceptions. The use of plants and plant verbs signifies sexual complementarity and equality; male and female activities are comparable for the Ilongots because both involve the production of food. Expressions used in the simile frame point, however, to an asymmetrical conception. Hunting is equated with killing, with the most focal of cultural traditions, and so men, because they are violent, may be seen as superior to women and the functions they fulfil.

Additional, less systematic, evidence permits us to complete our description. If hunting and agriculture are conceived to be in opposition, logical considerations alone would suggest that, as hunting involves life-taking, agriculture might well be associated with the giving, or creation, of life. No such association appears in the spells we have considered; moving from those to other kinds of cultural expressions, however, we find some suggestions of their availability in the repertory of Ilongot ideas.

(a) Ilongot gardeners identify their own life with the health and 'heart' of their rice crop. A woman who has begun harvesting will be reluctant, for example, to visit another's garden for fear that the 'heart' of her own rice will go to a neighbour's field. Again, after the harvest, the woman places some newly harvested stalks on her head, asking that the rice hearts live as long as she does, and that rice, like a woman, 'be big' where it is stacked.

(b) Earlier in the agricultural cycle, rice plants are treated like young children. While the plants are still growing, the woman bathes them—much as a mother bathes a new baby—to make them fat. When the

59

unripe panicles are full and almost ready to be harvested, they are described as 'pregnant'. And, finally, the harvester's bundle of collected herbs is combined with rice stalks, in a manner which suggests the 'rice baby' of freak ears used in Malay magic (cf. Endicott 1970), and it is 'given a body' with betel spit—which, in myths, has been known to give life to skeletons and bones.

Without further evidence, these suggestions of an equation between agriculture and childbirth must, of course, remain tentative; and the fact that the association is, at best, a weak one may itself be of importance (see below). If, however, we are willing to assume that Ilongot conceptions of subsistence activities are constrained by, and represent one variant of, a universally available pattern, we can diagram the metaphorical relations between hunting and gardening in the manner illustrated below (*Figure 2*).

Figure 2   Hunting and agriculture in Ilongot cultural conceptions

	Male (Life-Taking)		*Female (Life-Giving)*	
	headhunting	hunting	agriculture	childbirth
headhunting		A. good association, similes	B1	B2
hunting			A. strong association; plants	B3
agriculture				A. weak association

All 'A's' in the diagram indicate some kind of positive association—between agriculture and childbirth (or life-giving), hunting and killing, and, perhaps the strongest, between gardening and the hunt. We claim that this paradigm is an adequate representation of the relationships signified in Ilongot magical metaphors, and, similarly, that it characterizes a system of deep, pervasive, and widely ramifying cultural concerns. If this is correct, we would further expect to find expressions in Ilongot cultural practice which indicate the negative relations, or incompatibilities, of all combinations marked as B. In fact, these are available.

B1. Returning headhunters, wearing ornaments which indicate their success, are not permitted to enter a rice garden; through this prohibition, killing and gardening are opposed. Shedding blood in the garden —through leech bites, cuts, or even sacrifice—is also thought to endanger the growing rice.

B2. A myth suggests the incompatibilities of headhunting and childbirth. In it, a man takes his wife's head at her granary and then brings her to life. After they have lived together for a while, he sets off hunting, and instructs her to appear again at the granary—presumably to be killed—if she has not yet given birth. On returning from his hunt, the man sees that his wife is absent from the granary and tells it to fill itself with rice if the child is a female, and to be emptied if the baby is a male.

This episode occurs twice, and he has both male and female children. Had the wife failed to give birth in both instances, death rather than birth would have been the outcome, since she would have been beheaded.

B3. Evidence here (as with the positive associations between agriculture and childbirth) is weakest. Ilongots do, however, say that contact with women can damage a man's prowess in the hunt; the cure, in such a case, is the same as the ritual which is used to make a newborn baby grow. What is suggested here, though weakly, is that female fertility is dangerous; the ritual which promotes the natural development of a child is used to counteract a man's polluted state.

What does all of this tell us? Essentially, we claim to have identified a covert set of structural relationships which governs the selection of a variety of stereotyped cultural expressions, and which, in turn, is invoked every time a gardener or hunter performs an appropriate magical spell. The 'strength' of the various articulations of the model depends, in turn, on the strength of these associations in Ilongot culture. The evidence from plant metaphors is most powerful because these signify the symmetry and complementarity of men and women, an idea of equality pervading most aspects of Ilongot social life. The contradictory statement, of man's violence and superiority, corresponds to the fact that cultures universally recognize some form of sexual asymmetry;[7] male dominance, epitomized in headhunting, is, then, indicated in the similes used in these spells. The other relations, both positive and negative, were derived on the basis of less explicit evidence. This, we suggest, reflects the fact that, while they are available or 'present' in the Ilongot cultural system, they do not correspond to conceptions which Ilongots choose to stress. Ilongots place little emphasis on female sexuality or fertility; there are no rituals surrounding childbirth or sterility; menstrual taboos are absent as are any other explicit statements of woman's lesser status. Strong statements linking agriculture and fertility would, we suggest, emphasize woman's 'otherness', and, implicitly, her inferiority, and would therefore be incompatible with the egalitarian ethos which governs much of Ilongot life.

MAN THE HUNTER AND WOMAN

Anthropological tradition has nurtured the myth of an early 'man the hunter', the wilful creator of the first forms of culture and society. But just as man the hunter relied upon woman as food-gatherer, child-bearer, and companion, so conceptions of hunting enter a system of relationships which includes the activities of woman as well as man. Our analysis of Ilongot magical metaphors has shown, for one particular culture, that ideas about hunting and gardening are linked as terms of a fundamental opposition between life-giving and life-taking. Here, we will suggest that the structural principle underlying this set of cultural expressions is not unique to Ilongot culture, but governs cultural characterizations of the sexes around the world.

Beginning with the basic opposition of taking life and giving it, a set of logical connections can be constructed that relate the life-sustaining and life-destroying tasks of women and men. We can start with the place of hunting in this set. As a form of killing, hunting shares with warfare the act of destroying life and, like warfare, it is limited, with very few exceptions, to men. Cultural conceptions of hunting and warfare may be associated as male activities and subordinated under the rubric of life-taking, which in turn is defined in relation to cultural conceptions of its opposite, an exclusively female act, the giving of life through birth. Regardless of the degree of participation allotted to men by different cultural theories of procreation (cf. Leach 1961: Chapter I), women are indisputably associated with the birth and nurturance of the human infant; their bodies are the locus of earliest biological growth. If childbirth is the opposite of killing with respect to life, preparation of food may be regarded as the opposite of hunting with respect to economic productivity—that is, in its destructive aspect, hunting can be associated with warfare; in its productive aspect, with the gathering, growing, or preparing of food. The association of hunting and warfare is based upon the identity of the act of killing, as well as upon identical actors, men. The association of motherhood and the preparation of food is less direct. Metaphors may liken the preparer of food to the nursing mother, or compare the fertility of plants to the fertility of women. The ordering of relationships may be illustrated in the following way:

Life-giving	*Life-taking*
motherhood	warfare
cultivation, gathering, preparation of food[8]	hunting

In the remainder of this paper, we shall discuss how this paradigm and the possibilities for associations among its elements serve as a structural framework underlying culturally diverse representations of the sexes. This paradigm isolates as well some highly general, if not universal, considerations which lend an evaluative cast to symbolic statements about the relations of women and men. This evaluative aspect of our paradigm may best be illustrated by reviewing the Ilongot example.

In the analysis above, Ilongot metaphors were seen to build upon the complementarity of men's and women's contributions to production. Diagrammed in terms of the model outlined here, the Ilongot metaphors take the following form:

Figure 3

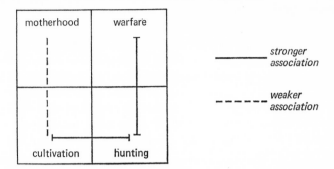

Because of their emphasis upon the commonalities of men's and women's economic contributions, we suggested that Ilongot magical metaphors reflect the relatively egalitarian relations of the sexes in the Ilongot social world. At the same time, we saw that men's hunting was distinguished from and elevated above women's gardening through its symbolic affinities with headhunting. Women's gardening, by contrast, was only weakly associated with childbirth. In fact, Ilongot culture provides almost no symbolic elaboration upon the themes of birth and biological fertility. As men's complements and near equals, Ilongot women come to view their social and productive roles in an idiom which minimizes their differences from men.

The Ilongot system would appear to represent one variant of a life-giving/life-taking opposition which we assume to be quite general. It is our contention that ties between male activities (and hunting in particular) and killing provide people everywhere with a symbolic idiom which ranks and differentiates the roles of women and men. The ways in which particular cultures elaborate upon the poles of the opposition reflect variations in the social relations and cultural valuations of the sexes: emphasis on economic complementarity suggests a relatively egalitarian system; emphasis on biological fertility, absent among the Ilongots, seems to be found in cultures where the sexes are seen as different and unequal by natural right. Though we are aware that women elsewhere gain ritual and social value through cultural recognition of their reproductive functions, we imagine that emphasis on these functions derives ultimately from an assumption of deep-seated inequality. The celebration of motherhood and female sexuality implies a definition of womankind in terms of nature and biology; it traps women in their physical being, and thereby in the very general logic which declares them less capable of transcendence and of cultural achievement than men.

To outline the beginnings of a comparative use of our model, we can now bring in evidence from some other cultures within the Malay Archipelago historically and linguistically related to the Ilongots, noting differences in the ways in which common symbolic elements are

63

integrated into particular cultural schemes. Though we know of no other studies for this area which present fully comparable sets of data, a few preliminary comparisons will highlight the appropriateness of the Ilongot analysis and illustrate the value of the analytical perspective developed here.

Drawing upon ethnographic accounts for the Philippines and Indonesia, we shall consider first the relations within the vertical columns of our paradigm, that is, between hunting and warfare, and between cultivation and motherhood, then treat relations between the life-giving and life-taking columns. As observed earlier, the relation between hunting and warfare (which includes headhunting and human sacrifice in this area) is based on the fact that both are forms of killing. In considering cultural metaphors for the two, it is often difficult to separate references to one from references to the other. Comparing a man to his arrow, as the Ilongot do, or to his spear or dagger as in a common Ngaju metaphor (Schärer 1963: 77), may connote hunting or warfare, since the weapons for both are the same. Allusions to shields (e.g. Barton 1930: 176) distinguish warfare from hunting; allusions to dogs (e.g. Ilongot, *supra*) seem more appropriate to the hunt. The point to be made is that the association between hunting and warfare is a very likely one, and one that is drawn by cultures in the area. The Ifugao, for example, make the same invocation to the same set of gods when setting out on a hunting expedition and when preparing for a head hunting raid (e.g. Barton 1930: 159; 1946: 105, 141). Ilongots perform a modified version of their headhunting ritual to celebrate a young boy's first successful hunt.

There appears to be more variation on the life-giving side of the paradigm among the cultures of island Southeast Asia. Indonesian and Philippine groups are largely nonunilineal in descent and relatively egalitarian in terms of sex roles—a fact which makes it unlikely that child-bearing and female reproduction will be of as much political and economic importance as they are for, say, some societies with unilineal descent. At the same time, childbirth and cultivation may be metaphorically linked. Explicit birth imagery in the context of agricultural rites is found throughout the area, suggesting that female fertility serves as an idiom for associating the women cultivators and their crops. Endicott (1970: 23, 133–136, 146–153), in his study of Malay magic, analyses the 'rice baby' practices of the Malay Peninsula. At the rice harvest in this area, a bundle of rice is collected ceremoniously and saved so as to preserve, it seems, the vitality of the rice for the coming year's crop. Generally it is the village midwife who collects these special stalks of rice and carries them like an infant to the owners of the rice field. The couple who own the field are called the parents of the rice baby and, at harvest time, the woman observes the prohibitions associated with childbirth. Both the rice baby and the human infant are protected from harm by an iron nail, which Endicott interprets as a barrier to keep the soul within the body and evil without. Similar rites are reported for cultures of Borneo (cf. Evans 1923: 19, 25–26). And, among many Philippine groups women perform special harvest ceremonies that suggest affinities to Malay rice rituals. We have mentioned already how Ilongot women bathe young rice plants as though they were infants. In the Davao district of Mindanao, the female shamans who lead the agricultural ceremonies are frequently midwives or celebrants of birth ceremonies as well (Cole 1913: 97, 174).

Women's fertility and plant fertility are symbolically related in other ways. Raats (1969: 29–30, 35–36) discusses a myth concerning the origin of rice from the body, often the dismembered body, of a dead woman; he cites occurrences of related myths among such varied groups as the Javanese, the Dusun of Borneo, the Manggarai of Flores, and the Bagobo and the Bukidnon of Mindanao. In a Moluccan version recorded among the Wemale of Ceram, root crops rather than rice grow from the woman's corpse. A variation of this theme from the Tempassuk district of Borneo tells of a creator couple who chop up their child, and bury the pieces, thereby causing rice and other edible plants to sprout (Evans 1923: 45–46). In all of these myths, the offspring of women's bodies become plant foods, not people; this image unites women's reproductive functions and their role as providers of plant food.[9]

In discussing cultural expressions of life-giving and life-taking in island Southeast Asia, we have focused thus far on relations between elements of the same column in our model; our earlier comments would suggest, however, that for any given culture the elements within a single column must depend upon the relations between columns as well. A comparison of Ilongot and Ngaju (South Borneo) metaphors for women and men neatly illustrates this point. Ilongot orators refer to a woman as rice, to a man as an arrow. Among the Ngaju, a spear or dagger is a common metaphor for a man; a woman is likened to a *lunok* or fig tree (Schärer 1963: 77). In both sets of metaphors, men are being compared to weapons, women to plants. In the Ilongot case, the primary illusion of the rice metaphor is to women's economic productivity. For instance, a suitor may state obliquely the purpose of his visit by saying he had 'come to borrow some rice seed' (M. Rosaldo 1971: 82–83). The meaning of this metaphor is bound up in women's role as cultivators. The import of the Ngaju metaphor appears to derive from an association between women's fertility and plant fertility; babies are said to fall at birth from the Tree of Life, represented by the *lunok*, and, should an infant die, its coffin is placed in a fig tree with the hope that its soul will be reborn to the mother as another child (Schärer 1963: 77, 85). Woman as mother is contrasted to man as hunter–warrior in the Ngaju metaphors; woman as cultivator is contrasted to man as hunter–warrior in the Ilongot metaphors.

This comparison is especially interesting in the light of the fact that

Figure 4

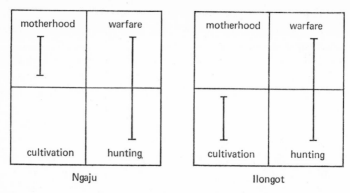

Ngaju   Ilongot

the Ngaju, more than other peoples in this area, show a striking concern with female fertility. Fertility pervades Ngaju religious thought. The female ritual specialists, the *balian*, are drawn from the ranks of slave women. Along with male transvestites, they preside at all the ceremonies, except those involving the sacred dead performed for headhunting, warfare, the clearing of new fields, or threats to the harvest (Schärer 1963: 147). What is more, the *balian* are conceptualized as representatives of the godhead, who embrace the sponsors of certain rituals as if they were babies (ibid: 137). *Balian* serve also as temple prostitutes (ibid: 58), thereby spanning the short gap between female sexuality and reproduction. The Ngaju priestess shares a name (*balian* is cognate with a word for female ritual specialists elsewhere in the area) and ritual duties with other female shamans in the Archipelago, but her role as prostitute carries further the explicit expression of life-giving through female fertility. At the same time, her low social status suggests that fertility, however important, is less valued than the warring accomplishments of men. The Ilongots, by contrast, seem relatively egalitarian; they build symbolically upon the economic complementarity of husbands and their wives.

That the symbolic expressions for the activities of both men and women should be taken together can be illustrated as well in regard to headhunting and human sacrifice. Since the days of Sir James Frazer, many scholars have assumed an automatic association between bloodletting and themes of agricultural fertility, or of death and childbirth (e.g. Hutton 1928). In fact, among a number of Philippine groups, headhunting is primarily a means for men to obtain prestige, and is not justified further as contributing to the welfare of crops or human life (cf. Jenks 1905: 174–5).

In the terms of our paradigm, possibilities range from complete segregation of headhunting from any association with women's life-giving functions, to a positive influence of headhunting upon plant and human increase; killing which grants fertility can be read as a statement of male dominance over women's productive lives. Three examples from Northern Luzon illustrate points along this continuum. Among the Ilongot, headhunting is segregated totally from both agriculture and childbirth. The headhunting rites of the Isneg, far to the north, have nothing to do with agriculture (Keesing 1962: 8), but show some affinities to motherhood. For example, the same ceremony is performed to celebrate the taking of a head and to prevent the death of a child (Vanoverbergh 1954: 233). The incompatibility of motherhood and killing is also suggested in Isneg culture. Women are forbidden to eat dog meat, which is the sacrifice of warriors (Vanoverbergh 1954: 248). Also, the Isneg mention a malady that may afflict a female shaman—always a married woman (Vanoverbergh 1954: 265)—filling her with a desire to kill and driving her to wield a headaxe until she is forcibly restrained; death is sure to follow such possession (Vanoverbergh 1953: 559; 1954: 245). The Ifugao stand in contrast to both Ilongot and Isneg. For them, a conscious motive in headhunting is to contribute to the fertility of crops, women, and domestic animals (Barton 1930: 197). Headhunters pray for fertility and increase (Barton 1946: 146, 200). Mock headhunting rites may be performed to cure barrenness (ibid: 156). Women ambush men returning from a successful raid and compare the men's bravery in the headhunt to the greater bravery they themselves exhibit in giving birth to the men (Barton 1930: 169). Headhunters invoke the Gods of Reproduction (ibid: 158). In short, among the Ilongots, headhunting is segregated from cultivation and women's fertility; among the Isneg there are weak associations between headhunting and motherhood, and none between headhunting and cultivation; among the Ifugao, the headhunter asserts symbolic control over both forms of female life-giving.

Several important differences in social structure appear to support these differences in symbolic expression. The Ilongot and the Isneg are swidden cultivators and hunters; women are primarily responsible for rice cultivation, and men prefer to hunt. Due to the nature of swidden farming, villages move over time, and lasting property rights in land are not of great concern. The Ifugao, on the other hand, are wet rice farmers whose terraces represent years of human effort; rights in land are passed on for generations among kin. Ifugao women do a major portion of the agricultural labour, but men's social status is closely bound up in ownership of rice terraces and the size of their yields (Barton 1922: 400); in contrast, prestige for plentiful rice harvests accrues to the Ilongot woman who worked the field, not to her husband. Ifugao agricultural ceremonies are officiated by male, rather than female, priests, in contrast to the other two cases. The birth of children is a focal legal and economic matter in Ifugao life because of transmission of property rights—concerns that are absent among the Isneg and the Ilongot. Whereas Ifugao marriages generally dissolve if no children are born to the union (Lambrecht 1935: 174), it is not infrequent among the Isneg (Vanoverbergh 1938: 189, 220) and the Ilongot

67

that childless couples will remain married. These differences have their parallel in the fact that headhunting is separated from birth and agriculture among the Isneg and the Ilongot, but has direct implications for women's childbearing and economic productivity in the Ifugao case. For Ilongot and Isneg, there is, then, evidence of a separate and complementary relation between men's and women's spheres of activity in social relations and in symbolization; among the Ifugao, by contrast, men exert symbolic influence over women's productive and reproductive services, which, in turn, have immediate importance for men's political and economic careers.

From this brief review of some symbolic characterizations of men and women in island Southeast Asia, it can be seen that a number of different combinations of elements within our paradigm occur. Women's biological fertility is used by some cultures more than others as an idiom for women's life-giving activities; among the Ngaju this emphasis dominates religious conceptions of women; among the Ilongot it is developed only slightly. Female fertility is used in some cases—in the rice baby observances of the Malay groups, for example—as an idiom of women's association with their crops. The relations between women's life-giving and men's life-taking are spelled out differently as well in different symbolic expressions. Among the Ilongot, the biological opposition between the two is played down and the economic complementarity of cultivation and hunting is stressed. The Isneg case seems similar, but the biological opposition may be slightly more overt. In the Ifugao case, women's life-giving functions come under partial domination by men's life-taking ones; within the scope of our comparison, they appear to be a relatively asymmetrical case. Finally, the culture area which we have been treating is noted for its highly egalitarian relations between the sexes. Application of the paradigm outlined here to characterizations of women and men in other parts of the world, will show, we expect, even more elaboration of the asymmetrical functions of giving and taking life.[10]

CONCLUSIONS

At the start of this paper, we posed our concern for the place of general considerations in the analysis of particulars. Assuming that certain oppositional principles constrain and organize cultural expressions universally, we sought to understand their realization in one culture's symbolic schemes. By examining the metaphors which Ilongots use in magic, we showed how a wealth of diverse images provides a redundant and affectively laden statement of the meanings which Ilongots assign to the relations of the sexes. The vivid and concrete imagery of spells speaks directly to the needs and aspirations of Ilongot cultivators and hunters. At the same time, systematic connections among metaphors give sense and order to individual experience by relating it to more

abstract and generalized concerns. In interpreting the order underlying metaphors used in magic, we related them to an opposition between life-giving and life-taking, which, we imagine, provides a framework for conceptualization of the sexes in diverse cultural settings.
Consideration of this framework indicated, first, that magical metaphors
are systematically linked to other symbolic expressions in Ilongot
culture, and second, that symbolic characterizations of men and
women among the Ilongots represent a locally appropriate and intelligible articulation of universal themes. The general implications of our
approach were illustrated by a brief comparative analysis.

In our discussion, we have then assumed that symbolic characterizations of men and women in any culture are shaped by social and
ideological factors, and that representations of one sex are dependent
upon representations of the other. The particular symbolic expressions
found in a culture are in no way natural or inevitable. They are choices
from a number of possibilities expressed in the life-giving/life-taking
paradigm and conditioned by forms of social life. Furthermore, we have
assumed that the two sides of the paradigm are never equal. In all
cultures, men's spheres of activity are more highly valued than women's
(M. Rosaldo 1974); and, for this reason, it seems likely that emphasis
upon female biological reproduction indicates a sense of asymmetry
in status between women and men.[11] This assumption, of course,
underlies our claim that the most egalitarian possibility is one which
stresses economic complementarity. The Ilongots elaborate this mode of
expression, although they also highlight the importance of life-taking
in the hunt. Hunting, through its association with headhunting, is
elevated above the productive activities of women. At the same time,
the relative lack of emphasis on female reproduction minimizes a
sense of women's difference from, and implicitly, their inferiority to,
men.

But the question remains—in what sense is men's taking of life more
valued than women's childbearing? How can we assume that in a world
where men are killers, cultural emphases on the maternal role, female
fertility, and female sexuality in general, necessarily imply that women
are, in some sense, less than men?

The general evaluative implications of the life-giving/life-taking
opposition are suggested by the fact that killing and childbearing tend
to be represented asymmetrically; metaphors for men and killing, as
against those for women and childbirth, associate men with cultural
activities and women with natural growth.[12] Men may work in the
forest, but they do so in the name of culture, and while women are, in
our examples, compared to rice and fig trees, men are portrayed as
spears and arrows. Further, men, in many cultures, can assume female
reproductive roles symbolically, but women are almost everywhere
denied a positive role in taking life. In cultural forms as diverse as the
couvade, sub-incision, 'male menstruation', headhunting which grants

69

fertility, and initiations marked by imagery of birth, men engage in what appears to be a valued and auspicious androgynous existence. The converse—the assumption of life-taking roles by women—is generally regarded as unnatural and undesirable. Female killers are portrayed as sterile, virginal, and, so, incomplete as women, or as violent, childhaters, mockers of group integrity, and imagers of in-auspicious times. Athena and Artemis in Greek mythology, Amazons who amputate their breasts so as better to draw their bows, the Mother Snake of Arnhem Land who swallows her own children, Ndembu women dressed as hunters to symbolize sterility, Gogo women mas-querading as violent men to 'turn around' bad fortune—these diverse representations of women as killers derive their impact from the anti-thesis of motherhood and the violence of taking life.

Motherhood is incompatible with killing, but then men conceptual-ized as killers can, and often do, assume positively valued symbolic roles associated with giving life. To understand the roots of this asym-metry we need to ask two questions. First, why are men and women, who play diverse and important roles in economics, politics, and religion, regarded almost everywhere as killers and childbearers? And, second, why do the experience and meanings linked to these conceptions give them an opposed and evaluative sense? The answer to the first question must lie in an account of the social fact of sexual asymmetry, the fact that men in all known social systems have been allotted roles of authority, dominance, and prestige. The opposition between life-giving and life-taking provides cultural terms in which to conceptualize and rationalize social asymmetry. Considering these structural poles in terms of their potential as 'key symbols', we can see why this might be the case.

Killing, unlike childbirth, grants men wilful control over the pro-cesses of nature, and, in particular, over the natural processes of life and death. Such an association is made explicit for cultural interpre-tations of forms of killing as distinct as warfare in New Guinea (Gardiner, in Heider 1972: 75) and live burial among certain African groups (Lienhardt 1961). We would suggest, then, that the critical difference between giving and taking life is rooted in the fact that a man's killing is always an act of will, directed towards a body other than his own; giving life through childbirth, on the other hand, is a natural function of a woman's own body, and usually is something over which she has little intentional control. Men's life-taking, because of its intentionality, becomes a means of culturally transcending the biological; whereas childbearing, despite values attached to it as the means of perpetuating a social group, remains grounded in the 'naturalness' of women's sexual constitution. It has been clear, since the writings of Freud, that we cannot dismiss the notion that sexuality is problematic for humans. And because women conceptualized as childbearers are less easily dissociated from their sexual functions than

70

men are, the female side of the life-giving/life-taking model is likely to be one of cultural and psychological ambivalence.

The terms of our structural opposition are, then, by no means arbitrary. The very feelings and experiences which give universal plausibility to conceptions of the sexes as childbearers and killers also, we are suggesting, lend these conceptions an evaluative cast. In de Beauvoir's words, 'it is not in giving life but in risking life that man is raised above the animal; that is why superiority has been accorded in humanity not to the sex that brings forth but to that which kills' (1952: 58).

To this we would add only one qualification: the fact that the sexes have often been epitomized as life-givers and life-takers itself requires explanation—an understanding of the roots of sexual hierarchy in the human social world.

Notes

1. 'Ilongot' is the name which, since the eighteenth century, has been used in the ethnographic literature to designate a Philippine group of Malayo-Polynesian speakers who refer to themselves and their language as *bugkalut* (untranslated) or *qiruNut* ('from the forest'). In 1967–69, Renato and Michelle Rosaldo did the first systematic work on their social organization and culture (R. Rosaldo 1970a: M. Rosaldo 1971), the latter's research being supported by a National Institutes of Health Pre-doctoral Fellowship and Research Grant (5 FI MH-33, 243-02 BEH-A). Materials presented in this paper were collected during that study, and also by Jane M. Atkinson, who visited the Ilongots for some months in 1972, under the support of a National Science Foundation Graduate Fellowship. We would like to thank Michael Dove, Paul Friedrich, Caroline Ifeka, Bridget O'Laughlin, Sherry B. Ortner, Renato Rosaldo, and Arthur Wolf for their comments on an early draft of this paper, and Demetrio Mendoza, of the Philippine National Museum, for his identification of plants.

2. All varieties of magic are called *nawnaw*, and these are further distinguished as medicines (*sambal*), preparations (*qaimet*), and a few other kinds of spells; most informants consider headhunting spells (*kuiri*), along with spells for agriculture and hunting, a kind of *qaimet*. Within the category *sambal*, cures range from a few words and a simple plant recipe (like the tea for bloody diarrhoea) to complex metaphorical performances which are considered to be the real or 'true' *nawnaw*, to ceremonies accompanied by sacrifice and possibly trance. 'True' *nawnaw* used in medicinal contexts are formally similar to the spells discussed below.

3. Expressions in quotation marks are English glosses for Ilongot plant names. Expressions without quotation marks correspond to explanations offered in, or inferred from, Ilongot statements concerning the magical properties of these plants.

4. These plant names overlap with one another in their referents. For a discussion of the significance of this fact, see M. Rosaldo (1972).

5. The free access Ilongot women have to the forest and its plants may be contrasted to the prohibitions the Lele of Central Africa place upon women entering the forest, the scene of the hunt and the source of 'sacred medicines'. Although the forest is also the site of many of their daily tasks, Lele women are barred from the forest every third day as well as upon a variety of ritual occasions (Douglas 1954:4).

71

6. The argument that wild plants have an 'unmarked' status in the Ilongot repertory is supported by the following observations (cf. Greenberg 1966). *Raqek*,
the word for all plants used in magic, also has the following senses: it is the
superordinate designator of plant life in general; it means 'wild' as opposed to
'cultivated' (*sinanem*) species; within wild plants, it distinguishes 'herbs and
grasses' from 'vines' (*wakar*) and 'trees' (*keyu*). *Raqek*, as 'wild plant', seems
to be the unmarked member in the contrastive pair wild/cultivated, both
because it is retained in neutralization as the superordinate term and because
there is more differentiation within the wild than the cultivated category. Wild
plants appear, in other words, to 'typify' plant life in general. And we imagine
that magical plants are called *raqek* because they are typically wild as well.
The argument that 'forest' is 'unmarked' relative to 'garden' is less con-
clusive. That the two form a contrastive set is indicated in *Figure 1*, p. 56.
Distinctions within this set are 'neutralized', e.g. in the fact that both are associated with spells called *qaimet* and both with the disease *beut*. Our impression
is that Ilongots in speaking of either *qaimet* or *beut* will assume that they refer
to forest and hunting, unless further contextual information indicates that
garden and cultivation are concerned.
7. The claim that sexual asymmetry is, at present, a cultural universal, is documented in M. Rosaldo (1974) and Ortner (1974b).
8. For convenience, we shall refer simply to cultivation in the discussion that
follows because our examples will be drawn from agricultural societies.
9. P. E. de Josselin de Jong has interpreted such myths as expressing the
generation of life from death. Our approach which considers sex roles as important to the understanding of cultural meanings finds additional significance in
the sequence of these stories, namely the association of women's reproductive
and economic roles.
10. Victor Turner's analysis of Ndembu ritual provides an excellent illustration
of a more asymmetrical representation of the sexes. As Turner (1957: 25-28;
1967: 8, 280) observes, Ndembu ritual downplays women's economic contribution (subsistence farming), while it plays up hunting, the less steady and reliable
economic contribution of men. Of the Ndembu healing cults that are segregated
by sex, there are fertility cults for women and hunting cults for men (Turner
1967: 9-15). These two kinds of cults share symbols and medicines, such as the
musoli tree which is said to make game appear for hunters and children appear
for women (Turner 1967: 288-289; see also 1967: 42, 1957: 27-28). In one rite
an infertile woman is dressed like a hunter because, suggests Turner (1967: 42),
she is spilling blood, but not bearing children.
    Turner (1967: 280; see also 1957: 25-28) credits the symbolic emphasis on
men's hunting and women's reproductive functions to the societal tensions
between matriliny and virilocality; the emphasis upon women's biological
rather than economic production at once fits with the matrilineal theme of the
society and at the same time avoids calling attention to women's importance in
the economic sphere.
    Fitting Turner's material into our paradigm, we find a strong asymmetrical
association between hunting and motherhood, a weaker one between hunting
and cultivation (Turner 1957: 28), and a strong association between women's
crops and their children (ibid.). There seems to be an association of warfare and
hunting as well (e.g. Turner 1967: 42). The contrast between Ilongot and
Ndembu symbolic clusters is illustrated in the diagrams (*Figure 5*) on 73.
11. In arguing that cultural emphases on reproduction imply female inferiority,
we are not saying that women conceptualized as mothers may not have considerable social influence and value. The 'matrifocal' (cf. Tanner 1974) households and communities of Minangkabau, Atjeh, and Java—all within our area—
testify to the social and cultural importance which women as mothers can and

do achieve. From the point of view of women, cultural elaboration upon the themes of motherhood and fertility may well be a source of satisfaction. When, however, male and female roles and symbols are viewed in relation to one another, we tend to find that men are conceptualized as wise and disciplined killers, leaders, and ultimate authorities, and that women as mothers are barred from certain crucial and transcendent pursuits which are associated with men.

12. We are indebted to Ortner (1974b) for this observation and for many of the suggestions which follow.

Figure 5

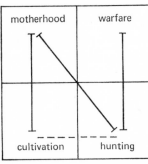

Ndembu

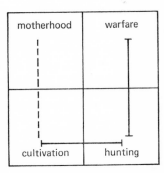

Ilongot

Bibliography

BARTON, R. F. 1922. Ifugao Economics. University of California Publications in American Archaeology and Ethnology **15**: 385–446.

— 1930. *The Half-Way Sun*. New York: Bewer and Warren.

— 1946. *The Religion of the Ifugaos*. No. 65, Memoir Series. Menasha, Wisconsin: American Anthropological Association.

COLE, FAY-COOPER 1913. The Wild Tribes of Davao District, Mindanao. Field Museum of Natural History, Publication 170. Anthropological Series, Vol. XII, No. 2, Chicago.

DE BEAUVOIR, SIMONE 1952. *The Second Sex*. New York: Knopf, original publication in French, 1949.

DOUGLAS, MARY 1954. The Lele of Kasai. In Daryll Forde (ed.), *African Worlds*. London: Oxford University Press.

ENDICOTT, KIRK M. 1970. *An Analysis of Malay Magic*. Oxford: Clarendon Press.

EVANS, IVOR H. N. 1923. *Studies in Religion, Folk-Lore and Custom in British North Borneo and the Malay Peninsula*. London: Cass, 1970.

FOX, JAMES J. 1972. Sister's Child as Plant: Metaphors in an Idiom of Consanguinity. In R. Needham (ed.), *Rethinking Kinship and Marriage*. London: Tavistock Publications.

GREENBERG, JOSEPH. 1966. Language Universals. In T. Sebeok (ed.), *Current Trends in Linguistics*, Vol. II. The Hague: Mouton.

HASTINGS, J. (ed.). *Encyclopaedia of Religion and Ethics*, Vol. II. Edinburgh: T. & T. Clark.

HEIDER, KARL 1972. *The Dani of West Irian*. Warner Modular Publications, Module 2.

HUTTON, J. H. 1928. The Significance of Head-hunting in Assam. *Journal of the Royal Anthropological Institute* **58**: 399–408.

JENKS, A. E. 1905. *The Bontoc Igorot*. Department of the Interior, Ethnological Survey Publications, Vol. 1. Manila: Bureau of Printing.

73

KEESING, F. M. 1962. The Isneg: Shifting Cultivators of the Northern Philippines. *Southwestern Journal of Anthropology* **18** (1).

LAMBRECHT, FRANCIS 1935. The Mayawyaw Ritual: 2. Marriage and Marriage Ritual. Catholic Anthropological Conference. Publications, Vol. IV, No. 2, pp. 169–325.

LANGER, SUSANNE 1942. *Philosophy in a New Key*. Cambridge: Harvard University Press.

LEACH, E. R. 1961. *Rethinking Anthropology*. London: The Athlone Press.

LÉVI-STRAUSS, CLAUDE 1970. *Tristes Tropiques*. New York: Atheneum, original publication in French, 1955.

LIENHARDT, GODFREY 1961. *Divinity and Experience*. Oxford: Clarendon Press.

MALINOWSKI, BRONISLAW 1966. *The Language of Magic and Gardening*. London: Allen & Unwin (first published as *The Coral Gardens and Their Magic*, Vol. II, 1935).

MUNN, NANCY. n.d. The Symbolism of Perceptual Qualities: A Study in Trobriand Ritual Aesthetics. Paper given at the Meetings of the American Anthropological. Association, New York, 1971.

ORTNER, SHERRY B. 1974a. On Key Symbols. *American Anthropologist*, in press.

— 1974b. Is Male to Female as Nature to Culture? In M. Rosaldo and L. Lamphere (eds.), *Woman, Culture and Society*. Stanford, Calif.: Stanford University Press.

PEPPER, STEPHEN 1942. *World Hypotheses*. Berkeley: University of California Press.

RAATS, P. J. 1969. *A Structural Study of Bagobo Myths and Rites*. Cebu City, Philippines: The University of San Carlos.

ROSALDO, MICHELLE Z. 1971. Context and Metaphor in Ilongot Oral Tradition. Unpublished Ph.D. dissertation. Harvard University.

— 1972. Metaphor and Folk Classification. *Southwestern Journal of Anthropology* **28** (1): 83–99.

— 1973. I Have Nothing to Hide: The Language of Ilongot Oratory. *Language in Society*, in press.

— 1974. Women, Culture and Society: A Theoretical Overview. In M. Rosaldo and L. Lamphere (eds.), *Woman, Culture and Society*. Stanford, Calif.: Stanford University Press.

n.d. It's All Uphill: The Creative Metaphors of Ilongot Magical Spells. To appear in A. Sanches and B. Blount (eds.), *Ritual Reality and Creativity in Language*. New York: Seminar Press, in press.

ROSALDO, RENATO I. 1970a. Ilongot Society: The Social Organization of a Non-Christian Group in Northern Luzon, Philippines. Unpublished Ph.D. dissertation, Harvard University.

— 1970b. Ilongot Kin Terms: A Bilateral System of Northern Luzon, Philippines. In *Proceedings* of VIIth International Congress of Anthropological and Ethnological Sciences, 1968. Tokyo: Science Council of Japan, 81–84.

SCHÄRER, HANS 1963. *Ngaju Religion*. Translated by R. Needham. The Hague: Martinus Nijhoff, first published in Dutch in 1946.

STRATHERN, ANDREW, and STRATHERN, MARILYN 1968. Marsupials and Magic: a Study of Spell Symbolism among the Mbowamb. In E. Leach (ed.), *Dialectic In Practical Religion*. Cambridge: Cambridge University Press.

TAMBIAH, S. J. 1968. The Magical Power of Words. *Man* **3** (2): 175–208.

TANNER, NANCY 1974. Matrifocality in Indonesia, Africa and Among Black Americans. In M. Rosaldo and L. Lamphere (eds.), *Woman, Culture and Society*. Stanford, Calif.: Stanford University Press.

TURNER, VICTOR 1957. *Schism and Continuity in an African Society*. Manchester: Manchester University Press.

— 1964a. Lunda Medicine and the Treatment of Disease. Rhodes-Livingstone Museum Occasional Paper No. 15. Livingstone: Rhodes-Livingstone Museum.

TURNER, VICTOR 1964b. Symbols in Ndembu Ritual. In M. Gluckman (ed.), *Closed Systems and Open Minds: The Limits of Naivety in Social Science.* Edinburgh: Oliver and Boyd.
— 1967. *The Forest of Symbols.* Ithaca: Cornell University Press.
VANOVERBERGH, MORICE 1938. The Isneg Life Cycle. II. Marriage, Death and Burial. Publications of the Catholic Anthropological Conference. *Publications,* Vol. III, No. 3, pp. 187–280.
— 1953. Religion and Magic among the Isneg Part II: The Shaman. *Anthropos* **48**: 557–568.
— 1954. Religion and Magic among the Isneg Part III: Public Sacrifices. *Anthropos* **49**: 233–275.
WITTGENSTEIN, LUDWIG 1953. *Philosophical Investigations.* (Translated by G. E. M. Anscombe from German, 1949.) New York: Macmillan; Oxford: Blackwell.

David McKnight

Men, Women, and Other Animals
Taboo and Purification among the Wik-mungkan

INTRODUCTION

In this paper I discuss taboos and purification rites among the Wik-mungkan, an Australian Aboriginal society. Kinship dominates the Wik-mungkan social world and, while it may not explain everything about it, there are few social activities and beliefs which can be understood without taking kinship into account. This is especially true of the subject-matter of this paper. As we shall see, certain acts make people and things *ngaintja* (taboo, see below) to those in particular relationships. Hence, to grasp the working of *ngaintja* and purification rites one needs some knowledge of the Wik-mungkan kinship and marriage system—conversely, since the taboos and purification rites are the kinship and marriage system in action, they help us to understand the latter which, *inter alia*, reflect the superiority of wife-givers over wife-receivers.

But there is another level of explanation which goes beyond kinship and marriage, and involves Wik-mungkan ideas about men and women, and their definition of man. Hence only in the first part of this paper is there much about kinship and marriage. Thus I first deal with the consequences of stepping over things and how one may deliberately make someone *ngaintja* by swearing a part of his or her body, and in this context I consider in detail how various kin and affines may or may not be affected. I then discuss faeces and menstrual taboos. Next I turn to the *ngaintja* beliefs surrounding the major *rites de passage* of death, birth, and initiation and I discuss Wik-mungkan ideas about the differences between men and women, and man's place in the animal world, and why men, taken collectively, are always *ngaintja* to women, or are more *ngaintja* than women. The term *ngaintja* is difficult to translate; but Thomson (1935: 483), who undoubtedly had a flair for languages, considers it to mean 'taboo'. McConnel (1935: 83), who also spoke Wik-mungkan, gives a similar translation, i.e. 'forbidden'. Certain places, people, substances, and actions, such as totemic sites, a man's mother-in-law, menstrual blood, a man defecating can be *ngaintja*. There are degrees of being *ngaintja;* the suffix *taiyin* is added to

77

indicate that something is very taboo or very forbidden, i.e. *ngaintjataiyin*. Sometimes there are unfortunate mystical consequences; sometimes not. People may be absolutely scandalized at even the suggestion of *ngaintja* act (as, for instance, a man going near the place where a woman gave birth), while other *ngaintja* acts may elicit no more than a surprised puckering of the lips. I consider that Thomson and McConnel have given a reasonable translation of *ngaintja*, but since it is a technical term I prefer to use the indigenous word.

The Wik-mungkan formerly inhabited much of the territory between the mouths of the Archer–Watson Rivers and the middle reaches of the Holroyd River on the west coast of Cape York Peninsula, in Northern Queensland. There are two main groups of Wik-mungkan: one of these traditionally resided around the Kendall and Holroyd Rivers, while the other, to the north of them, lived in an area between the Archer–Watson and Kendall Rivers. Although the two groups are socially similar, yet they differ in a number of significant respects, so I would like to emphasize that when I use the term 'Wik-mungkan' I am referring to the latter. Almost all of them, with others from closely related tribes, are now living in a Presbyterian Mission village at Aurukun, while many of the Holroyd River people reside in a Government settlement at Edward River.

STEPPING-OVER

Stepping over anything makes it *ngaintja* for persons in certain relationships. For example, a man may not eat food that his son or daughter has stepped over; to a woman her son is a possible source of making things *ngaintja*—she need have little fear of her daughter's actions. Generally speaking, while a man must be careful of both son and daughter, a woman must be particularly wary of her son's actions. Because of these *ngaintja* fears, children are soon taught not to cross in front of their parents, especially their father, but to step behind them. It is said that these taboos hold even for very small children, but the actions of a toddler are normally ignored. Although parents cannot cause things to be *ngaintja* for their children by this action, yet I noticed that most mothers and fathers avoided stepping over objects directly in front of their children. Nowadays, in the small European dwellings that many of the Wik-mungkan occupy, there is some rather awkward squeezing and moving about, particularly at mealtimes, in order not to step over things in front of other members of the household.

Among siblings the stepping-over taboo is more complex, for in their case age categories must also be considered. The Wik-mungkan make a distinction between elder brother (*wunya*) and younger brother (*ponta*) as well as between elder sister (*yapa*) and younger sister (*wila*). Anything that an elder brother has stepped over is *ngaintja* for his younger brother and sister, but what *they* have stepped over is not *ngaintja* for him. Similarly, an elder sister can make things *ngaintja* for her younger brother but not *vice versa*. Between sisters there is no fear of this type of taboo.

The superiority of wife-givers over wife-receivers is reflected in the *ngaintja* beliefs. Wife-givers can make objects *ngaintja* for wife-receivers, but not *vice versa*. Thus I may not take anything that my wife's brother has stepped over but he is not prevented from taking anything that I have stepped over. There is a similar pattern of behaviour with one's father-in-law and mother-in-law. Anything that they step over is *ngaintja* to me, but I cannot by this action make anything *ngaintja* for them. The Wik-mungkan make a distinction between mother's elder brother (*muka*) and mother's younger brother (*kala*). *Kala* is in the category of father-in-law, for in the Wik-mungkan marriage system one should marry the daughter of a mother's younger brother, albeit a classificatory one. But one should not marry the daughter of a mother's elder brother. The relationship with the two kinds of mother's brother is conceived as being different and this *inter alia* is illustrated in the Wik-mungkan beliefs about making things *ngaintja*.

Briefly, one may not eat, or use, anything that an actual or classificatory mother's younger brother has stepped over, sat upon, or handled in a sexually suggestive manner. In contrast, there is little or no concern about things being *ngaintja* between mother's elder brother and younger sister's child—particularly when they are in a classificatory relationship. Accordingly, while both mother's brothers may eat what their sister's child has stepped over, their sister's child may eat only what his mother's elder brother has stepped over. Both mother's brothers have a part to play in the relationship between their sister's child and sister's husband. They have the right to eat any food belonging to their sister's husband that his child has stepped over, and although others, such as the grandparents of the child—particularly mother's father (*ngechewut*) and mother's mother (*kemyiyu*)—may also eat such food, yet it is the child's mother's elder brother above all who has the main right. It is *muka* who is invariably claimed to be the one who should take the *ngaintja* food, while the rights of others, such as the grandparents, and even *kala*, are admitted as an afterthought. As one informant put it: '*Muk* is always there.'

Some hold that the act of stepping over something may be extended to include stepping over sideways so that the shadow of one's legs, in a sense, steps over the thing. Suppose that two men in the relationship of wife's brother (*kutth*) and sister's husband (*moiya*) are hunting in the bush, with the wife's brother in the lead. Should the sister's husband spot a hive, the wife's brother may argue that he has walked over it, i.e. the hive has passed between his legs, and hence it is taboo to his sister's husband. If, however, a sister's husband is in front and sees the hive first, or if the two hunters stand in a different relationship, such as

79

grandparent and grandchild, in which there are few taboos separating them, the one in front may not claim all the honey.

There is no fear of supernatural or mystical misfortune or of sickness should the stepping-over taboo be broken, though a shameless breach may cause a lot of trouble. People feel bad if they have stepped over things and others help themselves when they have no right to do so. If I step over something I am staking a claim to it; it is as if I were promising it to myself, with myself, with my sexual organs, and should someone such as my sister's husband ignore my claim then he is mocking me. For not only has he taken a wife from me, but now he also takes my food and possessions, whereas he should be giving me things, especially food, since he is the wife-receiver. In treating me thus, he would be taking everything from me and giving nothing but insults in return. Similarly, should he eat food that my sister's child has stepped over, he would be mocking both the child and myself. He would be mocking the child, since it is too young to fight for its own rights, and he would be mocking me, since it is I, and not the child's father, who have the right to eat what my sister's child steps over. If necessary I shall defend our rights to the point of fighting. I can also show my displeasure if my rights have been deliberately ignored by biding my time until I am present when the transgressor has stepped over something (or I may even deliberately place something in his path, and lie in waiting until he steps over it) and then rush up and make a show of carrying the thing off. If he should complain, I can argue that since he does not care for other people's rights they need not care for his.

Actions similar to stepping over can also make things *ngaintja*. Thus if a man throws something inadvertently and it lands on his daughter's or mother-in-law's lap he is forbidden to handle or eat it, for this touching of the lap, and to a lesser extent the leg, is considered suggestive of sexual intercourse. (There may also be the fear of contamination by menstrual blood.) This taboo can be used to prevent a man taking a disputed object by tossing it on his daughter's or mother-in-law's lap. In addition, as I have previously pointed out (McKnight 1973), if some foods, e.g. eggs, yams, mudshells, etc., have been obtained and prepared in what the Wik-mungkan consider to be a sexually suggestive manner, they are *ngaintja* for those in certain relationships such as father or sister's husband. One example may suffice. In digging up yams (*Dioscotea sativa*; Thomson 1939: 215) a woman may sit so that the yam is on her left side or directly in front of her. In the first case, the earth may be scooped so that it falls away from her, and in the second case it may fall between her legs and/or on her lap. If it falls on her lap, the yams are *ngaintja* for her father and a number of other relatives, but not if the earth is scooped to one side. The yams would also be *ngaintja* if she broke off their heads, since the heads are likened to the penis. To prepare yams for cooking they must be soaked in water so as to peel away the skin and rid them of their bitter taste. If a woman places the dilly bag of yams beside her and presses the water out with her hands there is no fear of them being *ngaintja*, but should she sit on the dilly bag so as to squish out the water they will be *ngaintja*.

SWEARING OF HANDS

Thomson (1935: 470) translates the Wik-mungkan word '*akan*' as 'swear' or 'oath'. The word 'swear' in English is often used in the sense of uttering obscenities or using bad language. In this sense in our society it is taboo to swear at people. But there is another meaning of swear which has a sacred connotation, such as to swear on the Bible or even to swear on one's mother's grave. These two meanings of 'swear' are also found in the Wik-mungkan word '*akan*'. And in this section I use it in its more sacred sense. I had thought of employing the word 'curse' to convey this second meaning, particularly as it is commonly used in anthropological writings. But I have rejected it because it has the sense of causing misfortune, which is not part of the meaning of '*akan*' as it is used here.

If one's kinsmen fail to fulfil their kinship duties one can deliberately make them *ma'angaintja* (*ma'a* = hand) by swearing their hands on someone's head or other part of the body. Thus if one swears A's hands on B's head, A may not give food to B, nor to B's close patrilineal kin, such as his father, father's sister, younger brother, and younger sister. This may seem straightforward enough, but problems arise over whose hands and on whose head one has the *right* to swear. I propose to examine the main categories of kin and affines to illustrate how the system works.

Once again we find that the rules differ according to the sex of the parents and the children. A father should not swear his daughter's hands but he may swear his son's. In contrast, while a woman should not swear her son's hands she may swear her daughter's. Normally a parent should only swear a child of the same sex—father swears son, and mother swears daughter. I was told that the reason why a man should not swear his daughter's hands, or a woman her son's, is because men are always *ngaintja* to women or are more *ngaintja* than women; interestingly enough, a mother's elder sister (*mukyiyu*) may swear the hands of her younger sister's son. This may seem incongruent with the ideal pattern of behaviour between mother and son, but the explanation is that a mother's elder sister is considered to be like a mother's elder brother (*muka*). Consequently just as a mother's elder brother (*muka*) may swear the hands of his younger sister's child (*mukaiya*), so may a mother's elder sister.

Why would a woman swear her daughter's hands? One reason is she may think her husband is taking too many things, particularly food, from their older daughter, and while arguing with her husband she may get angry enough to swear her daughter's hands on his head.

In this way she prevents her husband from obtaining anything from their daughter, and at the same time diverts the goods to herself. A husband is at a disadvantage if he tries to retaliate in kind, for he should not swear his daughter's hands (and even if he did this would not stop his wife from receiving food from her) and if he swears his son's hands, neither he nor his wife is allowed to eat their son's food. So if he wants to get even he has to cut off his nose to spite his face.

There is an exception to the rule that a parent should only swear a child of the same sex. A mother could stop her son from fighting by swearing his hands or spears on his daughter or brother's daughter. In a similar way a woman could stop her husband from fighting or taking something by swearing on his daughter or his younger brother's daughter. A husband in turn could stop his wife from fighting by swearing on her own brother's daughter, for she stands in the relationship of father to her brother's children, and just as his daughter is *ngaintja* to him so she is *ngaintja* to his sisters. If a husband and wife bicker about a particular piece of food it is enough for the wife to say their daughter's name to prevent her husband from eating the disputed food. So also may a man be stopped from taking something by saying his mother-in-law's name or by claiming that it belongs to his mother-in-law or father-in-law.

Although one should not swear the hands of a wife-giver, so as to stop him from giving things to other people, one can prevent him by indirect methods. Thus I may not swear my wife's brother's hands yet I may swear his children's hands and so effectively stop him from receiving anything from them. Since I am an actual or classificatory mother's brother (*muka* or *kala*) to his children, I have the right to swear their hands, and since I have sworn their hands, one of the persons to whom they may not give things is their father.

A woman should not swear the hands of her husband's eldest brother because, as the senior member of her husband's sibling group, he is like her husband's father, so she treats him like a father-in-law. She may, however, swear the hands of her husband's younger sibling. The Wik-mungkan say that it is all right for a woman to swear her husband's sister's hands, or her brother's wife's hands, since this is a matter between women and, unlike the behaviour between brothers-in-law, the inferiority and superiority of wife-receiving and wife-giving does not regulate their behaviour towards one another. A man may not swear the hands of his wife's eldest sister because she is a senior wife-giver (*wanch a:than*), but he may swear his wife's hands and her younger sisters'. An interesting consequence of this is that, although a son-in-law may not swear his father-in-law's hands, yet, by swearing his own wife's hands or those of her younger sister, he is able to block his father-in-law from receiving things from some of his daughters. A husband, however, may not stop his wife from receiving things from her younger sister.

Let us take the case of two men in the relationship of mother's father (*ngechewut*) and daughter's son (*ngecheyang*). The grandfather may feel that his grandson is neglecting him and is giving too much food to his parents and other relatives. So he starts to grumble, and in the ensuing quarrel he may swear his grandson's hands. By doing so he prevents his grandson's father, father's sister, and younger brother and younger sister from receiving anything, and so diverts the food to himself. Actually these relatives have not lost much, for ordinarily they do not receive many things from the grandson. But the Wik-mungkan emphasize that they are still even more isolated, for now they and some others may not even accept fire and water from him. As always, the mother's elder brother (*muka*) may still help himself to any food belonging to his younger sister's son. If pressed, the Wik-mungkan will concede that a father's father (*pulwut*), and even a mother's mother (*kemyiyu*), also have rights to his food. But one should bear in mind that, as the Wik-mungkan see it, the person whose hands have been sworn is *ngaintja;* he and his mother's elder brother are the main ones (besides the person who swore) who may touch or eat anything belonging to him until the taboo has been lifted.

Although swearing a person's hands on someone's head is no trifle, yet there are more powerful oaths, i.e. swearing on someone's blood, hot head, sexual organs, or anus, and even worse is to swear on something deep inside a person or on a man's spear-wounds. The worst oath of all is on a 'dead body'. The Wik-mungkan are extremely conscious of the rights of the recently deceased and of their surviving relatives. People say the living own the 'dead body'. Any form of disrespect to the dead man's relatives, or towards anything he owned, is sure to precipitate a quarrel. One quarrel I witnessed broke out when someone tried to stop a dog-fight by throwing a stick. One of the dogs belonged to a man who had recently died. His relatives complained that people were mocking the deceased and failing to respect their grief. Hitting the dog was regarded as hitting the deceased, or one of his relations. The dog was like a son to the dead man and indeed, among the Wik-mungkan, kinship terms are used for pets. Thus if I call a man father I must call his dog brother or sister (Thomson 1935: 458). So closely may a dog be identified with a person that I once heard a man complain that his affines were really directing acid comments at himself while pretending to talk to the family dog. This complaint was not without foundation, for it is *de rigueur* to speak (traditionally in an auxiliary language known as *ngonk wonka tonn*—see Thomson 1935: 474 n.22) to an affine through a third party, such as a child, and failing a child even a dog will do.

Swearing on a part deep inside a person, on his spear-marks, or on a corpse, is bound to cause physical violence. It is said that in the past such swearing could have ended in someone's death. Although one should not swear the hands, head, or corpse, etc., of a wife-giver, yet sometimes people become so angry that they disregard all the rules and impose taboos on people they have no right to treat in this way. The swearing is still effective, and how long the taboos remain in force depends on the intensity of the quarrel and swearing. Usually, if only hands have been sworn on someone's head, the taboos last for one or two weeks, but they may persist for a year or more if a corpse has been sworn.

To illustrate the purification rituals, let us take an example of a mild form of *ma'angaintja* caused by a woman swearing her daughter's hands because she thinks her husband has been taking too much from her. After a week or so, the mother may inform her daughter that she is willing to lift the taboo. The daughter makes a fire out of ti-tree (*Melaleuca leucadendron*: Thomson 1939: 218) and messmate bark, and places some cooked food near the fire. While she purifies her hands by rubbing them over the flames her mother's father (*ngechewut*), and/or mother's elder brother (*muka*), pours water over her hands until the fire is soaking wet. She then gives the cooked food to her mother's father, and mother's elder brother. After this she is allowed to give food to her father and other relations.

FAECES

It is believed that anyone who sees a man defecating becomes *ngaintja*. Thus if man A should inadvertently come too close to B while B is defecating, then, even if B should cough so as to warn him that someone is there, A is still *ngaintja*, he is in a state of *ma'angaintja;* he must tell his relatives what has happened, for while he is *ma'angaintja* he is restricted from handling any objects, particularly food, to many of them. People often make the sweeping statement that A may only give to B, but in fact he has greater freedom than that, for his mother's elder brothers, wife's brother, grandparents, and grandchildren may still take things from him. Nevertheless, B is the main person to receive things from A, and appropriately enough, A may also give things to B's mother's elder brother.

Only those who watch a man defecating suffer being *ma'angaintja;* there is no need to worry about seeing a man or woman urinating, nor does one become *ma'angaintja* by seeing a woman defecating. Furthermore, the relationship of those involved is immaterial, for in this matter a wife-receiver can cause a wife-giver to be *ma'angaintja* and so may a grandfather make a grandchild *ma'angaintja*. Since the Wik-mungkan are concerned with faeces pollution one might have expected them to impose strict rules as to where men and women should defecate. As Needham (1962: 254ff.) has indicated, the Wik-mungkan classify some things on dualistic principles, yet I could discover no way in which this played a part in the prevention of faeces pollution. There is no belief, for instance, that men should defecate to the east of a camp, and women to the west; or that the bush should be reserved for men and the beach for women. The most that is done at a camp is to make an *ad hoc* decision about which general area should be used by men and which by women.

If a person is able to make an instant payment when seeing a man defecating he or she can avoid being *ma'angaintja*. It is said that a woman could offer herself as payment. If immediate payment is not possible, then eventually the person who is *ma'angaintja* must place a good catch of fish, kangaroo, goose, or some prized food in front of the person whom he saw defecating and his mother's elder brother. He warms his hands over a small fire made out of ti-tree and messmate bark (both very common trees) while the other man and his mother's elder brother pour water over his hands until the fire goes out. After this he rubs his hands with the charcoal. Note that he purifies himself with fire, water, steam, and charcoal. Finally he gives food to the man seen defecating and his mother's elder brother and is released from being *ma'angaintja*.

MENSTRUAL BLOOD

Wik-mungkan men are very afraid of menstrual blood. A menstruating woman is a source of danger to all men, with the possible exception of her husband, providing that he is a *wutmantaiyin* (an old powerful man, an elder). Should a young husband have sexual intercourse with his menstruating wife he may fall ill, become lazy, and turn into a *yepin*— a poor hunter. It is said that, if a young boy came into contact with menstrual blood, his right arm would be weakened and that, when he matured, he would suffer pains in his right hand and shoulder and so be a poor hunter. In the past when a woman was menstruating she was secluded from the main camp to prevent men from coming into contact with her, or with anything that she had touched, either directly or indirectly. A menstruating woman had to be careful how she gathered food. She could only give yams to her father's sister if she took care that the earth did not fall on her lap.

Any act suggestive of menstrual bleeding makes things *ngaintja*. Thus if blood from an animal falls on a woman's lap, her father and many other male relatives may not eat it. If a young man carries meat on his back or shoulders (he should not carry meat on his head for it is believed that this will make him prematurely grey) so that the blood runs down between his buttocks this, to the Wik-mungkan, is too uncomfortably like menstrual blood to be ignored.

There are also taboos if sugarbag, i.e. honey, falls on a woman's lap. This is particularly the case with a sugarbag known as *mai kuyan*. Its entrance is said to be phallic; it protrudes a few inches from the tree trunk or limb and the tip is sometimes red with pollen carried by the bees which land there before entering the hive. Honey on a woman's lap is not only suggestive of sexual fluids as well as menstrual blood, but is also associated with grease or fat from a decaying body. My attention was drawn to the following equivalence: as the sugarbag is to the tree so the corpse is to the bark (for the corpse, like sugarbag, is wrapped in bark). Thus we could put it:

$$Sugarbag: tree :: corpse: bark.$$

Perhaps it is not without significance that, on the one hand, many hives are found in messmate trees and the bees gather much nectar from their blossoms, and, on the other hand, the bark from this tree is used to wrap corpses.

It is not surprising, therefore, to learn that, when men split open a hive or cut up flesh food, they make certain that women, especially their daughters, stand well away. Men will not even take fish from a daughter if she has caught it with a fishing line and pulled the line so that it falls on her lap. If a daughter should accidentally sit on her father's possessions then they are *ngaintja* to him.

To give a more rounded picture, though hardly a complete one, of Wik-mungkan beliefs concerning blood, I might add that blood from wounds is also considered to be *ngaintja*, though not to the same degree as menstrual blood. As I have pointed out, swearing on spear-marks, or on someone's head (where the hot blood rises), is not to be taken lightly. Moreover, to draw blood from a person's head in a fight is considered one of the worst blows. The injured man will always keep his eyes on the person who cut his head, in the hope of taking revenge. Although the Wik-mungkan have a sense of fair play, nevertheless, in these circumstances, so strong is the drive for revenge that the injured man will not hesitate to hit his enemy from behind while he is busy fighting someone else.

DEATH

In the past the Wik-mungkan used to preserve the bodies of their kin; they succeeded so well that even though the bodies were slung on a pole and carried wherever their owners went, they would keep for two years at least (McConnel 1957: 17; 1937: 346 ff.). Part of the treatment consisted in skinning the corpse, taking out the entrails, and then wrapping it in several layers of ti-tree and messmate bark. Eventually a mortuary feast was held, the body was cremated (it seems that each patriclan had their own cremation ground), the naming taboos were broken, and only then did the close relatives of the deceased investigate the cause of his death. As soon as a person has died his name may not be spoken, particularly in the presence of close relatives. To mention his name would be to mock both the living and the dead; for the dead cannot answer, and it would remind the living of their sorrow. The dead man's close relatives may threaten that, since others have called their 'dead body', they too will call the 'dead body' of others. At the mortuary feast a relative breaks the naming taboo by chopping ironwood (*Erythrophloeum laboucherii;* Thomson 1939: Plate XXII), and calling out with each blow the names of various objects, places, and people that sound like the dead man's name, and finally he cries out the name itself. After this anybody may say his name or any word which sounds like it.

The dead man's favourite camping-places are destroyed, by throwing the remains of his camp-fires into the water, or by burying them, or by strewing them about. There seems to be a systematic elimination of any trace of the deceased, for even his footprints are erased. Whereas formerly his shelter used to be burnt, this is no longer feasible, since most of the Wik-mungkan now occupy European dwellings. So they have compromised by 'smoking' them out. This consists of burning ironwood, which gives off a lot of smoke, in the house. It has the double effect of driving away the lingering spirit and of purifying the house. The smoking usually takes place a year or more after a death, and until it is done no one is allowed to go into the house. Most people even avoid going near it. However, I have recorded one case where the smoking took place only a few weeks after a death, but this shortened mourning period seems to have resulted from a particular constellation of circumstances: the deceased was very old, she had not actually died within the house, and the house was very much needed for a large family.

Traditionally, a dead man's personal possessions such as his spear, spear-thrower, gum (made principally from the roots of ironwood and used for binding things), and especially some of his hair, were kept at least until the cremation. The person who looked after these things was in a particularly vulnerable position and was not allowed to give anything to others, not even, according to some informants, to his own mother's elder brother (*muka*). This taboo was so strict that he was prohibited from acting as an intermediary. For example, any food a woman collects is regarded as her own, but, should she give it to her husband when he is looking after a dead man's things, he may not pass the food on to someone else. The person who looks after the dead man's things should not be a close relative, but someone in the classificatory relationship of wife's brother (*kutth*), sister's husband (*moiya*), mother's elder brother (*muka*), or elder brother (*wunya*).

The purification rituals for this person are very elaborate. First of all he rubs his hands over the flames of ti-tree and messmate bark (the same species of trees used to wrap a corpse). Then the dead man's mother's elder brother or, failing him, his father's father (*pulwut*) or mother's father (*ngechewut*), but not his mother's younger brother, pours water over the hands of the guardian of the dead man's possessions. He 'washes' his hands in the steam, and finally in the charcoal once the fire is out. Then the dead man's things are lit and completely burned, following which a third fire is made out of ironwood and leaves.

As its name implies, this wood is very hard and difficult to burn. Once again, the man purifies his hands by 'washing' them in the abundant smoke. The smoke and the smouldering flames from the ironwood are regarded as one of the most, if not *the* most, powerful means of purification. The person purifying himself must also warm his feet over the fire, so that when he goes hunting the dead man's spirit will not be able to follow him. The smoke will ensure that when he is searching for, say, honey, the spirit will not be able to affect his sight and make him unable to see the hives. By purifying his hands he will be able to throw straight, and be a successful hunter and so feed others. But if he does not purify himself he will have bad luck, for even if he throws his spear straight it will miss.

What we find, then, in this most elaborate purification ritual is that all the methods of purification—fire, water, steam, mud, charcoal, and smoke—are employed; in the other purification rites, only some of these methods were used.

HUMAN BEINGS AND ANIMALS

When I was doing fieldwork among the Wik-mungkan my main goal was to collect information about kinship and marriage, and to try to build up an understanding of the various patterns of behaviour of kin and affines. This material about *ngaintja*, *ma'angaintja*, and purification rituals is undoubtedly part of this system and it helps to illustrate the various rights and duties among kin and affines. Thus it is not difficult to understand why stepping over something makes it *ngaintja* for some relatives but not for others. Nevertheless, there are some aspects of this matter of *ngaintja* which cannot be explained in this way. For example, why should faeces but not urine be regarded as *ngaintja*? Or to put the question another way: why does one become *ma'angaintja* if one sees a man defecating, but not if one sees him urinating? In attempting to solve this problem, one must take into account that the Wik-mungkan are fascinated by the difference between the two waste products and by the way in which they are formed. Thus while drinking-water comes out of the body as a liquid, solid food is completely transformed. This may help to explain why faeces but not urine can make a person *ma'angaintja*, but it does not explain why it is that both men and women become *ma'angaintja* if they see a man defecating but not if they see a woman defecating. Any attempt to answer this question raises a host of problems. Why are men always *ngaintja* to women (or more *ngaintja* than women)? Why are women seldom *ngaintja* to other women? (As in the matter of defecation, and in the fact that a daughter is not usually a source of making things *ngaintja* to her mother, and as there is no concern between sisters of making things *ngaintja*.) Why are women *ngaintja* to men? (Although the power of men to make things *ngaintja* is greater, women, as we saw, may cause things to be *ngaintja* for men, and their menstrual blood is feared.) These questions cannot be answered in terms of kinship and marriage; the answers turn on Wik-mungkan ideas about men and women, the place of human beings in relation to animals, and the nature of being human.

Although it has been said *ad nauseam* of the Australian Aborigines that men are sacred and women are profane, there is nevertheless some truth in this generalization. To the Wik-mungkan, men are superior to women by their very nature, and they become more so because they are initiated and are taught about sacred things, and so have a greater understanding of the world. Women, in contrast, are not initiated and, in theory, they do not have much sacred knowledge. Let us examine these natural and cultural differences.

We know that there is an infinite number of possibilities open to a society as to how the world might be classified, yet we do not know why a society uses one particular axis of classification rather than another. Nevertheless, since Australia is south-east of the Wallace Line there is one striking feature of the Australian fauna: in the class Mammalia man is a placental in a predominantly marsupial world. I do not wish to imply by this statement that placentals are rare in Australia, for this certainly would be an exaggeration. There are many species of placental rats, as well as dogs (or dingoes), dugongs, and flying foxes. But in any one area there are many more species of marsupials than of placentals. Although in theory it is possible to ignore this, in practice the Wik-mungkan have used it as the intellectual cornerstone of their definition of man. The terms 'placental' and 'marsupial' which we use to distinguish two groups of mammals are really ill chosen, for marsupials also have a placenta, albeit a rudimentary one. Furthermore, although the word 'marsupial' means pouch, there are some marsupials, such as opossums, which are pouchless. It is because of the partial development of the placenta that marsupials are not as fully formed at birth as placentals and hence are kept in a pouch. By contrast, the placentals, such as ourselves, have a highly developed placenta and invariably lack a pouch. But to the Wik-mungkan it is not the placenta, nor the pouch, which marks the differences between these two groups of mammals. What they have singled out for special comment is the number and position of the orifices which make up the external sexual and excretory organs. I might remind the reader that in both sexes among marsupials, as is the case with a number of other kinds of animals and birds, the outlets of the bladder and intestines connect and discharge into the cloaca, consequently, unlike ourselves, they do not have separate orifices for eliminating urine and faeces. I would like to emphasize here that in the interests of simplicity I have tried to avoid technical terms. In doing so I may have oversimplified; if so, I ask the indulgence of those with specialist knowledge in zoology and anatomy.

Let us take the kangaroo as a paradigm of a marsupial. At birth the

89

neonate is extremely small, about half an inch long. It climbs up into the pouch and immediately starts to suckle, and it remains in this position for several months. The female has only one external orifice for excretion, copulation, and birth. The male kangaroo's external genital and excretory organs consist of testicles, penis, and anus. A cursory glance might lead one to conclude that, like the female, it has only one external orifice. But a closer examination reveals, as my informants recognize, that this orifice contains both the anus and the penis, the penis being separated from the anus by a thin membrane. Another anatomical phenomenon is that the testicles are pre-penial, i.e. above the penis. Hence when we compare human beings with kangaroos we find that a man is similar to a male kangaroo in having the same sexual and excretory organs, i.e. penis, testicles, and anus, yet they differ in the position of the testicles, which among men are post-penial. In contrast, there is a greater difference between a woman and a female kangaroo; since a female kangaroo has only one external orifice.

The Wik-mungkan are familiar with a few placentals, such as dog, dugong (more commonly known as sea cow), and flying fox. Of these three, the one that has really captured their attention is the flying fox. There are two species of flying foxes in this area—one red and the other black; the Wik-mungkan terms are *min wuk* and *min mukenbung*, while the European scientific terms are *Pteropus scapulatus* and *Pteropus gouldi* respectively (Thomson 1936: 378). As the popular English terms suggest, they are rather exceptional creatures. They are fruit bats, and in our system of classification they are classified as placentals (at one time in the Linnaean system they were classified among primates). They are undoubtedly an odd kind of placental since they fly. Their flight is not of a gliding kind like that of the sugar glider, which the Wik-mungkan are familiar with, but a sustained flight which they can keep up for many miles. Furthermore, they are nocturnal and migratory. They appear to breed outside the Wik-mungkan tribal grounds, for the Wik-mungkan claim never to have found a pregnant flying fox nor to have seen one giving birth. Surprisingly, they deny placental status to the female flying fox, for they claim that it has only one orifice, an anus, and that it lacks a vagina. On this basis it would be like a marsupial or a bird. For as a female marsupial has one orifice, as a bird has, there is some similarity between them. There is, however, the obvious difference of marsupials being viviparous, whereas birds are oviparous.

The question arises how do the Wik-mungkan classify the flying fox? Is it a bird? Although it flies, and hence has the major characteristic commonly associated with birds, the Wik-mungkan do not classify it as a bird. They advance many reasons for not doing so. It cannot be a bird, they maintain, because it has ears, which birds do not have; it has a mouth, while birds have a beak; it has teeth, which all birds lack. Nor does it have a nest or lay eggs. They therefore claim that it must be some sort of animal.

There is the related problem of the status of the emu (*Dromaius novae-hollandiae;* Thomson 1935: 468). Although it does not fly, nevertheless we classify it as a bird. Considering that it lays eggs, has a beak, and lacks ears and teeth, one might have assumed that the Wik-mungkan would also regard it as a bird. Although we regard an emu as a feathered creature, the Wik-mungkan claim that its 'feathers' are quite unlike the feathers of seagulls and willy wagtails, ducks and geese, etc. The feathers of these creatures are known as *pul*, while the feathers of an emu are known as *wu:tham*. This term, *wu:tham*, may only be used with reference to an emu. Because of this the Wik-mungkan conclude that an emu is *wi:wim*, which may be translated as: just itself or *sui generis*.

Some hold that a flying fox is also *wi:wim*, although it may be classified under the heading of furred animals because it is covered with light fur. Although the Wik-mungkan deny that a female flying fox is a placental, they do not withhold this status from a male flying fox. For they say, as we do, that it has a penis, testicles, and an anus. Furthermore, they recognize that a male flying fox differs from male marsupials but is like male placentals, particularly human beings, in having the testicles post-penial. We therefore find in Wik-mungkan thought, when human beings are compared with flying foxes, on which man models himself and makes himself sacred, men are the same, while women are anomalous. In addition, as we have seen, there is some similarity between men and male kangaroos but not between women and female kangaroos. This, to the Wik-mungkan, is the case with all marsupials. In short, as they see it, women do not fit into the natural world as well as men. To make matters more complex this anomalous creature, woman, shares in being partly male. For the Wik-mungkan, like ourselves, consider the clitoris to be analogous to the penis. This is regarded as one of the reasons why women can make things *ngaintja*.

INITIATION AND BIRTH

Even in the field I was puzzled by the odd structure attributed to female flying foxes. Although my knowledge of zoology is limited, I was nevertheless aware that flying foxes are placentals, and so I had some inkling that female flying foxes could not have the one external orifice of marsupials and birds. How are we to account for these beliefs? It is unlikely that the Wik-mungkan do not have a thorough anatomical knowledge of flying foxes, for these animals form an important part of their diet. It seems to me that what we must examine is the problem of the context of beliefs as formulated by Leach (1969: 85ff.) and Meggitt (1962: 273). Since we are dealing with sexual matters, not surprisingly the subject of procreation is pertinent. It is well known that there has been considerable controversy about what the Australian Aborigines believe about this subject. Leach flatly denies that they are ignorant of physiological paternity, or at least asserts that they are not as ignorant as some have supposed. He suggests that the misconceptions of some anthropologists are largely the result of their failure to recognize that their informants were making theological statements. He also claims that because the Trobrianders and the Tully River Blacks (an Australian tribe) know how animals reproduce, they must also understand human reproduction. Although I find myself much in agreement with Leach, nevertheless, like Spiro (1968), I think it unwise to extrapolate from animals to human beings. People's beliefs about animals are not necessarily identical with their beliefs about human beings. However, I have collected some puzzling information from the Wik-mungkan about the reproduction of kangaroos and flying foxes, and I can only conclude that they make theological statements not only about men and women, but also about animals.

Although the Wik-mungkan hunt kangaroos (*Macropus rufus* and *Macropus giganteus*; Thomson 1939: 215), and know a great deal about their natural history, e.g. about their diet and habitat, they say that kangaroos are born in the pouch; they claim never to have found an embryo in the stomach or uterus. They readily admit that this seems odd, but they fail to see how they can disbelieve the evidence of their own senses. Even more surprising is their belief about the birth of flying foxes, i.e. that they come out of the water or out of the belly of the Rainbow Serpent, *taipan* (*Oxyurenus scuellaptus*; McConnel 1957: 111). For a number of complex reasons the Rainbow Serpent is closely associated or even equated with water. As I have pointed out, flying foxes are migratory and they probably do not breed in the Wik-mungkan tribal area. My informants insisted they had never seen a pregnant flying fox, but that they had noticed females suckling the young. Although they know that they appear at certain times of the year, yet it is impossible to predict exactly where they will be. They suggested that if the flying foxes were hunted too industriously the Rainbow Serpent would swallow them and take them elsewhere. There are many taboos about hunting, cooking, and eating flying foxes. One may not hunt them late in the afternoon or when it starts to get dark. Old men may eat both kinds of flying foxes but young men may eat only the red flying foxes. There are said to be a few whiteish or piebald flying foxes which even the old men may not eat, for these specifically belong to the Rainbow Serpent. In the past, women were not allowed to eat any kind of flying foxes nor could the youths while they were being initiated. Before they are cooked the wings and legs must be broken and the male flying foxes must have the penis cut off. They should only be cooked in an earth oven. One may not whistle when hunting them, for this may attract the attention of the Rainbow Serpent.

It will probably be of no surprise to the reader to learn that the themes of flying foxes and birth occur in the initiation ceremonies. Uninitiated youths are identified with red flying foxes and older initiated men are identified with black flying foxes. There are two initiation ceremonies, *uchanam* and *winchanam*, and when the youths are taken away to be initiated (*nganwi*) they are said to be in the snake's belly, i.e. *tuk impanang*. The word '*impanang*' means belly or pregnant in the auxiliary language *nonk wonka tonn* (see Thomson 1936: 377). When the young boys reach puberty they are forcibly taken away from the women. The women try to hide the boys by covering them with leaves and branches and, although they strongly resist and may even pick up sticks, the older men push them to one side, and roughly grab the boys. Sometimes the men resort to a ruse by pretending to fight among themselves and when everybody rushes up to see what is happening they grab hold of the boys. Once the boys are caught there is nothing that the women can do; they turn and wail, looking in the opposite direction, just as the mourners do when a corpse is cremated.

During the initiation the youths are placed in a bough shelter, so not only are they like the flying foxes going into their camp but they, like them, are swallowed by the Rainbow Serpent. The initiation period is a hard time for the youths, for people say that when they come out they are thin. They are guarded and taken into the bush by the old men, just as the red flying foxes are surrounded by the black flying foxes. The old men blow a bamboo whistle, which is just like the Rainbow Serpent whistling for the flying foxes. During the initiation the boys are taught how to hunt, and they must remain in the snake's belly, i.e. bough shelter, for long periods. They must not whistle, or talk loudly, or eat large fish, birds, or animals which have sharp beaks, claws, and teeth. What is emphasized is that they are denied maternal care. The women may try to send them food but the old men take it for themselves and mock them for their concern. The women are not allowed to come near the initiation grounds. Hostility between men and women, and older initiated men and the young boys, is openly expressed. The old men claim that the boys have been pampered and spoiled by the women, who have allowed them to eat *ngaintja* foods, but now the boys belong to them and they will make men out of them. The initiates complain that the old men are greedy and mean.

The initiates are shown many important dances and carvings. Some of the dances are deliberately funny and obscene in an attempt to make the youths laugh. They are threatened with dire penalties if they do so and it is believed that a youth could in this way lose his hunting abilities, which could be taken by the older men. The youths are taught how to swing bullroarers, which in the Wik-mungkan mythology were first found by women but were taken away by the men. At the conclusion of the *uchanam* ceremony, the youths carry bow-shaped sticks which symbolize the Rainbow Serpent. These are stuck in the ground and the youths crawl through them, just as if they were passing through the Rainbow Serpent. At the end of the line, the older initiated men stand with their legs apart and the youths crawl through them as well. Hence the initiated men participate in giving birth, and as the youths face them it is as if they were born from the anus of the older men. McConnel (1934: 337) records that at the conclusion of this ceremony 'The women sit in a long row, with their backs turned to the initiates, who pass along the row touching the women one by one on their shoulders with their spears, saying as they do so, *Wikatauwala* or "you and I speak to one another".' And finally the women put their milk on the initiates' legs and give them food.

It is at their initiation that men obtain their unseen children. It is believed that every initiated man, particularly an older initiated man who has participated in the ceremonies a number of times, has an unseen child who may make others sick by causing stomach pains and swellings. The parallel between birth and initiation was well recognized by my informants. The former is the business of women, the latter of men. Just as men may not be present when a woman gives birth, so it is taboo for women to be present at the esoteric initiation rituals. During these *rites des passage* it is mystically dangerous for the opposite sex to be present. As a newly born child is formally presented to his father, so the newly initiated youths are presented to their mothers. The crucial difference between the two births is that women give birth to babies, but men give birth to adult human beings. I would emphasize that it is not surprising that flying foxes play such an important part in the initiation ceremonies, for these ceremonies are supposed to make men out of youths, and hence the question of what is man must form a central part of any male initiation ceremony. I would argue that, in the Wik-mungkan initiation ceremonies, the men are denying that the women have complete control over reproduction. Women may give birth to babies, but it is men who finally make them into adults.

CONCLUSIONS

A detailed analysis of the Wik-mungkan mythology, dances, initiation ceremonies, and system of taxonomy would obviously be desirable, but it is not possible to present this information here. I have not been able to follow up all the points that I would like to, nevertheless I think that with the material I have presented we can now interpret the Wik-mungkan beliefs about flying foxes [1] and understand why they claim that men are more *ngaintja* than women. The dogma of birth explains why they deny that female flying foxes are placentals and why they say that these creatures have only one orifice, i.e. an anus. There is no need, or no reason, for them to have a vagina for they do not give birth—they come out of the water or the Rainbow Serpent. Men too come out of the Rainbow Serpent but they come out as adult human beings.

Men are more *ngaintja* than women because they fit into the natural world better than women. This is particularly so when the Wik-mungkan compare themselves to flying foxes, which they consider to be the closest of all animals to men. Sociologically they are like men, for they live in groups, in camps. In these camps the females roost separately from the males. The parallel with male initiates and initiators who are separated from women was readily recognized by my informants and was offered as evidence that flying foxes must have their Rainbow Serpent too. Anatomically men have the same sexual and excretory organs, and in the same order, as male flying foxes; while women, it is claimed, have a different reproductive and excretory system. The Wik-mungkan (and this includes both men and women) claim that, outside the realm of kinship and marriage, men taken collectively are always *ngaintja* to women or are more *ngaintja* than women. This is so because of the anatomical reasons I have just mentioned and also because men alone are initiated. During the initiation ceremonies men see and perform the important dances, they see and make sacred carvings; this renders them particularly dangerous to women. But, as we have also seen, women too are to some degree *ngaintja*, and men are particularly frightened of menstrual blood. I think the answer to this lies in the fact that women also are associated with the Rainbow Serpent. The Rainbow Serpent is believed to be responsible for women menstruating. Thus in one myth (McConnel 1957: 115) we are told: 'Taipan's sisters are the red in the rainbow and Taipan is the blue. Seeing the rainbow and the red of the sisters in it people say: "Taipan has a sore inside", i.e. has her period' (see also McConnel 1936: 85).

I have mentioned one axis of classification based on reproduction and excretion, but there is another (somewhat less explicit) which we may term the container and the contained. Thus in discussing honey and corpses I drew attention to how honey could be equated with the decaying flesh of a corpse because they are both 'contained'—the honey in a tree and a corpse in the bark. Similarly we find that the body is a container, and the stuff which is *ngaintja* or which can make people *ma'ngaintja*, such as faeces and menstrual blood, the contained. So also in pregnancy and in initiation there are the contained and the container: unborn children are inside a woman and initiates are inside the Rainbow Serpent. Furthermore, children are born through the legs of women just as initiates are born through the legs of men and through the Rainbow Serpent. It cannot be fortuitous that what, in a sense, is passed through the legs in stepping over things can be made *ngaintja*. The axis of container and contained and the symbolism of pregnancy and birth appear to be important in Wik-mungkan rituals.

David McKnight

Note

1. The Wik-mungkan are not the only ones to have unusual ideas about flying foxes, for the Abelam of New Guinea (Forge 1965) go one better. They claim that all birds are female and although male flying foxes in their area have a prominent penis yet the Abelam insist that it is a breast, and so remain consistent in their claim that all birds are female. Apparently they consider that flying foxes are birds because they fly—yet the fact that a cassowary does not fly does not exclude it from being classified as a bird. I might also draw attention to an amusing passage in Francis Ratcliffe's delightful book *Flying Fox and Drifting Sand*. Ratcliffe carried out a scientific study of flying foxes in Queensland and while gathering information from the European settlers he was told by one old Queenslander: 'I wonder whether you have found out one very remarkable thing about flying foxes. They haven't got no fundament. I have looked for it everywhere, and there isn't a sign. I reckon that they must vomit up all they eat. That's probably why they stink so bad' (Ratcliffe 1963: 28–29).

Acknowledgement

I am indebted to the Social Science Research Council and the Australian Institute of Aboriginal Studies for funds enabling me to do fieldwork among the Wik-mungkan. I wish to thank Professors Lucy Mair, Edmund Leach, James Littlejohn, and Anthony Forge, as well as the participants of the Friday Postgraduate Seminar at the London School of Economics, for their helpful comments on earlier drafts.

Although I have not made specific references to the works of Professors Mary Douglas, Ralph Bulmer, Edmund Leach, and Claude Lévi-Strauss, and of Dr S. J. Tambiah, to name but a few, concerning taboo, pollution, and classification of animals, they have nevertheless influenced my thinking on these subjects.

I have a special debt to many Wik-mungkan who took much time and trouble to teach me about their civilization and the complexity of their cosmology. Even to this day some European Australians have doubts about the intellectual abilities of the Australian Aborigines; they find it difficult to believe that the Aborigines have anything to teach us. I hope this paper will convey some of the intellectual originality of one Australian Aboriginal society and how they approach the problem of what is man, which is a problem that concerns all of us.

References

FORGE, A. 1965. Art and Environment in the Sepik. *Proceedings of the Royal Anthropological Institute*.
LEACH, E. R. 1969. *Genesis as Myth, and Other Essays*. London: Cape.
MEGGITT, M. J. 1962. *Desert People*. Sydney: Angus & Robertson.
MCCONNEL, U. H. 1934. The Wik-Munkan and Allied Tribes of Cape York Peninsula, N.Q., Part III: Kinship and Marriage. *Oceania* 4.
— 1935. Myths of the Wikmunkan and Wiknatara Tribes. *Oceania* 5.
— 1936. Totemic Hero-Cults in Cape York Peninsula, North Queensland. Part II. *Oceania* 7.
— 1937. Mourning Ritual among the Tribes of Cape York Peninsula. *Oceania* 7.
— 1957. *Myths of the Munkan*. Melbourne: Melbourne University Press.
MCKNIGHT, D. 1973. Sexual Symbolism of Food among the Wik-mungkan. *Man* 8 (2).
NEEDHAM, R. 1962. Genealogy and Category in Wikmunkan Society. *Ethnology* 1.
SPIRO, M. E. 1968. Virgin Birth, Parthenogenesis, and Physiological Paternity: an Essay on Cultural Interpretation. *Man* 3 (2).

THOMSON, D. F. 1935. The Joking Relationship and Organized Obscenity in North Queensland. *American Anthropologist* **37**.
— 1936. Fatherhood in the Wik Munkan Tribe. *American Anthropologist* **38**.
— 1939. The Seasonal Factor in Human Culture. *Proceedings of the Prehistoric Society* (10), Cambridge.
RATCLIFFE, F. 1963. *Flying Fox and Drifting Sand.* Sydney: Angus and Robertson.

James J. Fox

On Binary Categories and Primary Symbols[1]
Some Rotinese Perspectives

... it is possible to imagine a purely formal lexicon which would provide, instead of the meaning of each word, the set of other words which catalyse it according to possibilities which are of course variable ...   R. Barthes[2]

INTRODUCTION

Structural analysis has, in its development, relied exceptionally on the use of dual categories or binary oppositions. Although forms of binary analysis may be traced to Vico in the eighteenth century[3] or to Bachofen in the nineteenth century, it is often argued that some vague analogy with the workings of the computer is primarily responsible for the recent impetus given these studies. Yet despite a vogue which this analogy may have created, binary analysis has its clearer basis in the programme for structural linguistics that emanated from Prague in the 1920s, and, although possibly derivative, in the literary studies of Indonesian social structure and mythology developed, independently, by Leiden anthropologists working in the 1930s. These two 'schools', Prague and Leiden, have been the chief inspiration for the two varying modes of binary analysis now advanced in social anthropology: Claude Lévi-Strauss's grand disquisitions on the nature of myth and Rodney Needham's precise two-column analyses of social and symbolic systems. Both contend that their analyses, in some way, tap certain fundamental features of the human mind.

Critics of these methods have not infrequently expressed puzzlement in attempting to disengage either mode of analysis from that which, it is argued, is supposed to be inherent in the materials analysed. More searchingly, however, it has been countered that whether or not one accepts the validity of binary categories, the same set of oppositions—male/female, right/left, raw/cooked, heaven/earth—recur with such monotonous frequency that they can hardly be expected to provide fresh insights into the ethnographic diversity which anthropologists study.

99

Those interested in reaching some deeper level of symbolic phenomena regard structural analysis as a poor resort for the problems they face. Thus, although the issue involves scholars of a whole range of differing opinions, it seems, at times, to divide those interested in the discovery of what are deemed to be a limited set of universals or near-universals in human cultures from those who feel themselves committed to the arduous task of recording the contextual richness of these same cultures.

More frequently, binary analysis, whether regarded as interesting or trivial, has tended to be accepted with some reservation. Paul Friedrich has recently stated this position: 'The so-called "principle of binariness", again in phonology and lexicology, may be categorically assumed or carefully guarded and qualified, but most scholars agree that in some form it is a major factor in empirical systems . . . and that it is often fruitful to assume that it is such a factor' (forthcoming).

This paper is intended to consider certain aspects of the use of binary categories. I take, as a starting-point, the 'principle of binariness' but my concern is to derive from it a means of going beyond this simple recognition towards a more systematic exploration of the complex use of these categories. In this paper, I attempt to set forth the initial methods and preliminary results of an analysis of the ritual system of a single society, that of the island of Roti in eastern Indonesia. In so far as my emphasis is on 'system' and 'complexity', I must insist on the tentative and partial nature of this present analysis. The first draft of this paper was written in Kupang on Timor during a respite from field-work on the island of Roti. During this further year's stay, I was able to more than double the textual basis for the analysis of the whole ritual system and was, for the first time, invited to perform, with other chanters, a major ritual—in this instance, the final mortuary ceremony for my close friend and instructor in ritual language, the eminent, long-dead chanter and 'Head of the Earth' in Termanu, S. Adulanu. Since it has taken several years of intermittent work to transcribe, translate, and analyse my previous corpus of ritual materials, I can only expect that it will take several more years to prepare these new materials. It was my distinct impression, however, while working among the chanters of Roti, that my earlier research was already sufficiently advanced to comprehend most of the new chants I encountered. Therefore, there appears to me to be some validity in describing this stage of my present researches. But rather than propound a set of conclusions, I can, at best, only outline a direction and venture a number of possibilities.

To generalize, however, from the symbolic system of one of the smaller islands of Indonesia to those of other cultures requires considerable justification. It is, therefore, necessary initially to focus attention on the widespread linguistic phenomenon of parallelism on which my methods of analysis are founded. It is this phenomenon that offers a possibility for the formal comparison of symbol systems.

THE PHENOMENA OF SEMANTIC PARALLELISM

The term 'parallelism' derives from the researches of Bishop Robert Lowth who, in the eighteenth century, made what was then the discovery that one of the major principles of composition throughout the Old Testament was a carefully contrived pairing of line, phrase, and verse. For this phenomenon, Bishop Lowth coined the phrase: *parallelismus membrorum*. Since Lowth's time biblical scholarship has continued to investigate this phenomenon and has shown that Hebrew oral poetry shared, with Ugaritic and Canaanite traditions, a standardized body of conventionally fixed word-pairs (cf. Newman & Popper 1918–1923; Gevirtz 1963; also W. F. Albright). It is the required pairing of set terms, according to the canons of the oral tradition, that gives rise to the careful balance of phrase and verse. Modern translations of the Bible often make clearer this parallelism than do the older translations more familiar in English traditions. The prophetic lines of Isaiah (2: 2–5) provide an appropriate illustration of this biblical parallelism:

> In days to come,
> The mountain of the Lord's house
> Shall be established as the highest mountain
> And raised above the hills.
> All nations shall stream toward it,
> Many peoples shall come and say:
> 'Come, let us climb the Lord's mountain,
> To the house of the God of Jacob,
> That he may instruct us in his ways,
> And we may walk in his paths.'
> For from Zion shall go forth instruction
> And the word of the Lord from Jerusalem.
> He shall judge between nations
> And impose terms on many peoples.
> They shall beat their swords into ploughshares
> And their spears into pruning hooks;
> One nation shall not raise the sword against another
> Nor shall they train for war again.
> O house of Jacob, come,
> Let us walk in the light of the Lord![4]

In these lines, the sets nations//peoples, ways//paths, word//instruction, Zion//Jerusalem, swords//spears give a translated approximation of the word-pairs of the original tradition.

The significance of Lowth's researches began to reach well beyond the field of Hebraic studies, when it was discovered, at first chiefly by missionary Bible translators, that in many cultures there existed similar traditions of parallelism (cf. van der Veen 1952; Onvlee 1953). And

101

there has gradually accumulated a considerable body of independently motivated research to indicate that parallelism, as a linguistic phenomenon, is of general occurrence among the world's oral literatures. Studies and translations have documented traditions of parallelism in ancient Semitic languages, ancient Egyptian, Chinese, Japanese, and early Greek as well as numerous 'folk' traditions found throughout south India and most of Southeast Asia, in Austronesian languages from Madagascar to Hawaii, in the various oral literatures of the Ural-Altaic area, in Turkic and Mongolian languages, and among American Indian languages, particularly in Middle America where these traditions reached a flowering in ancient Maya and Aztec literature. (Initial bibliographic sources on parallelism may be found in Jakobson 1966; Fox 1971a.)

Thus Isaiah, the *Popul Vuh*, ancient Chinese Festival Songs, Kachin *Nat* verse, and Hawaiian origin chants reflect similar principles in their composition.[5] And on this basis, it may not ultimately seem surprising that structural analyses of episodes from Genesis, or of the mythology of Borneo or of Highland Burma, or even a portion of American Indian myths should yield a rich array of binary oppositions, since this may—directly or indirectly—have been their composing principle. Conversely, it would suggest that a comprehending analysis of these forms of elaborate dualism ought to examine this underlying principle of composition.

ON ADDRESSING THE 'TEXT': A ROTINESE MYTH OF CULTURE

Of importance to this discussion is the selection of a 'text'. The problem is somewhat analogous to one a Rotinese chanter faces in preparation for a performance. The choice of a text is, by no means, a matter of unrestricted selection. There exists, for major rituals, a recognized repertoire of named chants: chants that each purport, by means of an idealized narrative structure, to 'explain', 'typify', or 'comment' upon a ritual situation (cf. Fox 1971a: 221). These chants resemble the *lakon* of the Javanese *wajang* tradition. Each is a self-contained episode in what appears to have been an epic drama. Close scrutiny of the genealogies that accompany the chants and identify their principal characters provide glimpses of the possible outlines of this epic, but among individual chanters and in the different dialect areas of the island there is a wide variation in the narrative structure of similarly named chants. Nineteenth-century references to bands of wandering poets (Heijmering 1843: 356–357), who would appear wherever major rituals were to be performed, suggest that the tradition may once have been more coherent than it is now. For the present, no Rotinese has attempted the Homeric task of resynthesizing the island's epic.

For a chanter, therefore, there exists a loose canon of relevant texts. From this canon, he is permitted his freedom to adopt, adapt, and embellish within certain limits the narrative structure that best fits the ritual occasion.[6] Judgements on his chosen text are made in terms of its 'appropriateness' to the situation rather than in terms of some unalterable, abstract standard. In a similar vein, I have chosen to summarize here a particular Rotinese ritual chant in strict parallelism. It is especially appropriate to a discussion of issues in structuralism and symbolic analysis because its subject-matter appears to be another transformation of the 'mythologic' traditions broached by Lévi-Strauss in *Le Cru et le cuit*. The chant tells of the hunting of wild pig, of the origin of fire and of cooking, and of the obtainment, by exchange, of the material implements of culture. It plays, at times subtly, at times openly, on the connotations of taste and the metaphoric equation of sexual intercourse and eating. And it goes on to explain the breach in the alliance that once ordered the primal powers of the world.

Properly speaking, this chant ought to be designated as the 'myth of the house'. Its chanting is reserved for the ceremonial consecration of a traditional dwelling. Those chanters who have recited this myth for me and those who have declined to do so agree in regarding it as the most 'heated' segment of Rotinese esoteric knowledge. It is the only chant, to my knowledge, that is intentionally distorted at its crucial juncture; in this case, to veil the crime that creates the house. Rather than adapt and embellish this chant as a chanter might, I intend instead to excerpt from and alternate between three separate versions of this chant from the domain of Termanu. (Complete translations may be found in Fox 1972a: I: 98—109; II: 110–120; III: 156–171. Version one is by the very capable chanter, P. Malesi; version two by the chantress, L. Keluanan; version three by the former Head of the Earth, S. Adulanu.) Together these versions comprise 677 lines of verse, which makes summary in this context a necessity. My intention is not to do a 'structural analysis', whatever that might entail, but to address these texts as a prelude to a discussion of their underlying symbolic structure.

The Rotinese epic involves the deeds of two opposing families: the descendants of the Sun and Moon (*Ledo do Bulan*) and the descendants of the Lords of the Sea and Ocean (*Liun do Sain*). Many of these deeds occur on earth and directly involve the men on earth. What gives the epic its social underpinning are claims by various lineages on Roti to direct descent from or ancestral association with figures in the chants. Most of the nobility of Roti, for example, claim descent, by separate lines, from the nine sons of the Moon, while other clan groups identify themselves with ancestors who allied themselves with the Lords of the Sea. And since both families intermarry in the epic, a putative link to one implies a relation to the other. The significance of this present chant is that it describes the first encounter of these two families—their mutual discovery and its consequences. The setting for the chant is the earth.

The sons of Sun and Moon, Patola Bulan and Mandeti Ledo, descend to earth, whistle for their dogs, Pia Dola and Hua Lae, and set out to hunt.

103

Ala sopu lai basa dae	They hunt throughout the land
Ala fule lai basa oe.	They track throughout the waters.
Leu Ledo lasi nana-papadak	They enter the Sun's forbidden forest
Ma Bulan nula nana-babatak	And the Moon's restricted wood
Ma lala meo dei pana-foe	And catch a pied-nosed cat
Ma kue dei iko-fula,	And a white-tailed civet,
Bulan kue nasa-mao	The Moon's fond civet
Ma Ledo meo naka-boi-na.	And the Sun's tame cat.

Immediately the Sun and Moon inform them of their error and assign them new regions in which to hunt. The hunt resumes but is unsuccessful.

Asu-la ta fue	The dogs corner nothing
Ma busa-la ta eko.	And the hounds encircle nothing.

They continue to where the land borders the sea and suddenly they encounter the Chief Hunter of the Ocean and the Great Lord of the Sea, Danga Lena Liun and Mane Tua Sain, who have come from the ocean depths with their dogs, Masi Tasi and Deta Dosa. It is essential to an understanding of this and subsequent passages to realize that Rotinese traditions personify the Lords of the Sea as Shark and Crocodile. These creatures can assume glistening human forms when they come up upon land. The hunters agree to combine their efforts. As version two makes clear:

Boe ma busa-la laka-bua	The dogs form a pack
Ma asu-la la-esa.	And the hounds join as one.
De ala fule kue	They track civet
Ma ala sopu bafi.	And they hunt pig.
De leo nula Kai Tio dale	Deep in the woods of Kai Tio
Ma lasi Lolo Batu dale	And deep in the forest of Lolo Batu
Boe ma asu-la fua	The dogs corner their prey
Ma busa-la use.	And the hounds give chase.

Here, instead of the forbidden pair, cat and civet, the hunters catch and kill the pair, pig and civet. What then follows is an exchange of invitations and a debate on whether to ascend to the heavens or to descend to the sea depths to eat the sacrifice of pig and civet. In the end it is decided to descend into the sea where the sons of Sun and Moon discover for the first time the taste of cooked food. Again the language of version two is clearer:

De leu, de ala fati bafi	They go and they eat the offering of pig

Ma fina kue.	And partake of the sacrifice of civet.
De ala tunu hai bei masu	They roast on a smoking fire
Ma ala nasu oek bei lume	They cook in boiling water
Nai lo heu hai ikon	In a house roofed with rayfish tails
Ma nai uma sini kea louk.	And in a home decked with turtle shells.

Patola Bulan and Mandeti Ledo secrete a leaf full of this cooked food and carry it off to the Sun and Moon, Bula Kai and Ledo Holo, who on tasting this morsel exclaim:

'Ladak ia nai be	'From where is this taste
Ma lolek ia nai be?'	And where is this goodness?'

And they are told:

'Ladak ia nai liun	'This taste is in the ocean
Ma lolek ia nai sain.'	And this goodness in the sea.'

Whereupon, in version one, the Lords of the Sea request the daughters of the Sun and Moon; in version two, Sun and Moon propose the marriage of their daughters. However, these daughters, Fuda Kea Ledo and Tao Senge Bulan, are already married. They must first be divorced before they can be remarried to the Lords of the Sea. Then begins one of the most significant passages in the chant, a passage that is virtually identical in all the versions I have recorded. The Sun and Moon begin to demand bridewealth payments:

Boe ala doko-doe fae-tena	They demand a payment of livestock
Ma ala tai-boni beli-batun.	And they claim a bridewealth of gold.
De ala fe lilo ma-langa menge	They give gold chains with snakes' heads
Ma ala fe kapa ma-ao foek.	And they give buffalo with crocodile-marked bodies.
Te ala bei doko-doe	But still they continue to demand
Ma ala bei tai-boni.	And still they continue to claim.
Besak-ka ala fe bo paä-bela	Now they give the bore-tool and flat-chisel
Ma ala fe taka tala-la.	And they give the axe and the adze.
Ala fe sipa aba-do	They give the plumb-line marker
Ma ala fe funu ma-leo.	And they give the turning-drill.
Te hu ala bei doko-doe	But they still continue to demand

Ma ala bei tai boni.	And still they continue to claim.
Boe-ma ala fe nesu maka-boka buik	Then they give the mortar whose thudding shakes its base
Ma alu mata-fia tongok.	And the pestle whose thrust blisters the hand.
Te ala bei doko-doe	But still they continue to demand
Ma ala bei tai-boni.	And still they continue to claim.
Besak-ka ala fe kutu-ana naü-poin	Then they give the little flint-set with loose tinder grass
Ma una-ana ai-nggeo.	And the little black-sticked fire-drill.
Besak-ka ala lae:	Now they say:
'Dai te ta dai	'Whether enough or not enough
O nai ta dai liman	What's in our grip is enough in our hand
Ma nou te ta nou	And whether sufficient or insufficient
O nai kuku nou nen.'	What's in our fingers is sufficient in our grasp.'
Besak-ka lenin neu poin	Now they carry everything to the Heights
Ma lenin neu lain.	And they carry everything to Heaven.

With minor variations and the change of a few names, versions one and two of this chant are remarkably similar. There exists, however, a third version that offers a significantly different interpretation, developing more explicitly, through its play on words, the connection between the eating of cooked food and marriage. Version three follows version two to the point where the hunters enter the sea with the catch of pig and civet and then focuses on the lighting of the cooking-fire:

Boe ma ala diu besi no batu	They strike iron on stone
Ma ala una ai no ai.	And they rub stick on stick.
De ala tao kutu naü poi	They work the tinder-top flint-set
Ma tao una ai nggeo.	And work the black-sticked fire-drill.
Boe ma ala pila nuli neu bafi	They burn and roast the pig
Ma ala masu ndalu neu kue.	And they smoke and fire the civet.

At this point, the sisters of the Lords of the Sea appear. They are

Lole Liuk and Lada Saik, literally 'Ocean Goodness and Sea Tastiness'. Immediately the chant begins its verbal allusions. Now that the pig and civet have been roasted, the Lords of the Sea ask their sisters:

'Te bafi sao no bek   'With what do you marry pig
Ma kue tu no hata?'   And with what do you wed
                                     civet?'

Boe te inak-ka Lada Saik   The woman Lada Saik
Ma fetok-ka Lole Liuk nafada And the girl Lole Liuk speaks
nae: saying:
'Te dengu doli no bafi   'Stamp rice with pig
Ma tutu lutu no kue.'   And pound millet with civet.'

Native exegesis on these lines directly identifies the verb, *sao*, 'to marry' with the verb, *naä*, 'to eat'.

The feast then proceeds and, at its conclusion, the Lords of the Sea themselves suggest that the sons of Sun and Moon take food to the heavens. On their return journey, they discover the sweet–sour taste of lontar palm juice, a staple Rotinese food. They remark:

'Seok-ka sain liun lalun-na   'Indeed the sea-ocean's beer is
  malada-hik: tasty:
Kei-kei ma kekeë.   Sweet and sour.
Bulan no Ledo lalun-na so   While the Moon and Sun's
                         beer is
Na namis ma makaleëk-ka.'   Insipid and tart.'

Thus along with cooked food, the sons of Sun and Moon return to the heavens with sweet–sour lontar juice. On tasting this food, the Sun and Moon's first response is to wage war on the sea to obtain more:

'Malole ata lea tafa neu sain   'It would be good if we extend
                         a sword to the sea
Ma loe dongi neu liun.'   And lower a barbed spear to
                         the ocean.'

The sons reject this proposal as impossible and, instead, propose that they marry the women, 'Ocean Goodness and Sea Tastiness'. Sun and Moon react to this by warning their sons that they ought not to attempt to supersede their elders. So Sun and Moon themselves marry the sisters of the Lords of the Sea. This version of the chant thus reverses the relations of the two powers: instead of being wife-giver, the heavens become wife-taker from the sea. In the chant, bridewealth is left unmentioned while all the cultural goods named as bridewealth in the other versions are brought by 'Ocean Goodness and Sea Tastiness' as part of their dowry. The same end is achieved but by altering marriage relations.

With the acquisition of tools from the sea, Sun and Moon order the construction of their house. Chanters regard this as the most critical

107

segment of the narrative and those who have recited it for me admit to obscurity at this point. Version two is the clearest.

The trees whose wood is required for the house are the 'two-leaved *keka* tree' (*Ficus* spp.) and 'three-leaved *fulihaä* tree' (*Vitex* spp.). These are to be made into the *toa*-poles and *sema*-beams: the ridge-poles and support-beams of the house. Various builders are called to work on the house but they are unable to erect the main beams. The chant explains:

Te laka-ndolu nai lain	When they work above
Na ana kekeak leo dae mai	It tilts towards the ground
Ma laka-ndolu nai dulu	When they work on the east
Na lai leo muli neu.	It leans to the west.
Te laka-ndolu nai muli	But when they work on the west
Na soko leo dulu.	It slants to the east.

The secret of the chant is that the house requires a model for the layout of its beams and poles. Shark and crocodile, the Lords of the Sea, the original benefactors of the Sun and Moon, are invited from the ocean, killed, and their skeletal structure used as a model. Thus the structure of the Rotinese house is that of a crocodile, with its head in the east and tail in the west, its rib cage forming the sloping roof beams. (More than once some old Rotinese, in the heat of explanation, has bent down on all fours to demonstrate this outstretched layout of the house.) Version two describes this:

Touk Danga Lena Liun	The man Danga Lena Liun
Ma taëk Man' Tua Sain	And the boy Man' Tua Sain
Ala taon neu uma dii	They make him into the house posts
Ma ala taon neu eda ai.	And they make him into the ladder tree.
Besak-ka kalu kapa ledo haän	Now the sun heats his 'buffalo sinews'
Ma dui manu au teë-na	And the dew moistens his 'chicken bones'.[7]
Ala tao(n) neu sema teluk	They make him into the three *sema*-beams
Ma taon neu toa duak.	And make him into the two *toa*-poles.

Finally true masterbuilders arrive, a species of spider and a giant stick-insect.[8] Laying out the dried bones of the shark and crocodile, they build the house.

Besak-ka Didi Bulan mai	Now Moon Stick-Insect arrives
Ma Bolau Ledo mai.	And Sun Spider arrives.
De lae: 'Deta ape.	They say: 'Dip spittle.

De deta ape neu be	Where the spittle is dipped
Fo lolo neu ndia.'	There lay the planks.'
Boe te Bolau lolo ape neu be	So wherever Spider lays spittle
Na ala solu limak neu ndia	There they then rest the arms
Ma Didi deta ape neu be	And wherever Stick-Insect dips spittle
Na ala fua lolo neu ndia.	There they then place the legs.
Besak-ka sema teluk-kala dadi	Now the three *sema*-beams are made
Ma toa duak-kala tola.	And the two *toa*-poles appear.
Besak-ka ala soe saike ikon	They incise a tail-design
Ma tati solo-bana langan.	And they cut a head-pattern.

And as version one concludes:

| De kue luü nai ikon | A civet crouches at the tail |
| De fani tai nai langan. | Bees nest at the head. |

This, I submit, is the kind of myth that structural analysis was developed to elucidate. Similar myths have been searchingly scrutinized. It offers literally hundreds of binary oppositions to tantalize the analyst and develops a major Southeast Asian mythic motif: a primal alliance whose inevitable, creative rupture establishes disorder and imbalance in the world. The myth is intimately connected, as well, with other Rotinese myths that recount the various causes of enmity between men and the Lords of the Sea: how, for example, the shark and crocodile, after forcibly marrying women on earth, are ambushed as they return to the sea, and their body-parts—blood and guts—are strewn out and then copied to become the motifs for Rotinese cloths. The very conventions of the tradition, the use of doubled names and the common (though not always consistent) stylistic alternation of singular and plural forms defy simple, straightforward translation and contribute syntactically to the overriding duality of composition.

The myth is also replete with seemingly minor details for which native exegesis provides no hint: the 'civet–cat', for example, occurs first as a pair with 'cat' whose hunting is forbidden, then with 'pig' whose flesh may be eaten, and finally with 'bees', domesticated as a design carved on the ridge-pole of the house. But since this myth is a detailed charter, there is a question of how much 'extra' information is needed to inform its analysis. Furthermore, there is the additional problem of the various versions. Version three is a radical departure from versions one and two and it completely avoids mentioning the sacrifice of shark and crocodile. Yet when confronted with these alternative interpretations, Rotinese, with whom I have discussed these matters, do not seem disconcerted. Each chanter has his opinion and obviously any of the versions would be adequate for the performance of the consecration of a house. Significance does not seem to reside wholly or even primarily at the message level of the narrative structure.

It is considerations of this sort that lead one to question the usefulness of any single myth analysis or series of analyses. If one takes as axiomatic that myths and their symbols are meaningful as part of a whole it would seem that any single myth or group of myths is too inadequate and truncated a cultural production to be acceptable on its own. What ought to be a goal of analysis is something far more systematic and yet at the same time, as has been argued, some principle or set of principles that orders the system.

RITUAL LANGUAGE AS A CULTURAL CODE

Among linguists, Professor Roman Jakobson has most frequently drawn attention to the phenomenon of parallelism, noting both its 'pervasive' and 'compulsory' qualities and arguing that the existence of a thoroughgoing canonical parallelism provides objective criteria for the study of native correspondences (Jakobson 1956: 77). A dyadic language of the kind used by Rotinese in their rituals is a formal code comprising the culture's stock of significant binary relations. It is a complex code, not arbitrarily restricted to a particular 'domain' of natural language and it is relatively stable.[9] In appearance, the code gives indication of being an open-ended, focused system of semantic interconnections, what linguists since Trier have designated a semantic field. Furthermore, it is capable of formal study, since it is itself a formal system.

To utilize the terminology I have adopted in previous discussions of Rotinese ritual language (Fox 1971a; 1974), each dual category or binary opposition is a dyadic set. As such, each dyadic set is a unique semantic grouping that brings into conjunction two separate elements, thereby 'affecting' their individual significance. What is more, an element that forms part of a dyadic set may pair with other elements to create new dyadic sets. Thus whereas these binary categories may be considered as ordered pairs, they are not exclusive pairs. A ready example is civet–cat in the previous chant. Civet forms dyadic sets with 'cat', 'pig', and 'bees', each set signalling an altered significance for its constituent elements. This feature makes possible the study of these relations, as a system, because any element may have a whole range of elements with which it forms a set and these elements, in turn, may pair with still other elements, creating an extensive network of interlinkages. In fact, the present stage of analysis suggests that the code for Rotinese ritual language can be displayed as a large constellation of complexly interrelated elements with only a limited array of unconnected elements.

What is more, these interlinkages cross-cut conventional grammatical categories, such as verb, adverb, preposition, and noun, joining elements instead by what seems to be some other underlying system of semantic values. Tracing relations among these semantic elements—the chains and cycles along edges of what is a symmetric graph—provides a glimpse of the structuring of the cultural code of the Rotinese.

THE SYMBOLIC ANALYSIS OF A CULTURAL CODE

Any form of symbolic analysis must confront the problem of complexity. A prerequisite to this particular analysis is, therefore, the compilation of a relatively large corpus of ritual texts covering an entire range of ceremonial situations. The present analysis is based on 25 lengthy chants and a small collection of short chants, the equivalent of just under 5000 lines of verse.[10] These chants are all in the Rotinese dialect of Termanu and Baä. A corpus of translated texts from other dialects, particularly from Thie, has not yet been studied. In addition, I estimate that my recent fieldwork has doubled the size of my total corpus from all dialects. Thus, again, I must emphasize the tentative nature of this stage of analysis.

A dictionary of ritual language, based on first texts, has been compiled.[11] It includes slightly over 1000 dyadic sets, but does not yet include names which form a large and important subset of additional dyadic sets. In total, the dictionary comprises more than 1400 entries. In the dictionary, each element or lexical item is translated and has listed, for it, all other elements with which it forms dyadic sets. The dictionary is thus an initial tabulation of relations among elements in the language.

A number of formal methods involving, for example, graph theory, matrix manipulations, or a variety of multidimensional scaling techniques, can be usefully employed in studying these relations. At the moment, as work on the dictionary progresses, I am experimenting with various different procedures. A formalization of these relations would be premature and is, therefore, not intended here. Rather, this analysis is primarily intended to indicate what appears to constitute the present core of this ritual language, to trace certain of its symbolic coordinates, and to consider its implications.

To define a core among interrelated elements is a matter of degree. Any 'core' may be as large or as small as one may wish to define it. In this case, I have selected all elements from the dictionary that have a range of five or more sets. There are currently 37 such elements. A range of five, it must be realized, is an arbitrary figure. Choosing a range of six would, for example, decrease the selection of elements from the present dictionary by more than one-third, while the choice of a range of four would nearly double them. A range of five establishes a key group of elements of sufficient size and complexity to illustrate the argument. The total number of links of these key elements to other elements comes to 250. But since many of these links are internal links, we can perform a further selection by eliminating those elements with less

111

than two links to other elements in the key group. Two links is the minimal number necessary to permit cyclical relations.[12] The resultant core forms a semantic network consisting of those elements with a total range of five or more, possessing at least two links in common. Although it could have been defined either more exclusively or more inclusively, and will most likely, by the application of the same criteria, become—as the dictionary develops—a larger and even more saturated network, nevertheless this core locates the area of greatest semantic density and connectivity in the ritual system. The core consists of 21 elements from a possible 1400 dictionary entries. The full list of these terms, with glosses and their links to one another, is given in *Table 1*.

Table 1   Core terms

Element	Glosses	Links
1. Ai:	'plant, tree, stick, wood'	Batu, Boa, Dae, Do(k), Naü, Oe, Tua
2. Dae:	'earth, land; below; low, lowly'	Ai, Batu, Dulu, Loe, Muli, Oe, Tua
3. Batu:	'stone, rock'	Ai, Dae, Lutu
4. Boa:	'fruit; counter term for small objects'	Ai, Hu(k)
5. Do(k):	'leaf; counter term for objects in strings'	Ai, Hu(k)
6. Naü:	'grass, tinder; the quality of being soft, gentle'	Ai, Oe
7. Oe:	'water, semen, juice, liquid'	Ai, Dae, Naü
8. Tua:	'lontar palm (*Borassus flabellifer*), the lontar's products'	Ai, Dae
9. Lutu:	'pile, ring or other arrangement of stones; to pile, erect stones; the quality of being well worked, smooth, refined; ritual name for millet.'	Batu, Hu(s)
10. Hu(-k,-s):	'trunk, base, root, origin; counter term for trees; designation for males in the maternal line of affiliation; term for clan origin festival'	Boa, Do
11. Ei(k)	'foot, paw, leg'	Hu(k), Langa, Lima
12. Lima:	'hand, arm; five'	Ei(k), Langa, Tei(k)
13. Tei(k)	'insides, stomach, womb; lineage'	Langa, Lima
14. Langa:	'head'	Dulu, Ei(k), Lima, Iko, Tei(k)
15. Iko:	'tail'	Langa, Muli
16. Dulu:	'east'	Dae, Langa, Muli
17. Muli:	'west; youngest child, i.e. last-born'	Dae, Dulu, Iko
18. Loe:	'to descend, to lower, to be low'	Dae, Tai
19. Tai:	'to balance, to cling (to an edge), to border, to be on the edge'	Loe, Luü, Saë
20. Luü	'to sink or settle down; to lie down (particularly of crocodile and waterbuffalo half-submerged in water); to brood (of a bird); to request a woman in marriage'	Saë, Tai
21. Saë	'to ride on s.t.; to perch (of birds); to rise (of water)'	Luü, Tai

What this core includes are directional coordinates, the words for 'earth', 'water', 'rock', and 'tree', terms for plants and plant-parts, body parts, and a peculiar collection of verbs of position involving ideas of balance, border, ascent, and descent. What is significant, however, is not merely the listing of these elements but their relations to one another. A graph of these interconnections is as shown in *Figure 1*.

Figure 1   Core terms

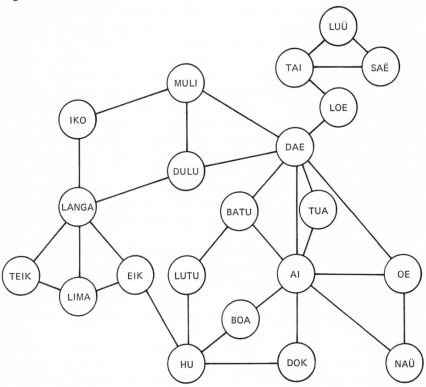

SPECIFIC INTERPRETATION OF THE RITUAL CORE

An interpretation of the significance of these core terms within the ritual system would require lengthy discussion. For my part, this analysis seems to confirm, at a formal level, certain of the far less formal interpretations I have previously made of Rotinese ritual. In an article on 'Sister's Child as Plant' (1971b), I argued that a major premise of Rotinese rituals is the symbolic equation of man and plant. Rituals are cast in a botanic idiom and specific plants are manipulated as icons to define the precise purpose of each ritual. Their general intent is always life-giving, that is, to provide for the care, cultivation, and conduct of a 'plant', even to a point beyond death when, for example, outstanding

113

individuals may be identified with some large hardwood tree which is then ceremonially surrounded with stones (*lutu*) to form an enduring megalithic monument. The occurrence in the ritual core of 'tree' (*ai*), 'fruit' (*boa*), 'leaf' (*dok*), or trunk (*huk*) is therefore revealing. Simple glosses on these terms, however, can be misleading since they function senantically in a complex way. They serve as counter terms for differently shaped objects and form compound semantic labels for parts of the human body: (*k*)*ai-usuk*: 'rib-case', *use-aik*: 'navel cord', *boa-deëk*: 'kidney', *langa-dok*: 'human hair', *dii-dok*: 'ears', *difa-dok*: 'lips'. My original argument (1971b: 240) was that there were a sufficient number of these composite semantic labels to permit native speculative exegesis to create the necessary correspondences between man and plant on which the rituals depend. It would now seem, on the basis of this present analysis, that this native exegesis is itself a secondary elaboration of a more fundamental semantic relation. In this regard, the term *hu* appears to function as a crucial linking node. *Hu*, as 'trunk', is a counter term for trees. *Hus* is the term for the annual clan feast and, via its links with *lutu*, refers to those origin celebrations of 'stone and tree' that are performed around a ring of smooth stone 'seats' at the base of a tree. *Hu* is also the designation for particular individuals of the maternal line of affiliation, *toö-huk*: 'mother's brother', and *bai-huk*: 'mother's mother's brother' who are the chief actors in all rituals of the life-cycle. Furthermore, *hu*, in its link with *ei(k)*: 'foot', serves as direct semantic bridge between plant-parts and body-parts.

The inclusion of a single specific plant, the lontar palm, *tua*, is particularly pointed since this tree is the one indispensable source of subsistence for the Rotinese, the virtual 'tree of life'. This large, dioecious palm—the female marked by clusters of large, hanging fruit, the male by drooping ithyphallic flowerstalks—is, I have argued (1971b: 245–246), a focal icon of the Rotinese.

Similarly, in an article on Rotinese symbolic inversions (1973), I suggested that a further premise of Rotinese rituals is an ordering of symbolic space that associates the parts of the body and the directional coordinates. 'East' (*dulu*) is linked with 'head' (*langa*); 'west' (*muli*) is linked with 'tail' (*iko*). The universe, the island of Roti, and the Rotinese house are all represented with a 'head' rising to the east and a 'tail' descending to the west. According to different exegeses, this shape is that of the crocodile, a sacrificial waterbuffalo, or even a man. But whatever its specific shape, the essential system is preserved invariant. In accordance with this system, the term *kona* is both 'right' and 'south'; *ki* is 'left' and 'north'. A series of symbolic syllogisms ('The east is as broad as the west, but the sun comes from the east, therefore, the east is greater than the west', etc.) provide a means of ranking the directions and then, upon this basis, there is constructed a host of symbolic associations. Thus, for example, native exegesis associates *uluk*, 'firstborn', with *dulu* (east) on the analogy that *mulik*, 'last-born', derives from the root *muli* (west).[13] What this present analysis indicates is that the initial logic of the system is founded on the relations and equations of ritual language. In the graph of the core terms, 'head', *langa*, serves as a key node linking body-part terms and the directional coordinates.

Close inspection suggests that there may be several discernible foci within the core of the ritual system. Plant terms are linked by *huk* to the words for body-parts, which are, in turn, linked by *langa* to the directional coordinates. The root *dae*, as noun for 'earth', as a directional coordinate 'below, beneath', and as a common adverbial term, 'lowly', serves as another crucial connecting node, both to the chain of positional verbs and to terms for the natural elements, 'water', 'rock', and above all, 'tree, plant'. In terms of their internal links, *ai* (tree, plant), *dae* (earth, low, lowly), *langa* (head), and *hu* (trunk, base, origin) account for 22 of a possible 31 edges in the graph. The problem is, however, that the elements in this core are highly connected in a complex fashion. In addition, it must be remembered, each element is itself the organizing node to an expansive network of semantic elements within the total system. The simple inspection of a reduced graph or the piecemeal examination of various subgraphs of the system are insufficient, on their own, to provide an understanding of the whole.

SEMANTIC NETWORKS AND COMPUTER CLASSIFICATION

The alternative to an intuitive inspection of either a simplified or an enlarged graphic representation of the elements of ritual language must, it seems, be some method of computer classification. The question is not whether to adopt such a strategy, for the complexity of the system leaves little choice, but rather what form of sorting strategy to adopt amid the numerous, diverse, and ever-increasing number of available methods. For this question, there is no simple answer. Theoretically, it is possible to argue for different methods in terms of the properties of the measures one wishes to consider; pragmatically, it is possible to experiment with several methods to see which provides more 'useful' results. In this regard, there can hardly be a 'true', 'natural', or 'necessarily best' method. The temptation is to mistake these methods for what they are not: to allow the arbitrary to assume the appearance of the natural. The gain in the adoption of any of these methods is one of intelligibility in the face of complexity and, for comparative purposes, the means of a standard procedure for treating different systems.

The core terms—or the relations among any number of elements in ritual language—can be conceived of as a graph and represented by the $N \times N$ incidence matrix of that graph. The range of any element—the incidence of that node in a graph—consists of all its positive entries with other elements of the matrix. To determine a measure of similarity among a set of such elements, it is necessary to decide on the properties that constitute the semantics of the system. Several properties would seem to be extremely important: (1) Every element should be considered not merely in terms of its link with any other element, but also in terms of the other pairwise links it may possess, together with that element, to additional elements in the system. This, in effect, involves considering all dyadic sets and matching elements by the sets they form with each other and via third elements. (2) Every element should be considered as a link with itself since this will permit the incorporation of invariant terms, i.e. terms in ritual language that have no pairs and functions as a repetition of themselves. In other words, the diagonal of the incidence matrix ought to consist of positive entries. (3) Since elements have different ranges of association, some account ought to be taken of the varying total range that any two elements possess. (4) The coincidence of all positive matches in the matrix should be counted as more significant than the coincidence of an absence of a match. With these properties in mind, we can adopt, from among the formulae that have been devised to provide a measure of similarity or what is called, in numerical taxonomy, the coefficients of association (Sokal and Sneath 1963: 128), a formula that consists, roughly speaking, of the intersection of the range of A and the range of B over the union of the range of A and the range of B. Formally, similarity is defined [14] as follows, where $x_{ij} = 1$ if element i pairs with element j; otherwise 0:

$$\text{Sim}(i, j) = \frac{\Sigma(2x_{ik} \cdot x_{jk})}{\Sigma(x_{ik} + x_{jk})}$$

This establishes a first stage—a reasonable measure of pair-to-pair similarity. On this basis, we can derive a new interelement similarity matrix, and from this matrix, it is possible to devise a variety of intergroup orderings depending on, as always, the measures one adopts. Among the more sophisticated, readily available, and economic sorting strategies for such intergroup similarities are the agglomerative or aggregative hierarchical clustering techniques. There are any number of these and their properties vary with the measures utilized (Lance and Williams 1967). But because of the relative economy of these techniques, it is possible to develop a programme that will, in a single run, submit the same data to a clustering process by a number of different measures of cluster distance or size. A programme of this kind has been developed at Harvard (Olivier 1973). It begins with N single-item clusters and merges pairs of clusters iteratively to form a single N-item cluster. Input is a N × N symmetric matrix of similarity (or dissimilarity) measures for the set of N items. Output is a tree-diagram with an added column of 'values' for each cluster depending on the particular method. Using this programme to experiment on the matrix of core terms and studying the clustering obtained by various measures,[15] I concluded that the measure of distance between clusters

A and B defined as the mean of the similarities between points A and B gave the closest approximation of my own intuitive understanding of the relations among the core terms. *Figure 2* is the tree-diagram of the aggregative hierarchical clustering of the core terms by mean distance. It may be compared with the graphic representation of these same terms in *Figure 1*.

Figure 2   Tree diagram of aggregative hierarchical clustering

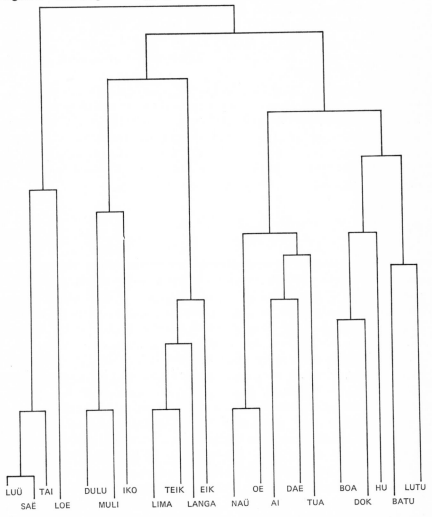

The point of this exercise has been to indicate a method that may be used to study the semantic relations of ritual language, noting that, as the complexity of the system increases, it becomes more difficult to decide upon criteria for distinguishing among the results of these methods. Implied in this discussion is the suggestion that a possible strategy would be to adopt the method that, on a limited scale, gives the best approximation of some intuitive understanding and to assume that, on a larger scale, it will continue to do so. This leaves 'intuition' as a foundation. Yet it is evident that, whatever my intuitions may be, they are based on present-day Rotinese practice and the insights and interpretations provided me by Rotinese elders and chanters. And it is also evident, at a theoretical level, that the semantic networks of ritual language are sufficiently complex to permit a variety of practices and, as I myself have frequently noted in my ethnographic descriptions, alternative interpretations of the same practice. What this seems to imply is that, however one approaches it, ritual language is a lived-in symbolic structure, incapable of exclusive comprehension by any monotypic representation.

But this does not mean that the exercise of comprehension is useless. In fact, proceeding from binary oppositions to semantic networks highlights a fundamental aspect of these semantic relations: that certain elements have a range of pairs, that these create networks, and that a core, however it is defined, of multiconjugate nodes within the network act as primary symbols in the system. This involves a consideration of the implications of hierarchy within ritual language.

HIERARCHY, TAXONOMY, AND POLYSEMY

Structural analysis, of the form we began by considering, is epistemologically a theory of oppositions. For Lévi-Strauss, this analysis consists in the theoretical modelling of the possible combinations and permutations of some defined set of oppositions. Structure is represented as a model that pertains to certain 'strategic' levels of reality and it is the task of the investigator to discover that 'order of orders' which by transformation encompasses these separable autonomous levels of structured reality (Lévi-Strauss 1953: 528–529, 547–548). Semantically, what this appears to imply is that all binary oppositions are generally autonomous, isomorphic, and equal in so far as they are the product of the same ordering logic. Needham, on the other hand, makes the consistent assertion that only certain societies—those of prescriptive alliance—are characterized by a pervasive concordance of complementary oppositions. The ordering of dual categories in all other societies is theoretically an open question. Hence, except in the proposed special test-case of prescriptive alliance societies, what is lacking in this epistemology, as critics, particularly Marxist critics (cf. Terray 1972: 40), have noted, is any articulated concept of hierarchy. The possibility of transformations between strategic levels is not the same as a hierarchy of levels nor does it seem to involve a hierarchical ordering of elements at any specific level. In any semantic theory, opposition without hierarchy can only lead to endless manipulations.

By contrast, the strength of American ethnosemantics has been in the elucidation of hierarchy via paradigms, taxonomies, tree structures, developmental sequencing, and flow-charting. In these investigations, however, lexical 'contrast' has generally involved the notion of 'inclusions' and thus resulted in the construction of bounded hierarchic structures ordered horizontally by differentiation and vertically in terms of a subordinating continuum of the particular to the more general. Applying these notions to the construction of folk taxonomies of natural language raises, as the theoreticians of these methods quickly realized, a variety of so-called 'special problems': multiple and interlocking hierarchies, extrahierarchic relations, synonymy, homonymy, and polysemy (cf. Conklin 1962, reprinted 1969: 41–57). It was in response to these hierarchic special problems that Charles Frake first proposed the study of *interlinkage* (1964, reprinted 1969: 123–137) criticizing, in the process, the concept of bounded semantic domains based exclusively on a hierarchy of inclusion:

> ... any concept is interlinked by a variety of relationships to a large number of other concepts, which, in turn, are interlinked with still other concepts. If a semantic domain is a set of related concepts, then it is clear that there is no one way to separate the conceptual structure of a people into a finite number of discrete, clearly delimited domains. Rather, we have a network of relations whose links enable us to travel along a variety of paths from one concept to another (1969: 132).

The problem involves the relation of hierarchy and interlinkage and requires a careful and lengthy consideration. Here only a few remarks can be made. Of its total vocabulary, we have seen that Rotinese ritual language has a relatively small number of primary symbols which, by their range of linkages, 'organize' other elements, which similarly organize still others to form what appears to be a hierarchy of symbols. If one accepts this understanding of hierarchy, then clearly this linguistic hierarchy does not resemble the previous taxonomic structures proposed for the study of folk classification. However one may attempt to interpret the higher-level, primary symbols in the light of ritual practice, they comprise a seemingly odd and certainly non-obvious collection of lexical items. *Ai*, 'plant, tree,' for example, would—in a standard plant taxonomy—appear as the maximal taxon and perhaps again at the next level of contrast, whereas *tua*, 'lontar palm', would occur at or near the lowest contrastive level. But in ritual language, *ai* and *tua* are linked and, because they both possess an equal range of linkages, they have the same hierarchical value. In this hierarchy, it is not taxonomic generality but polysemy—the property of a symbol to relate to a multiple range of other symbols—that becomes the criterion for hierarchical inclusion. To judge from the study of other ritual systems, there seems to be good empirical justification for this kind of criterion. Turner has elegantly and subtly argued for a similar criterion (1967: 48–58). No

James J. Fox

less than the *mukula* of the Ndembu, the all-important *tua* palm of the Rotinese can invoke a nexus of symbolic associations.

The implications of this hierarchy for the understanding of change are considerable. Change in a structure conceived of as equal, autonomous dyads can only proceed partially and by piecemeal. Change in a system of hierarchically interrelated combinations of dyads can only be appraised by examination of the point at which this change occurs. Change in this system is a dialectic process but not all change is equally significant. The rupture, resolution, or synthetic engagement of elements with a limited range of associations in some peripheral dyad may have little effect on the total system, while a similar change among any of the higher-level elements would have immediate and systemic effects throughout the language. The hierarchy of certain symbols—their position within the hierarchy—governs the particular manifestation of the whole.

We need not discuss these notions of change abstractly but can consider what is occurring at present on Roti in terms of ritual language. The majority of Rotinese have comfortably become Protestant Christians without rejecting their former traditions. But a small majority is evangelically engaged in a polemic against these traditions, contemptuously referring to the rituals as a 'religion of rock and tree'. Thus they have chosen a key dyad of primary symbols as the focus of their attack. On the other hand, the introduction of the Malay Bible, and particularly the Old Testament with its elaborate tradition of parallel verse, has provided unintended support for Rotinese ritual language. The roles of chanter and preacher are not incompatible, and a modern ritual can interweave chant segments, psalms, or quotations from Isaiah without apparent contradiction. Furthermore, what seems to have begun is a local-level retelling of the Bible in ritual language.

The chanter Peu Malesi, who provided me with version one of the myth of the house, was among the first chanters to offer to recite for me on my return to the island. Now, with the full and unchallenged power of a mature talent, he proposed to tell me what he described as an ancient Rotinese myth about the origin of death. This myth, which he told me before an assembled group of Rotinese, was about the ancestral pair, the man Teke Telu and the woman Koa Hulu, who lived in a walled and forbidden garden at the beginning of time. The woman, Koa Hulu, was tempted by an 'eel and snake' to pluck and eat a 'fruit sweet as lontar syrup and a leaf honied as bee's water' and by this act brought into being the tools for 'hewing a coffin and digging a grave'. And thus, according to the standard formulaic phrase, there arose 'the death of the spirits and the decease of the ghosts'.

This unmistakable Rotinese version of Adam and Eve was delivered in flawless ritual language. As such it was readily accepted by those who heard it, not as something new, but as something extremely old—a carefully guarded segment of the esoteric knowledge that proved the often stated Rotinese contention that the Bible is another version of Rotinese tradition. This kind of retelling transforms the seeming challenge of biblical Christianity into the means of maintaining the essential distinctions of the ritual language code. It would be foolhardy at this point to predict what changes may occur within the system of ritual language in its encounter with Christianity but it is possible to appreciate how, in a lived-in system of this complexity, a simple relational change of primary symbols can have far-reaching unintentional effects.

EXPLORATIONS ON RITUAL LANGUAGE

The initial impetus for the study of the semantic networks of ritual language was comparative: to establish recognizable procedures for the analysis of different ritual systems. Many societies in eastern Indonesia —on Sumba, Timor, and Flores—possess traditions of parallelism similar to those of the Rotinese. An adequate corpus of parallel texts already exists for the Atoni of Timor (Middelkoop 1949) and research is presently being conducted among the Mambai of Portuguese Timor to gather another.[16] Rotinese, Atoni, and Mambai are closely related languages which may, therefore, be considered to form a special field of study. But it is also possible to begin this comparative venture by a micro-analysis of the different semantic relations between dialect areas of Roti. Beyond eastern Indonesia, large collections of parallel verse exist for Nias, a number of Dayak groups in Borneo, and for the Sa'dan Toraja of the Celebes (Fox 1971a: 217–218). Gradually it may be possible to advance comparisons on the symbol systems of these widely separated linguistic groups and conceivably from Indonesia to similar systems in Southeast Asia and elsewhere.

A further research possibility of semantic networks is to consider their expansion and to trace the formal associations on any selected node within the system. Essentially, the exploration of these networks is the converse operation to that of defining a core. Whereas any element may be chosen as a starting-point, it is of particular interest in dealing with verbal and adverbial elements since the referential approaches to the study of semantics are generally inadequate to deal with this vast array of lexical items (cf. Fox [1974] for a discussion of the network of verbs of 'speaking' in Rotinese). In this connection, we may consider the associations on the term *loe*, 'to descend, to lower, to be low, lowly'. The chain of associations emanating from *loe*, through *tai*, *saë*, and *luü*, comprises a network of 90 elements, excluding all links to other core terms. To simplify this large network for purposes of this discussion, we can exclude all links from *loe* to other core terms, including *tai*, *saë*, and *luü*. This still constitutes a sizeable network of 21 elements. The list of these elements with their glosses and links is set out in *Table 2*.

Table 2   Formal associations on *loe*

Element	Glosses	Links
1. Loe:	'to descend, to lower, to be low'	(Dae), Dilu, Leä, Nggolo, Peu, Sai, Sali, (Tai), Teë
2. Dilu:	'to bend over, to turn down'	Loe, Sesu
3. Sesu:	'to bend, break, or cut at a joint'	Dilu
4. Leä:	'to stretch, measure, extend, pull, tug, drag; to divine (by stretching spear: Leä Te)'	Hela, Kani, Loe, Nole, Nuni, Tona, Tuluk
5. Hela:	'to pull, to tug, to pull out; to divorce (in the compound Hela-Ketu)'	Leä, Nole
6. Nole:	'to carry s.t. so that it hangs down, to drag; to divorce (in the compound Nole-Ladi)'	Hela, Leä
7. Kani:	'to hang down loosely; to divine (by the hanging stone method: Kani batu)'	Leä
8. Nuni:	'to pull, to lead (a horse, for example, by a rope)'	Leä
9. Tona:	'to push forth; to master, to overpower'	Leä
10. Tuluk:	'to shove, to push'	Leä
11. Nggolo:	'to protrude; a protuberance, promontory, snout (of an animal)'	Loe
12. Peu:	'to jut forth, to stick out (esp. of trees or the branches of trees)'	Loe
13. Sai:	'to appear, to arrive, to come upon a place; to fall (of rain)'	Loe
14. Sali:	'to pour out, to overflow; overflowing'	Doko, Loe
15. Doko:	'to hang, to droop, to recede; receding'	Benu, Sali, (Tai)
16. Benu:	'to balance, to be balanced; balanced or balancing'	Doko, Leo
17. Leo:	'to circle, to go round; circling, surrounding'	Benu
18. Teë:	'to rest, to stand still, to place on end; to erect'	Hani, Loe
19. Hani:	'to wait, to watch over, to tend (animals)'	Bafa, Hulu, Teë
20. Bafa:	'to wait in ambush, to hide'	Hani
21. Hulu:	'to draw in; to gather (animals) together'	Hani

The graph of their associations appears in *Figure 3*.

Here *loe* can be seen as a point of articulation for a variety of verbal forms. Some, like *nggolo*, *leu*, and *sai*, occur in a limited, specific orbit with *loe*. Some, like *dilu*, *teë* and *sali*, lead outward in a chain of associations, allowing us to follow, for example, the by-no-means obvious Rotinese associational logic that one attempts to encapsulate by glosses on descending, pouring out, drooping, balancing, and surrounding. Another, *leä*, forms a further point of articulation for a new orbit of associations.

Analysing these networks solves certain problems but raises others—

Figure 3   Graph of formal associations on *loe*

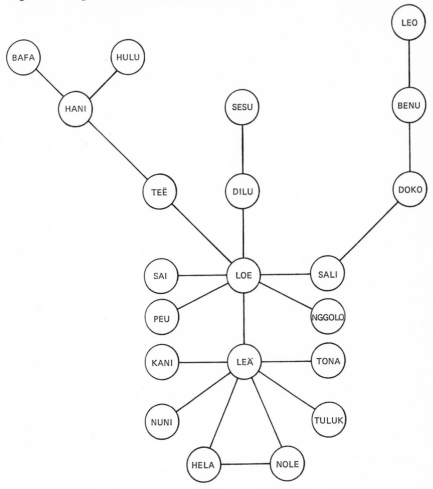

particularly in regard to homonymy. To take one instance, *bafa* in Rotinese has the meanings: (1) 'to wait in ambush, to hide' and (2) 'opening, mouth, beak, gully', and since these two occurrences of *bafa* sort themselves out in different regions of the semantic network, they can easily be recognized as homonyms. On the other hand, *doko*, although on its own it does not link with *tai*, does so in a compound term: *doko-doe//tai-boni*. This dyadic set is used specifically in the context of bridewealth negotiations to indicate the persistent prodding or gentle demanding that is supposed to characterize these negotiations. One could formally treat *doko* and *doko-doe* as separate, but associational links of both *doko* and *tai* with *loe* suggest that however difficult it may be to divine the association of 'demanding' and 'drooping' there would appear to be some relation.

But there is still another major exploratory possibility in the study of

123

ritual language. Roman Jakobson called attention to the investigation of parallelism within the context of an important discussion of what he described, in *Fundamentals of Language*, as the 'twofold character' of language: selection and combination. Developing distinctions established in linguistics since Saussure, Jakobson identified the associarive, the paradigmatic, the selective aspect of language with 'metaphor' and the syntagmatic, the combinative aspect with 'metonym'. (Lévi-Stauss's adaptation of these notions has given them currency in the anthropological literature.) In this terminology, the phenomenon of parallelism relates exclusively to 'metaphor'. In the case of Rotinese ritual language, the delineation of certain of the parameters of metaphor may make it possible to focus attention on metonymic creation.

The issue can also be posed in a different fashion. Rotinese ritual language consists of parallel verse that occurs in grammatically similar lines. In theory, one chanter responds to another by supplying the appropriate second verse to a verse given him by the first chanter. In practice, this is true only of chanters who are acquainted with each other; newly acquainted chanters, in my experience, require a considerable amount of cueing before they begin to respond properly to one another. In theory, the circle of Rotinese dancers is supposed to answer, in chorus, each line of verse initiated by the chanter in its midst. In practice, a chanter sings both verses before the chorus picks up the second verse (although this is said not to have been the case formerly). In theory, therefore, when the whole of the ritual language dictionary has been computerized, it would be an extremely instructive goal—as well as a methodological test—to develop a Response Programme that would answer any line of Rotinese verse with a correspondingly correct line. The problems to this are formidable but grappling with them may elucidate what is involved in metonym.

We may take two lines of verse from the myth of the house as illustration. The first verse presents no problem whatsoever:

(1) Ala fe sipa aba-do   They give the plumb-line marker

Ala (they) and *fe* (give) are invariant elements so that all that is required is the conjunction *ma* (and) or *do* (or)—either is permissible—and a search in the dictionary for what pairs with sipa aba-do (listed as a compound since this is the only way it occurs). The answer is a single link: funu ma-leo, so that the only possible correct response is:

(2) Ala fe funu ma-leo   They give the turning-drill

It is apparent, however, that since an element may pair with as many as ten or more other elements, the permutations and combinations of elements that must be considered to obtain a proper response are potentially enormous. Furthermore, there exists the question of what constitutes a proper response and whether there could be more than one such response. Consider the following line:

(3) Ala fe lilo ma-langa   They give gold chains with snakes'
    menge   heads

The response to this in the myth is:

(4) Ala fe kapa ma-ao foek   They give buffalo with crocodile-
                         marked bodies.

There is something strikingly 'mythological' about a correct response that attributes 'crocodile-marked bodies' to waterbuffalo. One must first comprehend that, according to the mythology, all buffalo originated from the sea as a gift of the crocodile. Then one must realize that in Rotinese *foe* is both the word for crocodile and the term used to refer to flecks of white skin pigmentation on men and animals. Etymologically, there is evidence that these two usages of *foe* are derived from different roots, but it is more important to be aware that, in Rotinese folk etymology, they are identical. Other animals may have white markings: the 'cat and civet' mentioned in the first lines of the myth of the house are described as 'pied-white nosed and white-tailed'. But it is when a buffalo has similar markings that it is considered a throw-back which shows evidence of its origin. Folk etymology based on mythology provides the essential means of linking snake-headed chains and crocodile-marked bodies on buffalo.

This 'correct' response appears even more interesting when compared with other possible responses. *Lilo* pairs with seven other elements; *langa* with eight, so that there are altogether 56 possible responses according to the following table:

		Batu		Alu	
		Besi		Ao	
		Buna		Dulu	
Ala Fe		Haba	Ma-	Ei	Foek
		Kapa		Fude	
		Lusi		Iko	
		Pota		Lima	
				Teik	

The majority of these combinations produce nonsense:

(5) Ala fe besi ma-dulu foek*:   They give iron with crocodile's
                         east

(6) Ala fe buna ma-fude foek*:   They give a flower with crocodile's
                         froth

(7) Ala fe lusi ma-alu foek*:   They give copper with a crocodile's
                         pestle.

But the following possible responses raise interesting questions.

(8) Ala fe kapa ma-ei foek*:   They give buffalo with crocodile's
                         feet

(9) Ala fe haba ma-iko foek*:   They give braided gold strings with crocodile's tails

(10) Ala fe batu ma-ao foek*:   They give rocks with crocodile's bodies

Line (8) creates a confusion in Rotinese classifications. The crocodile, like the monkey, is considered to resemble man in that its forelegs are *lima* (hands, arms) and hind legs are *eik*. A waterbuffalo, on the other hand, has four *eik*. So a crocodile-footed buffalo would be an anomalous creature.

Line (9) is a plausible response but describes a nonexistent cultural object. For centuries, Ndaonese craftsmen have braided gold strings for the Rotinese and many of these end with reptilian 'heads' but no one—to my knowledge—has fashioned a corresponding 'tail' to these strings, though this would certainly be within the symbolic conventions of the artistic tradition. But the question would remain: why this object should be identified by its 'tail' rather than its 'head'.

Line (10) poses further problems since it describes a common object on Roti. There are numerous rocks of varying sizes that are described as the solidified remains of former crocodiles. The island of Roti, as a whole, is said to be one such enormous rock. The response is perfectly sound, mythologically acceptable, but a rock may be inappropriate as bridewealth.

As a first-level approximation, what is needed is an understanding of the syntagmatic compound terms, irreversible binomials, and ritual formulae, of which there are many, to eliminate the most unlikely and nonsensical combinations. By further reflecting upon the networks of ritual language, it may be possible to develop a canon of accordance that would account for still more combinations. But this is clearly not the same immense task that the generative linguist sets himself in determining the logical, syntactical, inferential, and contextual rules that underlie well-formed, meaningful sentences. For one, the investigation is directed towards a definable segment of possible Rotinese utterances. Second, it is not concerned with generating new sentences but with matching appropriate sentences to already given ones by specific lexical rules. Furthermore, ritual language—although not context-free—is a special speech form of formulaic devices whose patternings make chants applicable to a variety of ritual situations. But still, in the process of this investigation, it is probable that there will occur an abundance of engaging responses that will have to be discussed directly with the chanters of Roti to involve them in the explication of their art.

COMMENTS AND CONCLUSIONS

In this paper, I have discussed various operations and analyses that may be performed in and on Rotinese ritual language. At this point, I would like to shift perspective and comment briefly on ritual language in relation to the whole of Rotinese verbal culture. It seems evident that a symbol in ritual language—'earth', 'rock', 'tree'—is related to but yet *differs in its use* in, for example, the Rotinese stock of dream omens and consequences, in proverbs, in folktales and in the genealogical narratives, in the oral codes for legal decisions at Rotinese courts, in ordinary conversation, and in baby-talk. Each of these usages, speech forms, or genres—and more that could be enumerated—I would label a 'language stratum', following Friedrich Waismann in what he announced as 'a programme for the future'. Already in 1946, Waismann was calling on those interested in linguistic analysis to reverse a traditional approach. Instead of defining words by their referents and then analysing referents by their subject-matter—material objects, sense data, vague impressions—he urged the examination of linguistic strata to determine their subject-matter:

> If we carefully study the texture of the concepts which occur in a given stratum, the logic of its propositions, the meaning of truth, the web of verification, the sense in which a description may be complete or incomplete—if we consider all that, we may thereby characterize the subject matter. We may say, for instance: a material object is something that is describable in a language of such-and-such structure; a sense impression is something which can be described in such-and-such a language; a dream is ——, a memory picture is . . ., and so on (1965: 246).

In the same discussion, he pointed to the 'systematic ambiguity' that words take on as they are used in different strata. On this evidence, the propositions of symbolic logic would be, for instance, an inappropriate means for the study of the symbolism of dreams.

Following this lead, I would argue that symbols in Rotinese do indeed change sense—in ways I would be unable adequately to describe —as one proceeds from baby-talk or ordinary conversation to the verses of ritual language. But I would go further and make explicit what is implicit in my earlier discussion; I would argue that there is a hierarchy of linguistic strata in Rotinese and that this hierarchy involves—to adopt an inadequate metaphor—a 'tightening' of the logic of relations among symbols. I would also see this hierarchy as dependent on a progressive learning process—the gradual comprehension and systematization of a culture. Ritual language is the recognized culmination of this learning, and for this reason, with the exception of a few gifted individuals, it is the special preserve of the elders. When Bea, the little girl who lived with us, used to refer to the sun as 'moon two' she had embarked on the Rotinese path of learning that, in a few instances, can lead to profound understandings like those of the Head of the Earth in Termanu who, before he died, had ceased to be referred to by any other name than that of his clan: Meno.

127

There is a further social aspect to this argument. When we consider all the situations on Roti when ritual language may be used—greetings and farewells, petitions, courtship overtures, preludes to negotiations, and the ceremonies of the life-cycle—they are all moments of formalized interaction that call for a clear statement of shared premises. The social effect of symbols at this level, one may hypothesize, has to do with both the clarity of their expression and the density of the semantic network they invoke. The formal simplicity of dichotomous thinking and the continuous partition of all things by two offers the most efficient means to this end.

Comparative evidence, I believe, would lend support to this position. A survey of some of the major instances of pervasive canonical parallelism in its distribution throughout the world's oral traditions suggests that this speech form or language stratum is reserved for special situations: for the preservation of past wisdom, for the utterance of sacred words, for determining ritual relations, for healing, and for communication with spirits. The litanies of the priests of Nias, the Book of Counsel of the Quiche Maya, the poetry of the Old Testament, the prayer chants of the Hawaiians, the spirit verse of the Kachin, the cosmological speculation of the Ngaju, and the epic deeds of gods and men recorded in the *Kalevala* retain, by their parallelism, idealized statements of a specific cultural order.

This has many implications both for an understanding of binary categories and for an analysis of them. The curious feature of the dyads in elaborate traditions of parallelism is that they make—though commentators on parallelism have attempted to make these distinctions—no distinction between similars and opposites. Complementary, contrary, and contradictory terms have in common their *relation* to one another as a pair. So that possibly, at a first-order level, there is a fundamental unity of similars and opposites, a primacy in polarity. Thus the creation of a semantics of relations would be a prerequisite to a semantics of reference. Binary analysis would, therefore, be an essential tool in this investigation, but its field would be more clearly delimited. Roman Jakobson has repeatedly argued that the binary principle appears to underlie much linguistic expression and most poetry. Systems of parallelism are clearly extreme and relatively transparent developments on a binary principle and for this reason suitable for such analysis. But by this same reasoning, it would seem unlikely that other aspects of culture would be equally suited for binary analysis.

In advancing the investigation of binary categories, we may be able to broach a speculative question posed by Mauss and Durkheim, implied in Lévi-Strauss's *Mythologiques*, and directly formulated by Needham: whether there exist 'certain things in nature [that] seem to exert an effect on the human mind, conducing to symbolic forms of the most general and, even universal, kind' (Needham 1964: 147). This is to ask whether certain instruments of the natural world offer themselves as a prevalent means to conceptualization and thereby form the material basis for the primary symbols of man.

Notes

1. The research on which this paper is based was originally supported by a Public Health Service fellowship (MH-23, 148) and grant (MH-10, 161) from the National Institute of Mental Health and was conducted in 1965–66 in Indonesia under the auspices of the *Lembaga Ilmu Pengetahuan Indonesia*. The continuation of this research was again supported by a NIMH grant (MH-20, 659) and carried out in 1972–73 under the joint sponsorship of LIPI, and the University Nusa Cendana in Kupang, Timor. The paper is a product of two specific influences: discussions with Rodney Needham in Oxford in the summer of 1963 while he was working on an as yet unpublished monograph on Ngaju symbolism and I was preparing for fieldwork on Roti, and later discussions at Harvard with Roman Jakobson after I had returned from Roti and had begun the analysis of the island's ritual system. To both of these scholars I acknowledge my personal indebtedness. In preparing the final draft of this paper, I have benefited from the assistance and comments of Steve Fjellman, Paul Friedrich, David Maybury-Lewis, Rodney Needham, Donald Olivier, David Schneider, John Sodergren, and John Whiting. I regret that fieldwork commitments in eastern Indonesia kept me from attending the ASA Decennial Conference for which this paper was prepared and submitted.
2. This quote is from Roland Barthes's *Elements of Semiology* (1967: 70). Barthes continues with the added observation that the 'smallest degree of probability would correspond to a "poetic" zone of speech' and then quotes Valle Inclan: 'Woe betide him who does not have the courage to join two words which have never been united.' This conception of poetry as implying undaunted freedom of composition is radically unlike traditions of formulaic oral poetry. Whereas one may imagine a formal lexicon of the sort that Barthes describes and, in fact, begin to construct one, it is my intention in this particular paper to indicate that, in the case of this oral poetry, the poetic zone corresponds to the highest, not the smallest, degree of probability.
3. Edmund Leach has called attention to this aspect of Vico in his article 'Vico and Lévi-Strauss on the Origins of Humanity' (1969).
4. This translation is taken from *The New American Bible*. It is worth comparing with Popper's translation (Newman & Popper 1918: 215–216) of these lines in his famous study of parallelism in Isaiah. He translates the lines of the second verse:

   Thereto all the nations shall stream,
   And many peoples shall flow, saying: . . .

   The set, stream//flow, makes clearer the underlying parallel metaphor of the verbs involved.
5. I am indebted to a number of scholars who have responded to my first survey of the literature on parallelism (1971a) by referring me to further sources: (1) Professor F. Lehman, who has informed me of his own researches on parallelism in Burmese; (2) Professor M. Edmonson, who has recently completed a new verse translation of the *Popol Vuh* (1971); (3) Professor E. Leach, who has referred me to the Introduction to the first edition of Hanson's *Dictionary of the Kachin Language* (1906); (4) Professor P. Voorhoeve, who has directed me to Kern's *Commentaar op de Salasilah van Koetai* (1956); (5) Professor K. Hale, who has written on a Walbiri tradition of antonymy

(1971); (6) Professor G. Sankoff, who has been studying the use of lexical pairs in Buang poetry from New Guinea; and (7) Professor W. Davenport, who has referred me to *The Kumulipo* (Beckwith 1951) of the Hawaiians.

6. To explain some of the factors that this entails, it is best to provide examples. In 1966, two chanters alternated in leading the chorus of the funeral dance for a young, unmarried noble girl in Termanu. Both chanters chose as their text the chant, *Meda Manu ma Lilo Losi*, but each, as the evening progressed, developed his own separate version in distinctive ways. Later I had the chance to ask one chanter about his intentions in the performance. *Meda Manu ma Lilo Losi*, he explained, is the appropriate text for a virgin girl who dies 'unripe'. But it contains no reference to a noble origin, implying in effect that the girl is a commoner. In this situation, the text was not entirely appropriate so that what he did was to make Meda Manu and Lilo Losi (chants are usually named after their chief characters) into a noble character. Some time before this funeral, an important male elder of this same noble lineage died. The leading elder of the royal lineage of Termanu, the foremost chanter in the domain at this time, came to honour the deceased. The lineage of the dead man originated as a client line of the royal lineage and as it prospered had given to the royal line a succession of enormous bridewealth payments to establish its independence and near equality of rank. The text chosen by this royal chanter was *Ndi Loniama ma Laki Elokama*, a chant appropriate for someone who dies with great wealth. It is among the most interesting of all Rotinese chants in that it praises the proper use of wealth, honouring the deceased for his generosity and his ability to attract a loyal following. What is more, it places in the mouth of the dying man an admonition to his descendants and heirs to act as he has in life. The narrative of the text, however, makes no reference to nobility and the royal chanter in performing added none. Although this could have been taken as a studied insult, it was regarded as appropriate between equals, the royal chanter's presence being sufficient to signify his good intentions.

7. 'Buffalo sinews//chicken bones' (*kalu kapa//dui manu*) is the standard formula in all rituals for bones disinterred from flesh.

8. The *Didi* (reduplication of *di*: 'pole') is a species of giant stick-insect of the order/suborder *Phasmida*. These insects are at least eight to ten inches long and resemble a mantis in form. They become active only at night and are especially visible in the light of the full moon, hence their association with the moon. The set 'spider//stick-insect' (*bolau//didi*) is illustrative of the translation problems one encounters in dealing with ritual language. On my first field trip, I never saw a *didi* and when I asked what this word referred to, I was told by several informants that the *didi* was an insect, 'like the spider'. One night on my second field trip, I discovered the *didi* was actually a stick insect: its being 'like a spider' had nothing to do with its shape or appearance, but only its co-occurrence in the same set.

9. In 1965 I recited to various Rotinese the untranslated text (Jonker 1911: 97–102) of a funeral chant gathered before the turn of the century. On hearing it, those who did not know where I had obtained it assumed it to be one that I had recently gathered. Its structure, pairings of lexical items, and formulae are indistinguishable from other chants in my corpus from this dialect area. This point is important since my analysis, in part, relies upon the relative stability of ritual language.

10. The collection of these texts is in multilith form: *Rotinese Ritual Language: Texts and Translations*, and is identified throughout this paper as Fox 1972a.

11. This dictionary is also in multilith form: *Dictionary of Rotinese Formal Dyadic Language* (270 pp.) and is identified in this paper as Fox 1972b.

12. My point is that either 4, 5, or 6 may serve to define an initial selection of elements. A range of 7, however, would define a selection too small to be of

particular interest and a range of 3 one too large to constitute a proper core. In the second-stage selection, two internal links appear to be justified because the application of this reduction proceeds by eliminating elements with only one link to any other element of the key terms. Elimination of this element also eliminates its link, which cannot be counted as one of the required two links for some other element. A rule requiring three internal links would systematically eliminate all the elements of the key group while a rule of one would only eliminate a few terms.

13. I am grateful here to Professor Meyer Fortes whose studies on the ritual importance of the first-born, presented at a colloquium at Harvard (November 1973), have helped me correct my confusion of the Rotinese distinction between 'first-born'/'last-born' and 'elder'/'younger'.

14. The particular application of this formula as an estimator of node similarity has been recently discussed in Sodergren (1973). I wish to thank Mr Sodergren for his assistance on this section of the paper.

15. Relying on the Olivier programme, I used four measures to cluster the matrix of core terms: the measure of distance between clusters A and B defined as (1) the minimum, (2) the mean, and (3) the maximum of the similarities between points A and points B and also as (4) the increase in total size due to merging A and B into a single new cluster, C (Olivier 1973: 3-6). The pairwise 'similarity' of many terms (Batu/Lutu, Boa/Dok, Lima/Teik, Ai/Dae, Luü/Sae, for example) was consistent for all methods at the lowest level of clustering, whereas differences appeared expectedly at higher levels of ordering. These differences by methods 2 and 4 occurred only at the two highest levels of clustering, and it is therefore worth pointing out that, according to Olivier, these two methods 'give useful results over an especially broad range of applications' (1973: 7).

16. Miss Elizabeth Traube of Harvard University has been doing this research on the rich and varied oral traditions of the Mambai.

Bibliography

BARTHES, R. 1967. *Elements of Semiology*. London: Jonathan Cape.

BECKWITH, M. W. 1951. *The Kumulipo*. Chicago: University of Chicago Press.

CONKLIN, H. C. 1969. Lexicographical Treatment of Folk Taxonomies. In S. Tyler (ed.), *Cognitive Anthropology*: 41–59. New York: Holt, Rinehart and Winston.

EDMONSON, M. S. 1971. *The Book of Counsel: The Popol Vuh of the Quiche Maya of Guatemala*. New Orleans: Middle American Research Institute, Tulane University.

FOX, J. J. 1971a. Semantic Parallelism in Rotinese Ritual Language. *Bijdragen tot de Taal-, Land- en Volkenkunde* **127**: 215–255.

— 1971b. Sister's Child as Plant. In R. Needham, (ed.), *Rethinking Kinship and Marriage*: 219–252. London: Tavistock Publications.

— 1972a. Rotinese Ritual Language: Texts and Translations (Multilith, 303 pp.).

— 1972b. Dictionary of Rotinese Formal Dyadic Language (Multilith, 270 pp.).

— 1973. On Bad Death and the Left Hand. In R. Needham (ed.): *Right and Left: Essays on Dual Symbolic Classification*. Chicago: University of Chicago Press.

— 1974. Our Ancestors Spoke in Pairs. In R. Bauman and J. Sherzer (eds.), *Explorations in the Ethnography of Speaking*. Cambridge: Cambridge University Press.

FRAKE, C. 1969. Notes on Queries in Ethnography. In S. Tyler (ed.), *Cognitive Anthropology*: 123–137. New York: Holt, Rinehart and Winston.

FRIEDRICH, P. Forthcoming. The Lexical Symbol and its Non-Arbitrariness. In M. Dale Kinkade (ed.), *Festschrift in Honor of Carl Voegelin*. Peter de Ritter Press.

James J. Fox

GEVIRTZ, S. 1963. *Patterns in the Early Poetry of Israel*. The Oriental Institute of the University of Chicago, Studies in Ancient Oriental Civilization No. 32. Chicago: University of Chicago Press.

HALE, K. 1971. A Note on a Walbiri Tradition of Antonymy. In D. D. Steinberg and L. A. Jakobovits (eds.), *Semantics:* 472–482. Cambridge: Cambridge University Press.

HANSON, O. 1906. *A Dictionary of the Kachin Language*. Rangoon.

HEIJMERING, G. 1843. Zeden en Gewoonten op het Eiland Rottie. *Tijdschrift voor Nederlandsch-Indië.* **6**: 81–98; 353–367.

JAKOBSON, R. 1966. Grammatical Parallelism and its Russian Facet. *Language* **42**: 399–429.

JAKOBSON, R., and HALLE, M. 1956. *Fundamentals of Language*. The Hague: Mouton.

JONKER, J. C. G. 1911. *Rottineesche Teksten*. Leiden: E. J. Brill.

KERN, W. 1956. Commentaar op de Salasilah van Koetai. *Verhandelingen van het Koninklijk Instituut voor Taal-, Land-, en Volkenkunde* Vol. 19. 'S -Gravenhage: Martinus Nijhoff.

LANCE, G. N., and WILLIAMS, W. T. 1967. A General Theory of Classificatory Sorting Strategies: 1. Hierarchical Systems. *Computer Journal* **9**: 373–379.

LEACH, E. 1969. Vico and Lévi-Strauss on the Origins of Humanity. In G. Tagliacozzo and H. White (eds.), *Giambattista Vico*. Baltimore: Johns Hopkins.

LÉVI-STRAUSS, C. 1953. Social Structure. In A. L. Kroeber (ed.): *Anthropology Today:* 524–553. Chicago: University of Chicago Press.

— 1964. *Le Cru et le cuit*. Paris: Librairie Plon.

MIDDLEKOOP, P. 1949. Een Studie van het Timoreesche Doodenritueel. *Verhandelingen van het Bataviaasch Genootschap van Kunsten en Wetenschappen* Vol. 76. Bandung: A. C. Nix and Co.

NEEDHAM, R. 1964. Blood, Thunder and Mockery of Animals. *Sociologus* **14**: 136–149.

NEWMAN, L. I., and POPPER, W. 1918–1923. *Studies in Biblical Parallelism*. University of California Publications in Semitic Philosophy, Vol. 1, 2–5.

OLIVIER, D. 1973. Aggregative Hierarchical Clustering Program. (Manuscript, Department of Psychology and Social Relations, Harvard University.)

ONVLEE, L. 1953. Van Zang en Psalm. *De Heerbaan* **6**: 16–23.

SODERGREN, J. 1973. Matching Coefficients as Estimators of Node Similarity in Symmetric and Non-Symmetric Graphs. (Typescript: Department of Anthropology, Harvard University.)

SOKAL, R., and SNEATH, P. 1963. *Principles of Numerical Taxonomy*. London: W. H. Freeman.

TERRAY, E. 1972. *Marxism and 'Primitive' Societies*. New York: Monthly Review Press.

TURNER, V. 1967. Ritual Symbolism, Morality and Social Structure among the Ndembu. In *The Forest of Symbols:* 48–58. Ithaca: Cornell University Press.

VEEN, H. VAN DER. 1952. Gebruik van Literaire of Dichter-taal bij de Vertaling van Poetische Gedeelten van de Bijbel in de Indonesische Taal. *De Heerbaan* **5**: 211–240.

WAISMANN, F. 1965. Language Strata. In A. Flew (ed.), *Logic and Language:* 226–247. New York: Doubleday.

Sherry B. Ortner

Gods' Bodies, Gods' Food
A Symbolic Analysis of a Sherpa Ritual

SYMBOLIC ANALYSIS

Symbolic analysis, like a symbol, means a lot of different things to a lot of different people. In the present paper[1] I perform a symbolic analysis of a Sherpa ritual, to illustrate how at least one kind of symbolic analysis is done; in the conclusions I will make some general observations on the symbolic process, as revealed by the analysis.

The approach I use is derived from the work of Geertz, especially from the programmatic papers, 'Religion as a Cultural System' (1966) and 'Ideology as a Cultural System' (1964). Since Geertz has not been concerned to articulate his approach in any single clear-cut paradigm, it will be useful if I summarize its main points (as I understand them).

The fundamental assumption running through Geertz's work is that, in order for human beings to operate within any given reality, they must have an ongoing sense of what that reality is all about, what it 'means', how it is to be conceptualized and felt about, in order to be acted upon. Thus human beings in every society constantly generate models of their own situation, in order to orient themselves and hence function in an effective and satisfying manner within it. A 'culture' is the system of such publicly and collectively subscribed-to models operating for a given group at a given period of time—the system of terms, forms, categories, images, and the like which function to interpret a people's own situation to themselves.

This is what Geertz means by 'a system of symbols', although the term 'symbol' still tends to call to people's minds things in relation to which (other—of course) people have irrational reactions—unicorns, national flags, crucified saviours—rather than anything 'which serves as a vehicle for a conception' (Geertz 1966: 5). Rather than 'symbol', I prefer terms taken from more formal jargons—'model', 'map', 'programme', 'template'—which seem more apt for conveying the sort of process being called attention to—the process of providing *orientations* within and to the particular natural, social, and psychological realities of particular groups. 'A system of symbols' remains, however, the most comprehensive way of indicating what 'a culture' is and does.

The configuration of a cultural system at any given time is conditioned by many factors. One is certainly the tendency towards 'logico-meaningful' coherence which any system of meaning evinces (cf. Sorokin 1962; Benedict 1934), a tendency guided by the 'key symbols' (Ortner 1973b), 'core symbols' (Schneider 1968), 'root metaphors' (Pepper 1961), 'structures' (Lévi-Strauss, passim) and the like around which the system coheres. But this aspect of the conditioning of the culture's systemic form and content at any given time is not of primary interest to Geertz—hence his repudiation of treating culture

> purely as a symbolic system (the catch phrase is, 'in its own terms'), by isolating its elements, specifying the internal relationships among those elements, and then characterizing the whole system in some general way—according to the core symbols around which it is organized, the underlying structures of which it is a surface expression, or the ideological principles upon which it is based (Geertz 1973: 17).

—a passage which puts down structuralism, ethnoscience, and a number of other unnamed but implied approaches in one fell swoop.

Thus while these approaches are not necessarily invalid, Geertz is far more interested in two other sets of factors to which any particular symbolic structure may be said to be a response, *and in terms of which it must thus be explained.* These are, *first,* the actual social, historical, natural, and psychological realities present in the society at the time, and *second,* the (conscious or unconscious) strategic (what some would call 'ideological') orientations which render those realities in a certain light, or with a certain slant, so as to yield a programme for experience and action which in fact embodies those orientations. An example of a relatively conscious source of 'strategic bias' in a particular symbolic construct might be the 'interests' of the sub-group putting forth that particular construct; and an example of a relatively unconscious source of bias might be the tendency of a group to define its reality in contradistinction to that of a neighbouring group.[2] In general, it is at least fair to say that the 'ethos' of a culture, its particular style and bias in construing reality, is the product of complex historical development and is only partly amenable to synchronic explanation.

Geertz's 'model of/model for' distinction (1966) refers to the two dimensions of analysis noted above. The 'model of' aspect refers to how cultural symbols 'catch up' (Geertz 1972: 23) and attempt to render intelligible the immediate problems of social structure, economic structure, kinship, ecology, and the like—not to mention the more existential dilemmas of suffering, evil, and bafflement—in a given society. And the same symbolic models which 'represent' the complex realities of the group, represent them in such a way—the 'model for' aspect—as to provide for the respondents a reasonable way, a sensible way, a meaningful way in which to deal with them. Such cultural models, further, are *a priori* neither conservative nor radical—they may be anything from templates for simply regenerating the system as it is presently constituted, to revolutionary programmes which depict the situation in such a way as to reveal its evils and exhort people to destroy it.

The important thing to understand is that any given cultural symbolic complex is both a 'model of' and a 'model for'—these are two aspects of a single process. As a group represents its situation to itself and to the outside world, it uses terms and images which select and emphasize some aspects of that situation, which distort or ignore others, and which, *in the process*, render an implicit value judgement on all its aspects, thus orienting the respondents' attitudes and actions in line with that judgement, or at least making it difficult for them to 'see' and respond to the situation in a different way. As Kenneth Burke, discussing poetry and other 'critical and imaginative works', succinctly put it: '[They] size up the situations, name their structure and outstanding ingredients, and name them in a way that contains an attitude towards them' (1957: 3).

It follows from what has been said that what one asks in a cultural— a 'symbolic'—analysis is a three-part question: (1) What are the problematic realities of the culture to which the symbolic construction under analysis is addressing itself?—What is it a 'model of'? (2) What orientation (or reorientation) is it engendering towards those realities? —What is it a 'model for'? And (3) How, in its peculiar construction, does it accomplish its task in a powerful and convincing way, so that its respondents in fact accept it as an accurate rendering of 'reality', and adopt its implied orientation of attitude and/or action? It is the third question which actually demands the execution of 'symbolic analysis' as such, an analysis of the semantic structure of the symbolic complex which seeks to reveal how the themes or problems being dealt with have been portrayed and interrelated, by means of various semantic devices, so as to have cast the situation in the light in which it in fact emerges.

Without further ado, then, I shall apply this general approach to the analysis of a Sherpa ritual. The proof of the pudding (and the Sherpas would be delighted with the food metaphor) is in the eating.

THE SHERPAS AND THE RITUAL

The Sherpas are a group of ethnically Tibetan people living on the slopes and in the valleys of the Himalayas in northeast Nepal. Their economic base is a mixture of agriculture, dairying, petty trading, and cash labour. Salient features of their social structure, for purposes of the present discussion, include the following: The social organization of the village is based on a status hierarchy in which every individual is ranked; while there are no formal status distinctions of caste, class, title, or the like, the hierarchy is publicly visible at all collective events, where people are seated in strict rank order. Status emerges from a combination of wealth, piety, and the status (=wealth and piety) of one's kinsmen and ancestors; it is fluid and changeable, and can be gained or lost, although it tends to be viewed at any given moment as fixed. On the political dimension, Sherpa villages are noteworthy for their virtual lack of formal political structure—there are no recognized statuses of political authority, and virtually no institutionalized, collectively recognized, and systematically applicable mechanisms of political and social control. The primary effective unit of collective social functioning is an ego-centred mutual aid group (generally some segment of ego's lineage plus some neighbours, friends, and affines); ego's social world could be said from one point of view to be conceptualized in terms of 'those who help me' *v*. 'those who don't'. Finally, there is in Sherpa society a heavily emphasized formal category distinction between lay people and monastics. The lay/monastic dichotomy, as we shall see, resonates strongly with the those-who-help-me-*v*.-those-who-don't structure of the social world.

The Sherpas practise Tibetan Buddhism, which belongs within the Mahayana school. They adhere to the oldest unreformed sect, the Nyingmawa, which resisted for a long time the reforms which introduced celibate monasticism to Tibet. The Nyingmawa ultimately did adopt monasticism, although it retained its married 'lamas' in the villages along with the celibate monks in the monasteries (and nuns in the nunneries). The Sherpas adhere specifically to the Sang-ngak subsect, which concentrates on fierce rites of exorcising and destroying a vast host of voracious demons.[3] There are also shamans and a variety of lesser healers in the villages.

Aside from individual acts of piety and prayer, village religion consists of ceremonies conducted by the village lamas at both the household, private level and the temple, all-village level; the former are performed for the most part in relation to specific crises, events, and religious aspirations of the host household, and may be held at any time; the latter are generally calendrically determined. The full corpus of village rituals is rich and complex; some of its complexity will be indicated if I point out that (1) many rituals with the same form are said to have different functions; (2) rituals said to be performing the same function may take many different forms; (3) on different occasions the same ritual may be directed to different deities, and many of its elements will vary accordingly; and (4) any given ritual may be pared down almost to nothing, or expanded and compounded almost indefinitely, depending on the means and generosity of the sponsor(s).

In consequence of this complexity, it is very difficult to isolate a unit for analysis. Nonetheless, it is possible to extract at least two relatively stable points of departure. First, there is an unvarying minimal structure, or ordered set of events, which every ritual contains, and which has essentially the same meaning (though not the same emphasis or importance) in all rituals. And second, given the strong anti-demon orientation of the Sherpa subsect of Tibetan Buddhism, whatever else the gods are asked to do in any given ritual, they are asked to protect the religion and the people from the onslaught of demons. In this paper, then, I shall analyse not any particular ritual, but the general structure within which, despite the variation of form and occasion, the Sherpas seek the help, and especially the protection, of their gods. This basic ritual form, though also enacted by monks in monasteries, will be analysed specifically from the point of view of the lay people, who see it, describe it, and intend it in terms appropriate to their own situation.

The basic structure may be summarized as follows: The first stage is always a purification rite, a *sang*, which itself may take many different forms, but which consists most commonly of offerings to the rather touchy and changeable local spirits (not the high gods) to assure their good humour and benevolence, and hence (by way of a complex logic) to purify the area and the participants.[4]

Following the *sang*, attention shifts to the main altar, upon which are arrayed a set of offerings which have been freshly constructed and assembled by the lamas for the performance of the particular ceremony, and which will be disassembled and disposed of at the end of the performance. The altar items are collectively referred to as *chepa*, offerings; everything that goes on the altar is casually said to represent some worldly category of gift for the gods.

The presentation of the offerings is guided by and synchronized with the reading of a text appropriate to the god and the occasion.[5] At the opening of the service, the gods are invited to come and attend the feast which is being held for them. Loud music is played to attract their attention. Incense is flooded through the area, and grain and beer are sprinkled skyward, all as gestures of invitation and welcome. The sprinkling of grain and beer are also acts of offering in themselves, for the lower gods and spirits.

Following the invitation and welcome, the gods are invited to be seated in the *torma*, moulded dough objects which have been prepared to receive their presences. Then measures are taken to protect the ritual from the anti-religious demons: the torma of the gods of the four directions is set outside the temple or the house as a receptacle for and an offering to them, so they will guard the boundaries of the precinct; and the special torma for the demons (the *gyek*) is thrown out as food for them, to satisfy temporarily their greedy desires and divert them from trying to come into the temple and eat up all the offerings. This is invariably a dramatic moment—the music slowly rises to a crescendo as the ritual assistant picks up, then holds aloft the demons' torma; finally there is a cacophonous crashing climax, accompanied by demoniac whistles, as the assistant dashes out of the door and throws the torma hard and far from the ritual precinct.

Next the gods are presented with all their offerings (the entire altar) and urged to eat fully and enjoy themselves. While they are partaking of the offerings, the lamas read 'praises for the goodness and admirable qualities of the guests', i.e. the gods (Waddell 1934: 431), and recite the spells or *mantra* appropriate to the high gods of the group (ibid.). They then read 'prayers for favours immediate and to come' (ibid.), and during the course of these readings (I am not sure precisely when) representatives of the community approach the altar and perform prostrations, which signify apologies for past offences, and theoretically wipe out sins.

The conclusion of the ceremony is always the offering of the *tso*, an assemblage of cooked or otherwise immediately edible foods which have been laid out upon a bench at the foot of the altar. The tso is offered to the gods, and then divided up among all the people present and eaten on the spot. The lama reads a brief benediction (ibid.), and as he finishes reading he allows his voice to trail off, suggesting the departure of the gods. Afterwards, the altar is dismantled. The butter lamps are allowed to burn themselves out, any raw grain becomes part of the lamas' take-home pay, and the torma are generally given to children, taken home to a sick or elderly person, or fed to the village dogs.

This, in brief, is the minimal structure and sequence of most Sherpa ritual performances. It all seems rather unremarkable to anyone familiar with cross-cultural and historical religious data. The gods are contacted and given offerings, the people communally eat some of the offerings at the close of the ceremony. At least three things, however, make this a *Sherpa* ceremony of the genre, and give us entrée to its meaning in Sherpa culture. These are (1) those peculiar items, the torma cakes; (2) the special kind of help or benefit sought from the gods—protection against the demons; and (3) the cultural metaphor through which the rite is viewed—that of social hospitality and the host–guest relationship. I shall examine each of these elements as a way of arriving at some of the problems the ritual is dealing with, and then I shall return to the full sequence of ritual action to see how it deals with those problems.

THE PROBLEMATICS OF THE RITUAL

1 *'Torma' and the body problem*

A torma is a dough figure, basically conical in form, ranging from several inches to several feet in height. The basic form may be elaborated upon by moulding the figure itself, and by adding other dough elements. Some torma are left uncoated, while others must be coloured

red, black or white, using melted butter tinted with red vegetable dye
or charcoal, or left undyed for white. Each torma is also decorated with
bits of butter shaped into discs, dots, petals, flames, etc. All of these
variations in shape, colour, and decoration have significance (see
Figure 1).

Figure 1 Examples of *torma* (after Nebesky-Wojkowitz 1956, by permission of the
publishers, Mouton & Co.)

Although there are several different understandings concurrently held
in the culture, and several different levels of meaning, the primary
significance of the torma is an abstract representation of, and a temporary 'body' for, a god. Every god, from the lowliest locality spirit
to the Buddha himself, has a prescribed torma; conversely, every torma
has a name and identity from the god it represents. Whenever a god is
to be invoked in a religious service, a torma should be made for him
beforehand. Then, when his name is called, he comes and enters the
torma, where he remains through the reading, listening to man's
petitions and receiving his homage. Since the Tibetan pantheon is
enormous, there are literally hundreds of different torma forms, all
achieved by performing transformations on the little conical cakes of
dough.

The second significance of torma is as food for the gods. This interpretation is held most often by laymen, either together with the body
notion, or alone. But it was also explained by a lama that this is an
orthodox interpretation in some of the other sects of Tibetan Buddhism.

139

While a number of torma on the altar are designated specifically as food torma, in a general sense it is held that all the torma are food offerings for the gods to whom the ritual is directed.[6]

The same duality of meaning is expressed in exegesis on the decorations of the torma. When asked the meaning of the colour coatings, lamas often replied off-handedly that red is like giving the god a monk's robe, which is red in Tibetan Buddhism. On the other hand, the orthodox meaning, also articulated by the lamas, is that red coating is for a god who eats flesh and drinks beer, while white coating represents a god who follows the so-called 'Brahmin-Chhetri' purity rules, eating no meat and drinking no beer (and wearing white clothing). The two exegeses are of course utterly contradictory, since monks, in fact, despite wearing red robes, observe the dietary purity rules: a red robe and a meat-and-beer diet simply do not go together. In orthodox point of fact, all red-coated torma are for ferocious, meat-eating gods, but if one asks lamas what red coating means, without reference to any particular torma, they will frequently say that it represents monks' clothing.

It is noteworthy then that while 'gods' bodies' rather than 'gods' food' is the more orthodox meaning of the torma as such, the more orthodox significance of the coating of torma refers to the diet of the god, rather than his clothes, his bodily covering. Thus the lay view of the meaning of torma, while 'wrong' from the point of view of one aspect of orthodoxy, is 'right' from another.

Now, how a god appears in outward bodily appearance, and the diet which suits his taste, are related to one another as metonymic aspects of his mood or disposition. The interrelation between food, body, and mood will be important for subsequent analysis. For the moment, however, let us postpone the issues of mood and food, and focus on the issue of body which is raised exclusively by the torma and some of its immediately associated items on the altar.

Sherpa religion is ambivalent about the body. Their Mahayana heritage glorifies the bodhisattva, who has achieved salvation but returned to the world in bodily form to 'help' others find the way. The bodhisattva concept has been institutionalized in Tibetan religion more literally than among any other Buddhist group, in the figure of the *tulku* or reincarnate lama who is actually identified as a living, breathing bodhisattva available to the direct acquaintance of the members of the community. The image of the bodhisattva makes the point that the body is a good thing, in so far (*but only in so far*) as it is a vehicle for practising the religion—for learning, teaching, and exemplifying religious precepts, and for performing meritorious deeds. (Meritorious deeds include such things as saving lives of helpless creatures, circumambulating religious monuments, supporting monks and endowing the performance of religious ritual; material aid to the needy and downtrodden are not high priority sources of merit.) In all other respects the body is a bad thing, in that, according to teachings of classical Buddhism which have carried through into Sherpa religion, the body is the agency of desire for sensuous pleasure, which leads humanity into sin.

The religious ambivalence concerning the body is nicely illustrated by some verses from a fourteenth-century lama; he was not a Sherpa but his verses sum up Sherpa sentiment well:

> . . .
> Now listen, you who would practise religion.
> When you obtain the advantages, so hard to obtain,
>   (of a well-endowed human body)
> It is best to accumulate merit
> By practising religion and so put all to good use.
>
> . . .
> Wine and women, these two
> Are the robbers who steal away your good conduct.
> Keeping far off from loved ones like poison
> Let this be your protective armour!
>
> . . .
> The best way to good rebirths and salvation
> Is purity of personal conduct.
> So never demean it. Hold to it
> As dearly as the apple of your eye!
>
> (Snellgrove 1967: 159–160)

Thus, in this Mahayana tradition the body is considered valuable as a means of helping others, but the 'help' is primarily by the example of 'purity of personal conduct' and not by direct support of those with whom one is socially involved: '[Keep] far off from loved ones like poison. . . .' Any other use of the body, any other appreciation of it for any other purpose ('wine and women'), is bad, leading to sin, poor rebirth, and entrapment in the round of evil and suffering.

Other Sherpa beliefs, not derived from Buddhist orthodoxy, support the generally negative view of the body encouraged by Buddhism. Sherpa pollution beliefs stress the defiling propensity of the body, and its tendency to impair the mental (psychological, spiritual, moral, etc.) functions (Ortner 1973a). Even Sherpa commonsense notions chime in with the point that the body and its desires lead to children, who are felt to be a nuisance and who must be supported by hard labour. The body then is, as a sum of all these points, almost utterly negative in theory.

At the social level, the question refracts in a very important way through the major social category distinction of the culture: lay *v.* monastic. The only proper way out of the body problem, according to the religion, is of course to become a monk, i.e. to practise celibacy and denial of sensuality while devoting all one's energies to the religion. This remains a strong ideal for every Sherpa male; most boys think about becoming monks, although few do, while most older men wish they had. Yet despite (or possibly because of) this fact, there are indications of antagonism on the part of laymen towards monastics. One strong piece of evidence for this is that the charity system of giving to monks is in disarray. Sherpa monks do not even try to sustain themselves by begging; they are supported by their families or by endowments given to monasteries by a few wealthy people. A lama explained this by saying that in these evil times people think monks are lazy and so begrudge them food; the lama said it was to save the laity from the sin of their bad thoughts that Sherpa monks do not beg.[7]

More directly, village lamas would occasionally complain of the injustice of their relatively low status in the religious hierarchy. A village lama, they said, is constantly on call for the religious needs of the people. When there is a request for a ritual, he must drop whatever he is doing and respond to this request. A monk on the other hand does nothing but seek his own personal salvation; he does not respond to the needs of the people. And yet monks are defined as more worthy of respect than lamas; they sit higher than lamas when both are participating in a single ritual; and they gain infinitely more merit for their calling. The lamas in some of their bitter moments were obviously resentful of this state of affairs.

Conscious antagonism towards monks should not be overplayed; I never actually recorded disparaging remarks by lay villagers against monks. To some extent the cultural category opposition between 'the village' and 'the monastery' only emerges as a genuine conflict in Sherpa social thought through the analysis of the ritual material. The point I wish to make here is simply that the monk/lay opposition may be seen in part as the social corollary of the body problem. Monks dramatize the religious ideal of rejection of sensuality, of 'body', and as such are respected. At one level people are grateful for the merit monks bring to the world by their single-minded pursuit and exemplification (or, as Christians would say, 'witness') of the religious life. Yet at the same time monks appear, from certain points of view, 'lazy' and socially useless. In other words, while rejection of body is good for the individual (monk), and theoretically good for the community, in fact it has socially problematic implications. These will be seen more clearly, and developed more fully from a slightly different angle, in the discussion of hospitality. Before we get to that, however, we must add the emotional ingredient of mood to the discussion.

2 *Gods, demons, and the problem of moods*

The Sherpas and Tibetans have many myths concerning the original struggle to establish the religion among their people. The myths describe the chaos which existed before the religion came—people were constantly harassed by demons and were violent and anarchic among themselves. The myths imply that this would be the state of affairs were the religion allowed to lapse, and thus the primary type of help sought from the gods in performing the rituals is that they renew their primordial struggle against, and re-enact their original triumph over, the demons and the forces of anarchy and violence.

There are vast numbers, types and grades of supernatural beings in the Sherpa universe,[8] but I shall focus on the two extreme types—the high gods who preside, as it were, over the system (and over every ritual), and the demons who pit themselves against the system (and against every ritual).

The highest gods of the religion are defined as having achieved salvation and bliss. They are utterly fulfilled and self-contained; they 'need nothing' and are basically not interested in worldly affairs. Their general disposition is said to be benevolent to and protective of humanity, but they are self-absorbed; unless people actively keep in touch with them through offerings, they will, as suggested by a number of myths, withdraw even further and leave humanity at the mercy of the demons.

All gods designated as such (*hla*) have two mood aspects—*shiwa*, peaceful and benign, and *takbu*, fierce and violent.[9] The 'same' god in his different aspects usually has different names; the benign form is considered more basic, while the fierce form is said to be adopted for the purpose of fighting demons. Almost all the gods appealed to in Sherpa ritual are ferocious aspects of one or another of the high Buddhist gods they revere—Chenrezi, Opame, or Guru Rimpoche. The appearances of the two dispositional aspects of gods may be seen depicted with great realism and in great detail in scroll paintings and temple frescoes, both available for all to see. Gods in their benign aspect are usually shown in light colours, in calm postures, with relatively few limbs, and relatively pleasant expressions on their faces. Gods in their terrible aspect are depicted in dark and harsh colours, with snarling faces, in threatening postures, and usually with an excessive number of heads, eyes, teeth, arms, etc. A takbu god, further, is usually shown in sexual consort with a goddess, or he is at least depicted with an erect penis, while shiwa gods generally sit blissfully alone.

At the opposite extreme from the gods are the demons, all of whom are considered to be intrinsically evil, and aggressive towards humanity. Most are defined as greedy and voracious, constantly frustrated, hungry and angry, and randomly aggressive. They strike people with illness and death whenever they possibly can, as a way of getting food, or simply because it is their nasty natures to behave that way. Further, at the same time as being personally threatening, they are also a menace to the religion in general. They try to tempt lamas and monks into sin, to eat temple offerings, and to undermine the religion however they can. Every Sherpa can recount tales of the struggles of gods and great lamas

143

to subdue the demons and hence defend the faith. This dual aspect of the demons—enemies of the people, enemies of the faith—will be seen to be important to the successful symbolic outcome of the ritual.

The basic Sherpa rituals, then, ask for the help of the gods in combating the forces of evil. This involves essentially making the high gods 'happy', by feeding them, so that they will want to 'help us' by engaging in the struggle against the demons. Yet it would also seem to require, as we shall see in the analysis, making the high gods themselves a bit angry, so that they will be drawn down from their bliss long enough to engage in this struggle. The symbolism of the supernatural types, in short, seems in part to represent a complex commentary on the regulation of mood—the question of the optimum interrelationship between self-absorbed bliss, random aggression, appropriately focused anger, and active benevolence.

In what sense is regulation of mood problematic to Sherpas? While in day-to-day interaction they do not appear to manifest, like some other groups of the anthropological literature, rigid control of temperament—actually, they appear to a Western observer relatively spontaneous and open—nonetheless there are unmistakable indications that Sherpas experience chronic difficulty in dealing with anger and other bad moods.[10] There are of course all those demons to witness this point, and the fact that most of the gods with whom the Sherpas are most involved are ferocious takbu types. But one need not look beyond the human realm for such projection. The merest slight from a neighbour is taken to mean that he or she is angry with one, whereupon one immediately searches for some fault one may have committed. On the other hand, one's own bad moods (including lethargy as well as evil temper) are considered puzzling; one often puts them down to having encountered some pollution, rather than to an outside provocation. The feeling of the individual, in short, seems to be, 'If my neighbour is in a bad mood, I must have done something wrong, and if *I* am in a bad mood I must have done something wrong.'

All of this indicates a culturally engendered confusion, for the individual, about the locus, meaning, and sources of anger. I hesitate to postulate a single source of this problem. Surely some of it lies in socialization practices (cf. Paul 1970), which I am not competent to discuss. Further, one might wish to argue that anger for Sherpas is generated by the contradictions and injustices of their social system, and that the confusion experienced by actors over its locus is a result of various cultural 'mystifications' which prevent individuals from seeing what its 'real' sources are. There may be a great deal of truth to this view, and various parts of the analysis in this paper tend to support it, although I will not specifically elaborate upon it. Here I will simply draw attention to some aspects of Sherpa culture and social structure which, in a more obvious way, serve to reinforce and regenerate the problem of handling ill feeling for Sherpa actors.

In the first place, there is a religious prohibition on violence—killing, fighting, angry words, and even angry thoughts are all considered highly sinful, bringing religious demerit to those who so indulge, and hence hampering their chances for a good rebirth and for salvation. These indulgences are also considered polluting, so that they may undermine one's physical and mental well-being in the present life as well. Now Sherpas are quite scrupulous about not killing, but as for the rest, fighting, angry words, and angry thoughts are relatively frequent and commonplace. Thus the point is not that they do not have outlets for *expressing* anger—they do it all the time—but, consistent with the cultural prohibition, there are available no clearcut models for its expression in controlled and articulated sorts of ways. An angry Sherpa cannot challenge to a duel, mobilize his lineage for a vendetta, organize a war expedition, bring litigation, provoke a witch trial, participate in a collective confession, or in short have recourse to any culturally organized (secular) mode through which he and others can get to objectify, comprehend, and systematically restructure disturbing feelings within a culturally sanctioned context. Only one secular form seems at least intended to provide such a structure—the institution of 'joking' at parties (see below)—but it is often only partially successful.

Thus, when anger is expressed in the culture, in the absence of institutional forms for rendering it orderly, manageable, and comprehensible to both the angry party and the observers, it often takes the form of a tantrum. I witnessed several such outbursts, in which the individual (generally after drinking) simply went out of control and began to abuse and attack everyone in reach, ultimately to be dragged away, literally kicking and screaming, by kinsmen and friends.[11]

The situation is strongly compounded by a peculiar aspect of Sherpa social structure which has been noted by previous observers—the highly diffuse authority structure of the society. While Fürer-Haimendorf describes a number of formal authority roles in the Khumbu Sherpa villages in which he worked, he remarks that

> The function of each village official, however, is strictly circumscribed, and large spheres of social life lie outside the jurisdiction of these officials. The settlement of disputes relating to these spheres is left to private mediation, and the inability—or unwillingness—of the village community as a whole to assume authority in dealing with such matters, is one of the peculiar features of Sherpa social organization (1964: 104).

In the Solu Sherpa village in which I worked, the situation is more extreme: there are no formal leadership roles, no elected 'village officials'. At the same time, the pattern of community 'unwillingness' to deal with disputes in any systematic way holds true—there are virtually no formal mechanisms of social coercion, punishment, or redress. Of course there are informal processes—gossip, snubs, and so forth—

145

but if an individual has enough nerve and/or insensitivity to ignore these pressures and flaunt the rules anyway, the community is helpless.

As things now stand, then, Sherpa social structure does not provide channels for dealing systematically with socially disruptive behaviour. Further, tendencies towards such behaviour (as well as tendencies towards virtuous behaviour) are thought to be inherited personality traits, to run, as it were, in the family, and hence not really to be amenable to change. The upshot of all this is general social paralysis in the face of socially threatening situations. There is a feeling—all things considered, a quite realistic feeling—that nothing can be done, or at least nothing directly appropriate.

Thus, aspects of the social structure and cultural belief converge so as to produce no culturally available forms for the systematic comprehension and constructive transmutation of ill feeling. The angry gods and violent demons dealt with in the ritual signal the fact that the ritual is in some sense an attempt to deal with this problem. Part of the analysis, then, will be an attempt to show how the ritual tries to help its participants achieve a particular subjective orientation, consonant with the realities postulated by and experienced in this culture. In particular, for the Sherpas, it is a matter of understanding 'correctly' the nature and sources of one's moods and dispositions, and discovering appropriate, constructive, and comfortable forms and courses for them to take.

3 *Hospitality, anger, and body*

The Sherpas make the explicit analogy between the offering ritual and social hospitality. The people are hosts, the gods are their guests. The people invite the gods to the human realm, make them comfortable, and give them food and drink, all of which is meant to give them pleasure, 'to make them happy' so that they will want to 'help' humanity by providing protection from the demons.

According to the native model, all of the business of the ritual in relation to the gods is accomplished by the same mechanisms whereby human cooperation is obtained in hospitality practices. Thus the music, incense, and sprinkling of grain and beer with which the ceremony opens are described as 'invitations' and 'gestures of welcome' to the gods. The gods are then 'seated' in their torma, and the assemblage of altar offerings is served as one serves the food and drink of a party for the sensuous enjoyment of the guests. Thus aroused, pleased, and gratified, the gods, like one's neighbours, will feel 'happy' and kindly disposed toward the worshippers/hosts and any requests they might make.

Further, just as ordinary social hospitality involves thinly disguised coercion and manipulativeness on the part of the host, beneath the veneer of warm invitation, welcome, and generous disinterested presentation of well-prepared food, so does the ritual. In social hospitality the invitation takes the form of a disguised command which it is virtually impossible to disobey (Ortner 1970); similarly, the invitation portion of the ritual text contains mantra which do not ask but actually conjure the gods into coming. And the invitation to the gods is coupled with various sensuous temptations (music, incense, food and drink appetizers) which lure rather than merely invite the gods.

Second, the seating of a guest in ordinary hospitality has a culturally defined latent coerciveness—once he can be got into a seat, he must accept the proffered hospitality or risk gravely insulting the host. Once in the house and seated, in short, he has become a *guest* and must follow through in the appropriate ways. The coerciveness of the seat is also seen in funerals where, in order to make sure the soul does not wander off and miss the reading of the *totul* (the *Bardo Thödöl* or 'Tibetan Book of the Dead'), a special seat is prepared for the soul with a mystic design in the centre; the soul is conjured into sitting there and its presence is thus assured for the remainder of the reading. Similarly, then, the conjuring of the gods into their torma-seats is a coercive gesture which controls their presence and their availability for being fed, pleased, and petitioned.

And finally, just as feeding the guests is not only a hopeful gesture, but is seen as intrinsically manipulative and coercive in ordinary social hospitality, so the feeding of the gods is not only propitiatory but coercive in the ritual. In ordinary life—and this is a critical point—it is asserted that food and drink have certain *natural effects* upon people, so that, having been wined and dined, they become more open, friendly, and receptive to oneself and one's wishes. (The converse holds too—not feeding others automatically makes them angry and un-cooperative at the very least.) Drink in particular, through its intoxicating properties, is said to render the personality expansive and the resistance to various temptations and imprecations low. That analogous effects are expected to take place in the gods' dispositions is seen in the following passage addressed to the gods from one of the ritual texts: 'I am offering you the things which you eat, now you must do whatever I demand' (quoted in Fürer-Haimendorf 1964: 193). Thus, as in ordinary hospitality, the guests (in this case the gods) are not only being given pleasure in the vague hope that they will be kindly disposed towards their host. The various pleasurable offerings mask mechanisms of more direct control and manipulation.

The hospitality model is thus applied intact as the native gloss on the action and expectations of the ritual. And this extension makes perfect sense—a tried and more or less true procedure for gaining assistance in ordinary life is applied to an apparently similar situation in dealing with the gods. But how similar is the situation? The gods, unlike men, have no bodies and (hence) no sensuous desires; they are specifically said to 'need nothing'. If nothing else, then, this point serves to call into question the appropriateness and efficacy of the hospitality structure itself, which, perhaps, is exactly what it is intended to do. In other words, it may be that social hospitality *is* the problem, and that the ritual, cast in the idiom of social hospitality, is at least in part a device for dealing with it.

Let us say that social hospitality has at least two problematic dimensions: it is one of the major contexts of village life in which the moral implications of the body problem are most sharply highlighted; and it is the matrix *par excellence* where the issue of confusion over anger and other moods is most seriously raised.

First, the body problem: Hospitality raises the issue of body not as an abstract concern with relevance only for one's ultimate salvation, but as a conflict between religious ideal and the pragmatics of worldly social life. The religious ideal devalues the body, but social pragmatics indicate that sensuality is not only personally pleasurable but a socially constructive mechanism; it is the body with its weaknesses that renders others subject to social manipulation. The whole hospitality ethic dictates that it is a good and socially useful thing to give others sensuous pleasure, by providing them with food and drink, since when people are thus gratified they will, in a word which has great import in the culture, *help* one another. Without the hospitality procedures the Sherpas would be virtually at a loss for means of gaining social cooperation, especially in the light of the absence of authority structures and coercive mechanisms described earlier. Virtually the only way to get people to do something in the culture is to make them *want* to do it, or at least make them feel obligated to do it. Thus the whole hospitality ethic with which all villagers are so much involved virtually all of their non-working time, and upon which the whole integration of village social life could be said to depend, winds up putting people in direct conflict with the highest ideals (and even the lower-order beliefs concerning pollution and the like) of their culture and their religion.

The conflict between the religious devaluation of sensuality and the necessary social manipulation of sensuality finds much concrete expression. A cultural notion—fully borne out by experience—is that hostesses force one to eat and drink too much, making one drunk and lethargic, analogous if not equivalent to polluted states which signify an upsurge of the lower aspects of one's being (Ortner 1973a). In particular they are said to tempt village lamas with too much food and drink, undercutting whatever minimal gestures towards asceticism these clerics, falling short of full-scale monkhood, try to make. I have even seen a drunken father trying to force his monk son to drink beer. And local villagers who try to swear off drinking are subject to the most intense sorts of pressures by hosts and hostesses to take a drink. All of this serves to point up the vital importance of sensuous susceptibility for the smooth working of village life, and the conflict between that and the ideal of ascetic self-control stressed by the religion. Even the most minimal

148

gesture of asceticism, such as swearing off drink, is a threat to village social dynamics.

And these points in turn illuminate some of the meaning of the villagers' ambivalence about monks. Rejection of sensuality, while good in terms of ultimate salvation, seems virtually immoral from the perspective of village life—ascetic leanings represent social non-availability; sensuous susceptibility is the basis for real social help and mutual support.

As for the problem of mood, the Sherpa party is meant to make people happy, and it does that quite often and sometimes quite intensely. It is meant to pacify anger and create mutual benevolence, and it often performs these functions as well. But is also generates plenty of anger, anxiety, and ill feeling. Suffice it to say that a full-scale party is a veritable *mélange* of moods and feelings for all concerned. This is not to say that Sherpas do not experience the various moods in other contexts of their lives. But it seemed to me that often they experience all of them at the highest intensity, in the most complicated mixture, in a short period of time, and in a confined and rigidly structured social space, than on any other sort of occasion.

In the first place, there are cultural notions concerning both the angry host and the angry guest. From the point of view of the host, guests are thought to become angry if they are not adequately fed or if they are otherwise improperly treated. If one is a guest, on the other hand, the notion is that one must accept and eat all that is offered to one, or the host or hostess will become angry and take some sort of nameless retribution. (Much of the anxiety often seems to focus upon the hostess, who, it is thought, will send witchcraft against one and make one ill.) Yet it is clear from my own observations that a host or hostess whose hospitality has not been properly accepted suffers anxiety rather than anger, for he or she assumes that the guest's refusal is a sign that the guest is for some reason angry with the host household. The anxiety seems to be further encouraged by cultural etiquette, which prescribes that a guest make several refusals before accepting food and drink. The host is thus forced to urge his hospitality on the guest, never being sure whether a refusal is a polite gesture, a genuine indication of non-hunger, or a veiled indication of personal animosity. One plays it safe by assuming the latter, and presses the food relentlessly, which in itself sometimes irritates the guest.

Assuming that all goes well between host and guest in the serving and receiving of food, the mood development of the party can now take several courses. People may in fact, as they ideally should, simply feel pleased and gratified, and expansively benevolent. They may even move from that to genuine exhilaration, and end the evening with singing and dancing, so that all experience in the party context, and afterwards, a genuine surge of intense good feelings. On the other hand, as the Sherpas well know, drink does funny things to people. Another, not unexpected, development is that some of the guests will begin 'joking', which takes the form of nasty ragging of some other guest present, generally someone with whom there is already bad blood. Joking is not supposed to culminate in fighting—on the contrary, it is obviously meant to provide a non-violent format for the articulation and resolution of ill feelings. Yet it often becomes quite vicious, an intolerable provocation which culminates in a fight between the parties to the repartee. Then the feast may break up with bad feeling all around, leaving a residue of anger. Or a fight might not break out, in which case at least some of the guests spend the rest of the evening sulking and smouldering with anger. Or the fight may break out, but some friends will hustle the fighters off to their respective homes and the party will continue, but with the pall of the unresolved fight over it. All of these outcomes are at least as probable as the ideal of the bevy of happy and satisfied guests warmly in the host's debt at the end of the party.

Noe it is true not only that some large-scale parties turn out exhilaratingly well, but also that there are many instances of smaller-scale visiting and inviting in which both the chance of high exhilaration and strongly provoked anger are low. But it is also true that when a host invites a few people to a small party he often wants some particular favour from them, and these parties thus turn more on the anxieties of the host/guest relationship described earlier—the host's anxiety to be able to bring off his persuasion, the guest's feeling of being pressured and coerced, the fear of each of angering the other. Either way—large parties with highs of good feeling and lows of surliness and resentment, small parties with their smaller pressures and anxieties—the Sherpa hospitality situation is a matter of complex experiencing of a mixture of moods and feelings generated by sensuous pleasures and problematic social relationships.

Hospitality, then, is the situation in which the problems outlined earlier as pervading much of Sherpa thought and animating certain behaviour patterns and certain institutions are highlighted and intensified in various ways. It is fraught with contradiction. It is supposed to be a form for making people happy—stimulating the senses and feelings in positive ways, and soothing and pacifying aroused ill feelings—yet it often generates as much ill feeling as good. And it is the situation *par excellence* which highlights the contradiction between the standard ethics of village social life, which value the sensuous susceptibility of the body as a means of gaining social aid and cooperation, and the ideals of the religion which strongly oppose, as inimical to salvation, any pandering to sensuality. The guest-who-doesn't-eat may be such a charged notion precisely because it summarizes all these issues: not-eating means anger, not-eating means asceticism, both anger and asceticism mean (from different starting-points) social non-cooperation.

THE SOLUTIONS OF THE RITUAL

But there is more to diagnosis, either medical or sociological, than the identification of pertinent strains; one understands symptoms not merely etiologically but teleologically—in terms of the way in which they act as mechanisms, however unavailing, for dealing with the disturbances which have generated them (Geertz 1964; in 1973: 204).

Let us now return to the action of the ritual, to analyse the symbolic development and handling of each of the problematic issues outlined above. For the problems are not simply represented; they are dramatized in particular relationships to one another and modulated towards particular resolutions.

Social hospitality provides the metaphor, the outer form, as it were, in which the ritual is encased. We saw above both the surface analogy— invitation, seating, feeding—and the hidden analogy—the command beneath the invitation, the trapping underlying the seating, the intentional manipulativeness of the feeding. Yet it is clear that much more is going on in the ritual than this analogy allows us—and perhaps the participants—to see. Let us look more closely at the offerings and at the action surrounding them.

The structure of the altar platform is that of a series of steps. On the first, or lowest, step, are placed the *chinche*, the 'outside offerings' (also called, in Tibet, 'the offerings to accomplish drawing near' [Ekvall 1964: 166]). These include the so-called 'eight basic offerings'— water for drinking, water for washing, a flower for good smell, incense for good smell, a butter lamp for light, water for cooling, a simple uncoated torma for food, and cymbals for music.[12]

On the next step are arrayed the *nangche*, the 'inside offerings'. The nangche represent offerings *of* (not *to*) the six senses. There should be cloth, as clothing, signifying touch; a plain torma, as food, signifying taste; incense, signifying smell; cymbals, as music, signifying hearing; a mirror, signifying sight; and a sacred book, signifying the sixth sense, thought or spirit. The nangche level is often omitted in setting up simple altars, but it was stressed by the lama informant as conceptually important.

The next two steps comprise the *sangche* or 'secret offerings'. On the lower of the two are the torma of the lesser gods of the constellation being worshipped, the 'soldiers', 'helpers', etc., of the high god. On the right hand end of the row, as one faces the altar, stands the special torma which will be thrown out to the demons, somewhat separated from the others, usually with a butter lamp interposed. On the top row in the centre stands the large main torma, for the focal god of the text being read on this occasion. This is called the *torma che*, the 'senior' or 'head' torma, or the *khil-khor torma*. Khil-khor (Skt., *mandala*) means a

151

constellation of gods, of which the khil-khor torma represents the head god; it also means the palace and more generally the heavenly realm or abode of that god and his constellation. Khil-khor also refers to a diagram of this realm/palace/constellation, the minimal reduction of which is a complex geometric form combining in various ways circles and squares, each inside the other (cf. Ortner 1966; Tucci 1969; Snell-grove 1957). A khil-khor diagram should be placed under the head torma. (Ultimately, the Khil-Khor represents the entire universe.)

The main god is flanked with his two immediate guardian gods. To the gods' right goes the *dutsi*, a mixture ideally composed of all the foul ingredients of the world, said to signify semen, and usually represented by beer. The term dutsi literally means demon-fluid; Waddell (1934: 430) calls it 'devil's juice'. To the gods' left goes *rakta*, ideally menstrual blood, usually represented by tea.[13]

In front of the completed altar, a bench, lower than the first level of offerings, is set up. On this bench is placed the *tso* food, a set of cooked or otherwise immediately edible foods, which will be offered to the gods at the end of the service and then eaten by the people (see *Figure 2*).

The offerings are said to be presented in order from the bottom to the top of the altar, from the 'outside' to the 'inside' to the 'secret offerings. One exegesis I have presents the sequence as follows. The *chinche* or 'outside' offerings are 'for people'—the worshippers are transformed at the beginning of the action (probably by the prior performance of the purification ritual noted earlier) into (low-level) gods, and are propitiating themselves with the first-level offerings. Then the people/gods at the first level offer the *nangche* or 'inside' offerings at the second level to the *chepi hlamu*, the offering goddesses. The nangche offerings, it will be recalled, are composed of symbolic representations of the six senses. The offering goddesses in turn offer the *sangche* or 'secret' offerings of the top level to the gods of the ceremony, the holy offerings being the torma and the polluting liquids.

Following the presentation of the offerings, hymns of praise to the gods are read, prostrations are made by representatives of the worshippers, and prayers of petition for favours are entered. Finally, the tso feast is offered, said to be a party in celebration of the positive effects the ceremony has wrought—the gods are said to be in good moods as a result of receiving their offerings, and they join the worshippers in a party in which they and then all assembled consume the tso foods.

Let us now try to construct, in our terms, the sense being constructed by the ritual action. I suggest, first of all, that the rite may be read as an extended and systematic pollution of the gods[14] through a double process of embodying and, contrary to the native model which says they are being 'made happy', infuriating them, all, strangely enough, producing the positive outcome of triumph over evil. In the process, I will try to show, the participant is meant to experience a transformation of consciousness concerning both his body and his anger. And finally,

Figure 2 An altar

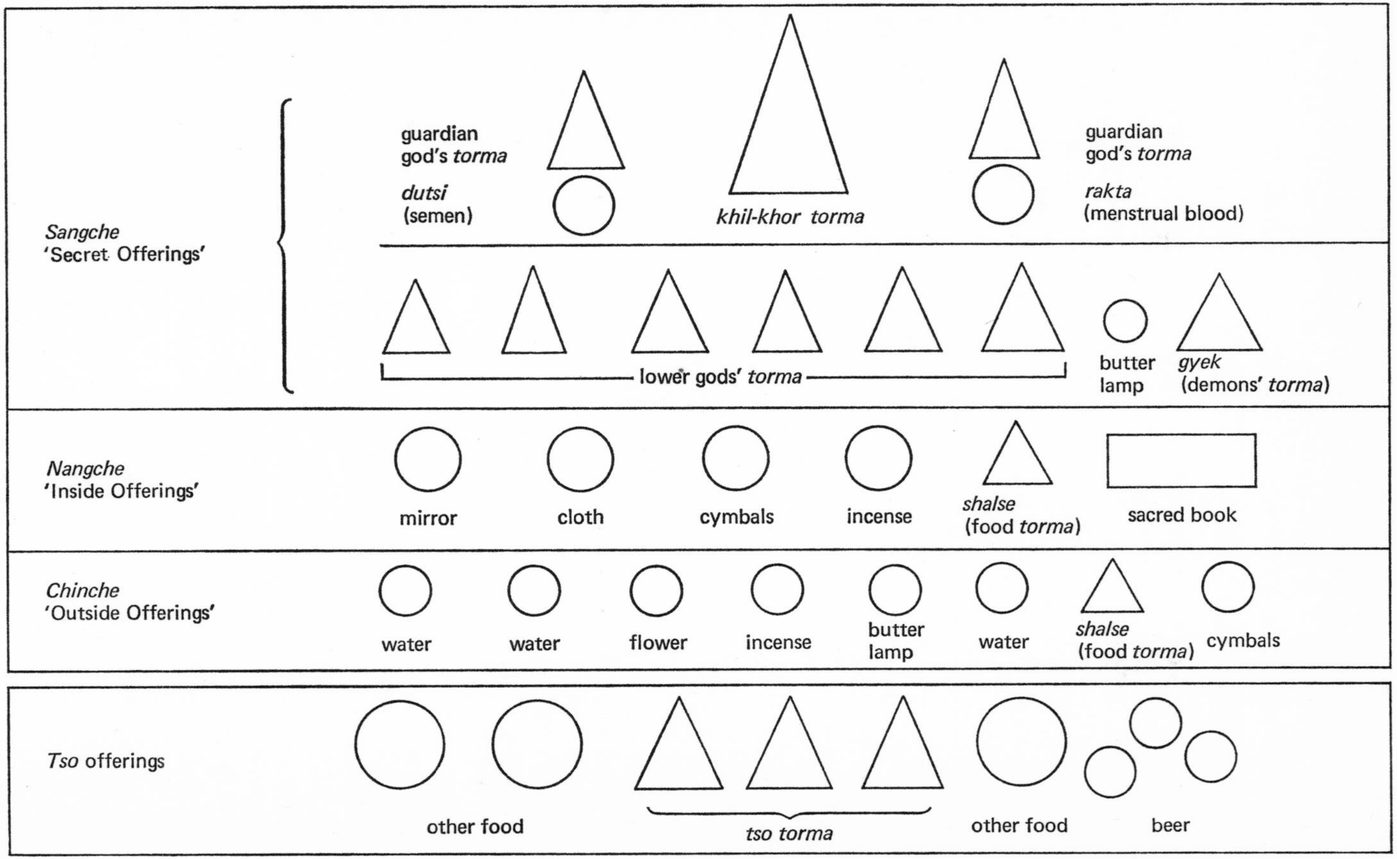

Sangche 'Secret Offerings'

guardian god's *torma*
dutsi (semen)

guardian god's *torma*
rakta (menstrual blood)

khil-khor torma

butter lamp   *gyek* (demons' *torma*)

lower gods' *torma*

Nangche 'Inside Offerings'

water   cloth   cymbals   incense   *shalse* (food *torma*)

mirror

sacred book

Chinche 'Outside Offerings'

water   water   flower   incense   butter lamp   water   *shalse* (food *torma*) cymbals

tso torma

Tso offerings

other food   other food   beer

all of this, by being encompassed within the hospitality framework, winds up reconciling the felt contradiction between social pragmatics and religious values. We must now look to see, as Clifford Geertz once said, how the trick is really done.

1 *Bodying the gods*

The rite can be read, first, as a series of symbolic acts and representations which encase the gods more and more tightly in more and more substantial forms, especially, though not exclusively, in bodies. If we turn the sequence of altar action upside down, and read from the top of the altar downwards, rather than from the bottom up, we see an interesting development of meaning. A justification for this analytic inversion is created—and perhaps the point is not lost on the worshippers either—by the hospitality structure of the ritual, which dictates that the first step of the action is the installation of the gods in their seats, the torma, which stand at the *top* of the altar. And the conclusion of the rite is always the offering of the *tso*, explicitly a party in the most festive sense, the tso foods standing at the *bottom*, actually below, the altar.

The very first move, then, in this reading, is to force the gods to take bodies at the 'secret' level of the altar. The body itself, as discussed earlier, is a pollution to the spirit; it is the source of semen and menstrual blood, both highly polluting, representations of which flank the senior torma on the highest level of the altar. Further, in the Sherpa view of human reproduction, the body is the product of semen and menstrual blood; conception occurs as a result of their being mixed. The torma body which the god is forced to adopt is thus both the source and the product of its polluting companions on the altar. It seems clear, then, that these items are not here for the god to eat, but as the generators and sustainers of the bodily form which he has been forced to adopt; they set up a self-sustaining system, like the poles of a battery, which keep his body powerfully charged, which in turn keeps him trapped inside it.

Beyond this, the torma have coatings of 'clothing', as we saw earlier, developing further the gods' physical encasement. And the head torma at least, which summarizes all the others, is placed on his khil-khor, the geometric representation of his palace and his realm. The khil-khor design depicts enclosures within enclosures—squares inside circles, circles inside squares. Thus each of these elements stresses ever heavier layers of physical encasement. The body encases the god's spiritual essence, the clothing encases the body, the palace encloses the embodied god, and the boundaries of the territory enclose the palace.

It is noteworthy that, according to various textual translations and exegeses, the verbal material at this early stage stresses descriptions of the physical appearances of the gods. According to a summary of a

154

text given to Haimendorf by a Sherpa lama, the invocation is followed by 'detailed descriptions of the gods' (193). (The 'informant thought that these were recited in order to prove to the deities, believed to suspect their worshippers of being ignorant of their true nature, that the lamas are well aware of their appearance and character' [ibid.].) A bit later, theoretically following the offering of the torma and the polluting liquids, 'the seat of the god is then described in detail' (194)—the seat presumably being his heavenly realm and palace, as signified by the khil-khor upon which he is also actually sitting. We also see, in a 'hymn of praise' from a different text, translated by Waddell, careful attention to mentioning details of the deity's physical appearance—face, hair, hand, foot—as well as his (actually 'her'; the hymn in this case is to a goddess) spiritual and magical powers (437). Thus there is great stress throughout the textual material, which accompanies and directs the symbolic action, on the physical forms which the gods have taken.

Having boxed the poor fellow in, as it were, the second level provides those important entries—the senses—to the now shielded interior of his being. We saw that the second-level offerings are representations of the senses, a point which is difficult to comprehend except in the context of the present interpretation. So the ritual action now gives him sight, hearing, smell, touch, etc., to render him susceptible to the further machinations of the worshippers.

Finally, moving down to the third level, the outside offerings, the ritual action stimulates and arouses the god with gentle sensuous delights. His body is caressed with cleansing and cooling waters, incense and flower scents are wafted before his nose, softly glowing candles flicker before his eyes (the Sherpas explicitly think of the light of butter lamps as a soft and gentle light), sweet music is sounded to his ears, and he is fed a bit of delicately prepared food (the food torma) and drinking water. At this point, too, hymns in his praise are sung, caressing his pride as well. Now, verily, he is at the worshippers' disposal.

For what has been done? He has been, it seems clear, turned into a human being, trapped in a body and suffused with sensuous desires. And to prove it, he is now invited to the *tso* feast, where the food is *real human food*, none of that torma and incense business, but cooked rice and vegetables, sweet corn, cane stalks and raw peas, oranges and bananas, even packaged biscuits from the bazaar, and big bottles of beer. The only indication of the divinity of the guest at this point is the fact that the cooked rice is formed into the conical torma shape (and it is called a *tso torma*), and the fact that the guest is courteously allowed to eat first.

2 *The moulding of anger*

The demons, as we saw earlier, manifest and signify capricious and unpredictable anger and violence. The potential allies of humans in the struggle against the demons are the gods, but they are problematic too. The *shiwa* gods, in their state of blissful fulfilment, are utterly detached from the world, and indifferent to its affairs. The ferocious *takbu* gods, on the other hand, are the more logical allies of the people, since they are by definition engaged in struggle with the demons— that is why they are ferocious. Yet if the takbu gods are already fighting the demons, why do people have to perform the ritual at all? To answer this we must recall that the takbu state is a special transformation on the shiwa state. *All* gods need nothing and are *fundamentally* fulfilled and blissful. Takbu gods are still gods; they presuppose and point to the fulfilled, self-contained state from which they came and to which they can return. The general tendency—the 'pull', as it were—of the whole religious system is towards shiwa bliss; the implied threat of the takbu gods (and hence the precipitating factor of the ritual), is that they will abdicate their struggle, subside into bliss, and leave people at the mercy of the demons.

In short, the problem for the ritual is less to get rid of the 'enemies' (indeed, the exorcismic element in this, compared to other Sherpa rituals, is marginal) than to stimulate the active support of the rather inert 'allies'. And this in turn, given the shiwa 'pull' of the system, seems to be a matter not of making the gods 'happy' (they are tending towards too much happiness already), but rather of making (or keeping) them angry. Indeed, as I will try to show in this section, we can observe over the course of the ritual a controlled and systematic arousal of— and, simultaneously, a particular shaping and formulation of—godly anger. I will return below to the difference between divine and demonic anger, to the doublethink of infuriating the gods while claiming to make them happy, and to the paradox of giving offerings to beings who 'need nothing'.

If we accept the notion that part of the problem is not only to combat capricious violence, but also to combat emotional detachment ('bliss'), then the whole first part of the ritual, in which the gods are, contrary to their natures, trapped in bodies, encased in heavy material forms, fed and otherwise polluted, can be seen as an attempt to infuriate the gods, to rouse them to passionate reaction. We must recall the general attitude concerning the body in Buddhist and Sherpa thought—it is the agency of desire ('attachments'), which is the source of frustration, which is the source of anger. Thus bodying the gods, and providing various things to sustain and fortify their bodies (the semen and menstrual blood, the food) must be assumed to anger them, if the sensuous desire→ attachments→frustration→anger logic has any force. And following the offering of the altar to the gods, the worshippers perform prostrations, theoretically as apologies for past offences, but conceivably as apologies for angering the gods within the ritual itself.

While the above points are somewhat speculative, or at least merely deductive, the arousal and shaping of godly anger can be seen quite clearly in the so-called Hymns of Praise, read while the gods are consuming their offerings. The one text I have at hand is actually to a shiwa (blissful) goddess, Drolma, the highest goddess of the pantheon and a deity of personal mercy rather than demon-killing. Even so, in it we see clearly the verbal shaping of the deity's anger and its orientation against the proper foes. The hymn begins, as is appropriate to Drolma, with praises to her mercifulness: 'Deliveress sublime', 'Rich . . . in pity's store', 'Soother of our woe', etc. But then it modulates into stronger dispositions, getting down to the business that people (at least the Sherpas, if not all Tibetan Buddhists) tend to be at least as interested in as mercy and pity: power and fury against the demons.

> Hail to thy *tut-tārā-huṅ* [her mantra]
> Piercing realms of earth and sky
> Treading down the seven worlds,
> Bending prostrate everyone!
>
> Hail! adored by mighty gods
> Indra, Brahma, Fire and Wind
> Ghostly hordes and Gandharvas
> All unite in praising Thee!
>
> Hail! with Thy dread *tre* and *phat* [15]
> Thou destroyest all Thy foes:
> Striding out with Thy left foot
> Belching forth devouring fire!
>
> Hail! with fearful spell *tu-re*
> Banishing the bravest fiends
> By the mere frown of Thy brows
> Vanquishing whole hordes of foes!
> (Waddell 1934: 437)

The text may be interpreted as a symbolic device for shaping and orienting the deity's anger, chanted while she eats the offerings. Even in these brief verses we can see that the goddess is read through a series of very specific modulations of her mood, each then directed against the various fiends and foes. First her mantra is said to 'pierce' evil—it is sharp; then she 'treads down' heavily; then she 'belches fire'—broadcasting rage; then—perhaps so focused and controlled now is her anger—she 'merely frowns' and it is enough to 'vanquish whole hordes of foes'. While one would certainly need to look closely at a range of similar texts, presumably they all have the same general form and intent.

Now it happens to be the case that most Sherpas, including the lamas, cannot understand the texts, but this does not negate the analysis. For the meaning is carried not only by the words, but by the other media of the ritual—the physical manipulation of the altar items and other ritual instruments [16] by the lamas, the prescribed hand-gestures (*mudra*) made by the lamas as they read, and the music which weaves through the reading. The music is probably of paramount importance, and unfortunately here I am not competent to offer an analysis analogous to the one just suggested for the text. The pace and intonation of the chanting vary with different parts of the texts; in some places there are recognizable and repeated melodies with which the lay people often hum along. The percussion instruments—large drum and bells—sometimes accompany the chanting, and again people seem to recognize and tap along with some of the rhythms. From time to time the full orchestra plays. The orchestral music is sometimes a series of extended chords, even in length and rhythm, and sometimes accelerating melodies which begin with long deep blasts upon the alpine horns, then build to a cymbal-clash climax. All of this, it may be argued, conveys to the worshippers the intent of the text concerning the development of the moods of the gods. Indeed, the music is probably the primary vehicle, for the unlettered layman, by means of which the divine mood conversions are understood and felt to be taking place.

It does not take much imagination to suggest that what is being manipulated here are the moods of the worshippers themselves. I have already described the culturally engendered problems the Sherpas have in dealing with anger; given the general prohibition upon its expression, there are few structures within which a Sherpa learns to comprehend and order his unruly feelings. The ritual points to these moods in pure archetypal forms—the absolute detachment and self-contained bliss of the gods, the absolute violence of the demons. It then proceeds to transform bliss itself into anger or violence, but of a controlled and focused sort which can triumph over the uncontrolled violence of the demons. The rite is hence both a 'model of' a complex emotional state— let us call it positive anger, or an anger of commitment—for which few models are provided in ordinary Sherpa life (or perhaps in any life), and a 'model for' achieving such a state.

It is important to be clear on this point: I am not saying that the rite simply provides some sort of symbolic outlet or catharsis for repressed anger which has no avenues of expression in the culture, although this may to some extent be the case. What I am saying is that, as I indicated earlier, although the Sherpas experience much anger, and in fact express it (or explode with it) not infrequently, they have very few resources for understanding or dealing with it in any systematic way. Both their own and others' bad moods, not to mention rages, are largely mysterious to themselves. The rite provides a symbolic vehicle not only for the expression of those moods, but for their structuring: one participates in a sequence over the course of which one's feelings are sorted, as it were, into the elements of a (morally approved) pattern, and the achievement of this patterning *is* the resolution of the 'problem of anger'. If this discussion is accepted, it would explain why the rite seems more concerned with *building* anger (in the gods) than with *destroying* it (in the demons). For it is at least as important, given this thesis, to experience how and of what one's mood is constructed, as to dissipate it; indeed, that is the condition for overcoming it.[17]

But this is not all that the ritual is about. It would distort it as much to reduce it solely to this 'subjective function' of providing a template for the structuring of emotional states, as to reduce it to a sterile social function of dramatizing (say) the proper relationship between monk and laity, although, as suggested earlier, it might be doing some of the latter too. We must not lose sight of the fact that this is a religious ritual; its religious import remains to be delineated.

3 *Hospitality: the dialectic between religion and the social order*

Let us say that, minimally, religion is that metasystem which solves problems of meaning (or Problems of Meaning) generated in large part (though not entirely) by the social order, by grounding that order within a theoretically ultimate reality within which those problems 'make sense'. At the same time it must be realized that religion, by the very fact of being a metasystem which is separate from and yet addressed to the social order, itself engenders paradox, contradiction, and conflict. When one says that religion is an autonomous element of a sociocultural system, one is not saying that it floats free of a social base; one is simply saying this: that while it is responding to (both 'reflecting' and attempting to solve) some problems, it is creating others.

By making offering to their gods in the idiom of social hospitality, the Sherpas are saying something about both their social order and their religious order. Sherpa hospitality, as we have seen, is a vital element of the Sherpa social process, yet it is also fraught with problems. It is a locus, for the participants, of complex feelings and moods which are disturbing in other areas of life, and disastrous in this particular context—a context intended to be pleasing, soothing, and productive of social cooperation. Further, hospitality has the problem of being implicitly denigrated by the religious devaluation of sensuality, a point which ultimately calls into question the entire morality of secular existence. At the same time, from that secular perspective, hospitality opens a serious question concerning the morality of the *religious* worldview and ethos, for it is hospitality which, according to the culture, renders people cooperative and mutually supportive, as opposed to a religious orientation in which it is every man for himself, pursuing his own salvation.

Actually, the religious critique of the social order, specifically of hospitality practices, and the social critique of the religious order, have more subtle and detailed dimensions. Let us look a bit more closely at both.

Even if we grant, as certain defenders of Sherpa religion might well

159

argue, that the religion does not utterly devalue sociality as such, it can at least be said to take the following stance. The trouble with the social order, as it is normally lived, is that people treat it as an end in itself. Entertaining, feeding, helping one's neighbours are not *ipso facto* wrong or irreligious, but they become so when used solely as means to personal self-enrichment and self-aggrandizement, and this is how they are normally used. What the religion might claim to be criticizing is only a certain *mode* of sociality, namely, 'interested' as opposed to 'disinterested' giving.[18] One should live the social order, enact its forms, in the name of some higher good; the ideal is to give with no thought of material gain, to give as a meritorious act. One's own merit will not only improve one's fate, but increase the general store of merit in the world and thus contribute to world salvation. The right kind of sociality, 'disinterested' benevolence, re-establishes one's contact with this higher moral order, regrounds one in the religious cosmos, and ennobles all one's words, thoughts, and deeds.

These points of the religious critique of the Sherpa social order clarify a number of issues about gods and demons. In the first place we can see that, among other things, the demons are bad because they represent the worst form of the wrong kind of sociality: they make demands upon others (by making people sick and demanding ransom for the patient's health) for their own trivial, personal ends—the pure pleasure of food and other gratifications. Second, we can see why divine *takbu* anger is 'good' while demonic anger is 'bad': takbu anger by definition is directed against the demons in their role of enemies of the moral system, while demonic anger represents petty rage at personal frustration. Takbu godly anger is universalistic, concerned with a relatively disinterested defence of the system (not totally disinterested, since the destruction of the system would bring the gods down with it); demonic anger is particularistic, since even their enmity towards the religion is based on the fact that the religion limits their activities and frustrates their desires. (The problem from the other point of view is that the takbu gods' anger, though more social and 'engaged' than the shiwa gods' bliss, is still too abstract; takbu gods defend the system but not the people. I will return to this in a moment.)

Finally, the distinction between interested and disinterested giving helps solve the central paradox of the ritual: we can understand how Sherpas could reconcile or at least rationalize giving offerings to beings who 'need nothing'. When one feeds people who are needy, one is potentially playing upon their need, and banking (almost literally) on their gratitude as insurance for future favours. When one feeds beings who need nothing,[19] one's aims are theoretically purer; one's gift is humble in relation to their wealth; it is more literally a sacrifice, and effaces rather than aggrandizes oneself. In fact, of course, this is not the spirit in which the ritual is conceptualized by the lay people, but technically it can be used, and was used by lama informants, to rationalize the paradox of offering material things to totally fulfilled gods.

From the secular point of view, on the other hand, the fine distinctions between good and bad—interested and disinterested—sociality which the religion might be claiming to make are probably largely lost. While secular criticism of the religion is, as I said, almost nonexistent, it seems clear from the analysis of the ritual that the religion may appear to the lay perspective utterly antisocial, and hence virtually immoral; it appears to devalue all those social forms which render men cooperative and helpful among themselves, and which in fact make Sherpa social life possible. If people and demons are too 'interested', the gods are too 'disinterested'. The significance of the gods, from this point of view, now becomes clear: they represent all of those tendencies of Sherpa religion to encourage the pursuit of one's own salvation while ignoring the needs of others, a salvation which, moreover, itself consists of utterly self-contained, asocial bliss. The gods represent everything from the doctrine itself, to the monks who live its tenets, to the villager who seems unresponsive to social forms and does not fulfil his social responsibilities.

The Sherpa ritual of making offerings to the gods, cast in the idiom of social hospitality, is an attempt to deal with all these problems. The symbolism of the ritual catches up and reworks the issues so as to render a different judgement upon each. Through the symbolic process of the ritual, as I will try to indicate in this final section, religion in the most general sense is shown to be less selfishly oriented than it, in pure dogmatic form, appears to be, while secular life is shown to be less sinful, self-interested, and mired in sensuality for its own sake than it, from the religious perspective, appears to be. The application of worldly forms—bodies, food, hospitality—to divine processes—engaging the gods to fight the demons—results in simultaneously rendering the religion more moral, and providing ultimate moral sanction for those worldly forms. The gods are rendered socially 'engaged' rather than self-absorbed, while the forms of human existence are shown to contribute to the preservation of cosmic order, by functioning as the stimuli and vehicles for defeating those enemies of the cosmic order, the demons.

The essence of this process would seem to lie in the relationships of encapsulation between the various levels of symbol-work in the ritual. The core of the ritual, the central dynamic, is the transformation of the gods' mood from abstract bliss (present in takbu rites as a tendency, and by implication) through abstract anger (defending the system) to a final state which has the dual properties of anger against the demons and/because of active benevolence towards humanity. That this emotional transformation is culturally, and not just analytically, the essential dynamic of the ritual, is evidenced partly by the fact that when one asks Sherpas why they do these rituals, the first answer is almost invariably 'to make the gods happy'. For a long time I treated this as an almost

161

phatic statement, but I came to understand that the mood changes of the gods form the premises upon which everything else depends: when the gods are happy, everything good will follow; when they are not, man is prey to every conceivable evil, the latter essentially symbolized by the demons.

The whole system of mood states and transformations in the ritual, in turn, is carried by (encapsulated in, represented by, and often engendered by) the body symbolism. The lama moulds the torma from formless dough to represent appropriate bodies for each of the gods of the ritual, and the decorations of the torma (the colour differences, and the different shapes of the butter elements) are the major loci of visual representation of the shiwa/takbu mood distinction. Further, the differential treatment of the gods' and demons' torma represents the difference between godly and demonic anger, and deals differently with the two types: the demons' torma is thrown out of the temple and smashed, a gesture which both portrays their indiscriminate and scattershot violence, and wards it off by forcing them to scatter and chase the crumbs; the gods on the other hand are invited into their torma, a move which portrays the more focused and responsive nature of their dispositions, and which actually (as we saw) begins the transformation of their mood. Finally, and most important, through the sequence of first enticing the gods into the torma/bodies, then endowing them with organs of the senses, then stimulating those senses with the delicate 'outside' offerings, the active anger of the gods, I argued, is aroused. This anger thus becomes available for shaping in line with human modes of emotional response, and in relation to ends with which humans are concerned. In short, most of the visual development of the mood process of the ritual is carried by the treatment of the torma, i.e. by the treatment of the body symbolism. And by having this critical symbolic role in effecting the success of the ritual, the body itself receives strong validation as a vehicle for moral action.

But the process is not complete. By endowing the gods with body, they are rendered human, or at least humanoid, but only in a very crude sense. They are still lacking that final critical dimension of humanity, sociality; they are still monads. The final transformation, then, is effected in two ways. In the first place, there is the performance of the *tso* as the conclusion to the ritual. It is at the point of the tso that the gods have been symbolically brought as far as possible to the human state of corporeality and sensuousness, since here they are feasted with real human food as opposed to the divine foods of torma, incense, and the like. And the tso foods stand beyond and below the outer offerings of the altar, again indicating the point that the gods have been almost fully brought to the human state. But the critical point is that the tso feast is actually shared with the gods by the human worshippers, whereas the other altar items are not made part of any social feasting. In the tso, in other words, with its most explicit social hospitality ('party') format, the gods have finally become social allies; only now can it truly be said that they have been humanized.

But the point of interest here is that, only at the point of the tso, when the gods have been as fully 'humanized' as possible, are they finally asserted to be 'happy'. The tso is always said to be joyous, an expression and celebration of the final transformation of the gods to a positive, benevolent, and expansive mood, ready and eager to help humanity by doing battle with the demons. This conclusion to the ritual thus dramatizes the point that the human bodily state is, ideally, also a state of active benevolence *vis-à-vis* others, and further, that both of these conditions—bodiliness and benevolence—find their fullest and best means of expression in the context of a party, the context of social hospitality.

But if the only representation of hospitality in the ritual were in the tso, the moral attitude of the ritual towards hospitality would remain ambiguous. If the transformation of the gods to a state of sociality and active alliance with human concerns were merely the closing act of the body-and-mood manipulation drama of the central part of the ritual, then hospitality would merely be the last of a string of clever tricks. The whole system of problems revolving around hospitality—its immorality from the religious point of view, and its challenge in turn to the ascetic ethic—would stand unreconstructed. But in fact the entire sequence of ritual action, from beginning to end, is encapsulated in an idiom of hospitality. The gods are cast as guests from the very outset of the ritual, and the development of their alliance with humans by the end is the product not (only) of cheap manipulation, but (also) of working through a full social event, from tense and slightly antagonistic invitation to the establishment of mutual respect and at least temporary mutual trust by the point of parting. And the torma are not just bodies, trapping, irritating, and manipulating the moods of the gods; they are also food, tokens of social exchange in the creation of bonds of mutual interest.

With this, the full statement of the ritual on the problems with which it is concerned can be articulated. The thrust of the ritual, through its many layers, is simply to make the gods 'human'—to make them corporeal, to make them susceptible to sensuous pleasure, to make them angry, to render them socially engaged, to get them to 'help'. The significance of this point is twofold: to validate the human modes of being and operating in the world, by showing their contribution to the preservation of cosmic order and not just to individual self-interest; and to 'humanize' the religious order, that is, to counteract its essentially antisocial bias, by literally turning the gods into human beings and forcing them to become agents of direct social help and support. Put in other words, the ritual figuratively humanizes the religion, by literally humanizing the gods, while at the same time sacralizing the apparently irreligious and sinful social forms by having them serve as vehicles for a collective moral struggle.

In the process of this double movement, however, the various aspects of humanness which play a role in the ritual are themselves transformed and restructured. Anger in the ritual is developed and then transcended in a controlled and satisfying way; it achieves a complex structure which is neither the frustrated rage of the demons nor the abstract moralistic crusade of the gods. It becomes an anger of social commitment, generated by identifying one's own needs with the needs of one's social allies, and hence moving to a more universalistic (but still not totally abstract) mode of emotional response. As for the body, the sequence of ritual action shows a similar movement from treating it as an instrument of personal pleasure, to celebrating it as a vehicle of collective triumph over the forces of evil. And finally, the fact that the gods respond to the hospitality procedures, despite needing nothing and having no use at all for paltry human offerings, provides a model of the spirit in which hospitality should ideally be treated and responded to: in a spirit of essentially disinterested benevolence. The gods enter into social partnership with the people not because they needed all that food and felt obligated for having been satisfied with it, but in recognition of the goodness of the act of giving itself.

In sum, the religious ideal of 'help' (as an abstract exemplification of The Way) is transformed downwards a bit, by being hitched into a system of real social alliance, while the lay social forms are transformed upwards and brought more in line with the religious ideal, by being rendered more universalistic, and stripped (ideally) of simple self-interest. The fragility of this compromise is attested to by the frequency with which it must be constructed and re-constructed, over and over, in the religious life of Sherpa villagers.

CONCLUSIONS: SOME GENERAL ISSUES

The analysis of this paper raises issues which go beyond its immediate scope.

First, and most immediately, it points to the rest of the enormously complex Sherpa ritual and religious system. The present analysis merely opens the discussion of that system; it is incomplete not only in the sense that much more could have been said about this particular ritual, but in the sense that the full meaning of this ritual will only emerge in relation to other rituals of rather different orientation. In particular, the various rites of exorcism, the largest of which take several days and constitute the most flamboyant festivals of the culture, focus much more directly and actively on the demons; that is where the demons really come into their own.

The second and more general area of concern to which this analysis speaks is the enduring question of the relationship between a 'high' religion and its popular practice. Confining the discussion to Buddhism (although much of it might, I think, be applicable to much of Christianity as well), it is well known that orthodox Buddhism coexists, in every Buddhist society, with popular cults whose content is not only different from, but often actually contradictory to, Buddhism. Further, since the inception of Buddhism, orthodoxy itself has undergone many changes; the most formally articulated of those was institutionalized as the Mahayana school, but a great deal of what falls within the confines of theoretically orthodox Buddhism today is heterodox to say the least.

There have been two sorts of explanations for these facts. One type departs from the 'remoteness' and human impracticability of orthodox Buddhism. The orthodox doctrine, it is argued, fails to answer to certain basic psychological needs (e.g. reduction of anxiety over immediate worldly problems), and the popular cults, or the changes in orthodoxy, function to fulfil those needs (Weber 1958; Spiro 1970). The other sort of explanation, derived from general considerations of the 'great tradition—little tradition' distinction, would argue that the various changes in orthodoxy, or accommodation to local religions, which the orthodox system undergoes in popular practice, are simply part of a natural process by means of which the sociologically (rather than substantively) remote religion is adapted to local situations. The high religion is simply particularized, or 'parochialized' (Marriott 1955), as part of the process of fitting itself to local social structures and local material conditions.

While there is no doubt a great deal of truth to the second sort of explanation, the first, couched in terms of substantive problems with the content of the religious doctrine, seems closer to the heart of the matter, although still inadequate. As the analysis of the Sherpa material at least indicates, Buddhism is indeed 'too remote' from ongoing Sherpa experience, but not (only) because it fails to respond to certain basic psychological needs. It is too remote not only because, say, ascetic self-control appears irrelevant for solving most of the problems with which people are faced in the normal course of life, but because, substantively, it is anti-reciprocity, anti-exchange, anti-marriage, and, in a word, anti-social. Let us say that Buddhism 'stands for' these things, in the sense that these points are part of its doctrinal platform, and also in the sense that it represents, connotes, *symbolizes*, this entire orientation. And in so far as Buddhism 'stands for' this anti-social orientation in the eyes of any Buddhist group, it must be problematic.

Historically, the Mahayana transformation of Buddhism seems to have been an attempt to solve this problem, with its central notion of the Boddhisattva who returns to the world to 'help' others achieve salvation, thus suggesting some element of personal relationship and support. The point that emerges from the Sherpa material, however, is that this transformation was still inadequate—incomplete, makeshift, unstable. The gods who adopt the takbu form and are available to help

165

people (under the proper conditions) always have the potential for subsiding into the shiwa bliss which they have already achieved, and to which they apparently have every reason (given its paradisical qualities) to return. What the Sherpa ritual seems to do, among other things, is reinvent, reconstruct, the Mahayana 'solution' to the problem of the remoteness and asociality of Buddhism. Just as the Mahayana Boddhisattva reincarnates in the world to help those who remain mired in the illusions of worldly existence, instead of dissolving in tothe nirvana to which he is entitled, so the Sherpa gods, with a bit of coaxing, incarnate in their torma to help the lay people in their struggle to lead a better, and hopefully also more moral, existence. I would expect the same interpretation, *mutatis mutandis*, to be applicable to many rituals in other Mahayana Buddhist societies.

Finally, this analysis of a Sherpa ritual suggests a number of points about ritual and the processes of symbolic action. What I should like to stress in particular is the constant intertransposition of form and content. Virtually every element of the ritual can be seen to function as both part of its problematic (its 'content') and part of its modes of solution (its 'form').

For example, consider the relationship between the mood aspect of the ritual and its other aspects. On the one hand, as noted earlier, we might see the whole anger development as functioning simply to engage the participant, by appealing to the more 'primitive' or emotional aspects of his psyche, more strongly with the 'real' (i.e. social and cultural) issues of the ritual; the anger development appears as a kind of device for drawing the actor through the ritual sequence, thus experiencing its resolution of the other issues. In this sense the mood aspect is part of the ritual's form, part of its repertoire of semantic mechanisms. On the other hand, we saw also quite clearly that anger is in fact culturally problematic for Sherpas; it is thus also part of the content, the set of substantive issues with which the ritual is dealing.

Similarly, both the body symbolism and the symbolism of the supernatural types are part of the form of the ritual in handling the anger problem as content: the body is used to engender and manipulate certain moods in the gods; the gods and the demons portray the opposition between certain kinds of emotional dispositions and the triumph of one over the other. But at the same time both the body and the gods are themselves substantively problematic in their own ways: the body traps people in drudgery, sin, and pollution; the gods raise the whole issue of social non-accessibility, both between lay neighbours and between the village and the monastery.

A final example of the intertransposition of form and content within the ritual is the point developed most explicitly in the body of the analysis. From the perspective of the religious ideology, worldly social forms are the problem, and engagement with the forms of religion the solution, while from the lay perspective many aspects of the religion are problematic, and the symbolism of a secular social form, hospitality, is employed to deal with these problems of the religion.

The lesson of this, I would argue, is the futility of any sort of reductionism in symbolic analysis. Every aspect of a complex symbolic form is both part of its structure and part of its substance, is both being addressed by the ritual and being used by the ritual in its process of addressing other problems. We cannot, if we understand the ritual fully, emerge with a clear-cut assertion of the primacy of the social or cultural or psychological dimension of its meaning. It is the ingenuity of ritual symbolism constantly to transpose these into one another, to solve problems in each mode by means of forms derived from other modes and thus to show, ultimately, both their irreducible interdependence and the means of moving between them. Effective symbolic analysis, like effective symbolic forms, must be genuinely dialectical, sustaining this sense of the interplay between relatively autonomous yet mutually interacting and interdependent levels of structure, meaning, and experience.

Notes

1. I am indebted to Clifford Geertz, Robert Paul, Michelle Rosaldo, Renato Rosaldo, Terence Turner, and Roy Willis for critical comments on an earlier draft of this paper.
2. In the case of this latter example, one can see at least one point at which structuralism might be coordinated with the symbolic analysis perspective.
3. I make no pretence of the orthodoxy of Sherpa beliefs and practices. Specialists in orthodox Buddhism or even orthodox Tibetan Buddhism will find many discrepancies between their understanding of the religion and the Sherpas', but I am describing local meanings, practices, and interpretations as recorded in first-hand fieldwork. The fieldwork was carried out between August 1966 and February 1968, through the generous support of the National Institute of Mental Health and the National Science Foundation.
4. For a discussion of some aspects of the *sang* ritual, see Ortner (1973a).
5. Since the texts are in archaic Tibetan, which I cannot read, the following account of their contents is pieced together from several sources: lamas' and laymen's statements about the content, usually given in an interview context removed from the time and place of the action; extrapolation from the observable physical actions which accompany the reading of the text; and several source-books on Tibetan religion which will be cited as I proceed.
6. The torma also has phallic connotations. These are not orthodox, but are nonetheless fairly overt in the culture (Paul 1970). This dimension will not be incorporated into the present analysis, although it would not, I think, be contradictory to it.
7. In the history of Tibetan Buddhism, celibate monasticism did not become a generally accepted ideal until the beginning of the fifteenth century, when there was a successful reform movement which called for a return to a purer Buddhism and which became institutionalized as the Gelugpa sect. The Nyingmawa sect resisted this reform for a long time, and continued to permit its lamas to marry and remain in the villages serving the lay people's religious needs. Later, however, this sect (still in Tibet) began to mimic the politically and religiously dominant Gelugpa sect's monastic system, while still retaining

the institution of married lamas (*banzin*). The whole thing has not fully sorted itself out even today, among the Sherpas; some Sherpa monasteries were celibate from their founding; some were 'married' monasteries, communities composed of 'monks' and their families; and there were and are married lamas in the villages. One 'married monastery' started a reform towards celibacy within the present generation; it now only accepts celibate candidates, and although the married monks have not actually been purged, they cannot sit on the same row of seats in the temple as the celibate monks.

8. For an extended discussion of the Sherpa system of supernatural beings, see Ortner (n.d.).

9. Actually there are four mood aspects: *shiwa* (ZHi Ba)—'mild'; *gyewa* (rGyas Pa)—'increasing or expansive'; *'ong* (dBang)—'powerful'; and *takbu* or *towu* (Drags Po)—'fierce' (Ekvall 1964: 169), but the Sherpas largely operate with the shiwa/takbu opposition.

10. For a discussion of this issue from another point of view, see Paul (n.d.).

11. There is actually some order and significant content even in these tantrums, but space forbids my going into that here.

12. This is the local understanding of these offerings. Variations include interpreting the drinking-water as being parallel to the ceremonial drink of beer with which one greets arriving high (human) personages; interpreting the butter lamp as food rather than as light; interpreting the cooling water as a serving of beer parallel to the serving of the food torma.

13. Shiwa gods, benign and pure, theoretically eschew these delicacies. Yet my notes show these items on altars of shiwa rituals too. Possibly their presence would be explained as offerings to the ferocious guardians of the shiwa gods. In any case, most Sherpa rituals are directed towards the takbu divinities, who demand this sort of fare.

14. Yalman (1969) pointed out that Ceylonese offering rituals involve polluting the gods, but his conclusions on the significance of this point are different from those I will be developing here.

15. 'Mystic spells used by wizards—*phat* means break or smash!' The hymn is translated by Waddell (1934: 437), including the footnote. He ends with 'etc., etc., etc., etc.'—obviously there is much more in the same vein.

16. E.g. the *dorje*, a mystical weapon against demons, which each lama has at his place.

17. It should be noted that Tibetan Buddhism, which is a highly psychologically sophisticated religion, does not miss this point in its esoteric practices. Advanced meditation consists of mentally constructing, bit by bit, detailed mandalas, which in turn become the source of mystical comprehension of cosmic unity: 'The mandala born, thus, of an interior impulse became, in its turn, a support for meditation, an external instrument to provoke and procure such visions in quiet concentration and meditation. *The intuitions which, at first, shone capricious and unpredictable are projected outside the mystic, who, by concentrating his mind upon them, rediscovers the way to reach his secret reality*' (Tucci 1969: 37, my emphasis).

18. See the chapter on charity in Ortner (1970).

19. Not just gods; the best, most meritorious objects of charitable giving are high reincarnate lamas, who are the objects of so much donation that they are generally quite rich.

References

BENEDICT, RUTH 1934. *Patterns of Culture*. Boston: Houghton Mifflin.
BURKE, KENNETH 1957. *The Philosophy of Literary Form*. New York: Vintage Books.

Gods' Bodies, Gods' Food

EKVALL, R. B. 1964. *Religious Observances in Tibet*. Chicago: University of Chicago Press.

FÜRER-HAIMENDORF, CHRISTOPH VON 1964. *The Sherpas of Nepal*. Berkeley and Los Angeles: University of California Press.

GEERTZ, CLIFFORD 1964. Ideology as a Cultural System. In D. Apter (ed.), *Ideology and Discontent*. New York: The Free Press.

— 1966. Religion as a Cultural System. In M. Banton (ed.), *Anthropological Approaches to the Study of Religion*. London: Tavistock.

— 1972. Deep Play: Notes on the Balinese Cockfight. *Daedalus*, Winter 1972: 1–38.

— 1973. *The Interpretation of Cultures*. New York: Basic Books.

LÉVI-STRAUSS, CLAUDE 1963. *Structural Anthropology*. Tr. by C. Jacobson and B. G. Schoepf. New York and London: Basic Books.

MARRIOTT, MCKIM 1955. Little Communities in an Indigenous Civilization. In his *Village India*. Chicago: University of Chicago Press.

NEBESKY-WOJKOWITZ, RENÉ DE 1956. *Oracles and Demons of Tibet*. The Hague: Mouton.

ORTNER, SHERRY B. 1966. Tibetan Circles: An Essay in Symbolic Analysis. Unpublished master's thesis, Department of Anthropology, University of Chicago.

— 1970. Food for Thought: A Key Symbol in Sherpa Culture. Unpublished doctoral dissertation, Department of Anthropology, University of Chicago.

— 1973a. Sherpa Purity. *American Anthropologist* **75**: 49–63.

— 1973b. On Key Symbols. *American Anthropologist* **75**: 1338–1346.

— n.d. The White-Black Ones: The Sherpa View of Human Nature. Forthcoming in James Fisher (ed.), *Himalayan Anthropology: The Indo-Tibetan Interface*. World Anthropology Series, The Hague: Mouton.

PAUL, ROBERT A. 1970. Sherpas and their Religion. Unpublished doctoral dissertation, Department of Anthropology, University of Chicago.

— n.d. Instinctive Aggression in Man. mimeo.

PEPPER, STEPHEN C. 1961. *World Hypotheses*. Berkeley and Los Angeles: University of California Press.

SCHNEIDER, DAVID M. 1968. *American Kinship*. Englewood Cliffs, N.J.: Prentice-Hall.

SNELLGROVE, DAVID 1957. *Buddhist Himalaya*. Oxford: Bruno Cassirer.

— (tr. and ed.). 1967. *Four Lamas of Dolpo*. Cambridge, Mass.: Harvard University Press.

SOROKIN, PITIRIM 1962. *Social and Cultural Dynamics*. New York: Bedminster Press.

SPIRO, MELFORD 1970. *Buddhism and Society*. New York: Harper and Row.

TUCCI, GIUSEPPE 1969. *The Theory and Practice of the Mandala*. New York: Samuel Weiser.

WADDELL, L. AUSTINE 1934. *The Buddhism of Tibet, or Lamaism*. Cambridge: Heffer.

WEBER, MAX 1958. *The Religion of India*. Glencoe, Illinois: The Free Press.

YALMAN, NUR 1969. On the Meaning of Food Offerings in Ceylon. In R. Spencer (ed.), *Forms of Symbolic Action*. Seattle and London: University of Washington Press.

Biographical Notes

ATKINSON, JANE MONNIG. Born 1949, St Louis, Missouri; educated at Bryn Maw College, A.B. (1971); at present a doctoral candidate in anthropology at Stanford University.
National Science Foundation graduate fellow, 1971–74.

FOX, JAMES J. Born 1940, USA; educated at Harvard University, A.B. (1962); University College, Oxford (Rhodes Scholar), Diploma in Social Anthropology (1963), B.Litt. (1965), D. Phil. (1968).
Visiting Professor of Anthropology, Duke University 1968–69; Assistant Professor of Social Anthropology, Harvard University, 1969–74; Fellow, Centre for Advanced Study in the Behavioral Sciences, Stanford, California, 1971–72; Associate Professor of Social Anthropology, Harvard University, 1974– .
Author of 'A Rotinese Dynastic Genealogy: Structure and Event' in *The Translation of Culture*, ed. T. O. Beidelman, 1971; 'Semantic Parallelism in Rotinese Ritual Language', *Bijdragen tot de Taal-, Land- en Volkenkunde*, 1971; 'Sister's Child as Plant: Metaphors in an Idiom of Consanguinity', in *Rethinking Kinship and Marriage*, ed. R. Needham, 1971; 'Our Ancestors spoke in Pairs', *Explorations in the Ethnography of Speaking*, ed. R. Bauman and J. Sherzer, 1974, and *A Clash of Economies* (forthcoming).

JACKSON, ANTHONY. Born 1926, England; educated at King's College, Cambridge, M.A.; Gothenburg, Ph.D.
Research assistant in Social Anthropology, Gothenburg University, 1963–65; Lecturer, Salford University, 1965–70; Lecturer, Edinburgh University, 1970– .
Author of *Elementary Structures of Na-Khi Ritual*, 1970; and several articles on the Na-khi.

MCKNIGHT, JOHN DAVID. Born 1935, Canada; educated at Bishop's University, Lennoxville, Quebec, B.A.; University College London, B.A.Hons. (1963), M.A. (1965).
Research Fellow, University of Queensland, 1965–68; Lecturer, University of Edinburgh, 1968–70; Lecturer, London School of Economics, 1971– .
Author of 'Extra-Descent Group Ancestor Cults in African Societies', *Africa*, 1967; 'Some Problems concerning the Wik-mungkan', in *Rethinking Kinship and Marriage*, ed. R. Needham,

171

1971; 'Sexual Symbolism of Food among the Wik-mungkan', *Man*, 1973.

ORTNER, SHERRY B. Born 1941, USA; educated Bryn Mawr College, A.B.; University of Chicago, M.A., Ph.D.

Lecturer, Princeton University, 1969–70; Visiting Fellow, Princeton University, 1970–71; Member, Anthropology Faculty, Sarah Lawrence College (no ranks); 1971– ; Member, Institute for Advanced Study, Princeton, 1973–74.

Author of 'A Kernel of Truth: Some Notes on the Analysis of Connotation', *Semiotica*, 1972; 'Sherpa Purity' and 'On Key Symbols', *American Anthropologist*, 1973; 'Purification Beliefs and Practices', *Encyclopaedia Britannica*, 14th edn, 1974; 'Is Female to Male as Nature is to Culture?', in *Woman, Culture and Society*, ed. M. Rosaldo and L. Lamphere, 1974; 'The White-Black Ones: the Sherpa View of Human Nature', in *Himalayan Anthropology*, ed. J. Fisher, 1974.

ROSALDO, RENATO I., JR. Born 1941, USA; educated Harvard College, A.B. (history and literature) and Ph.D. (social anthropology).

Author of 'Ilongot Kin Terms: a Bilateral System of Northern Luzon, Philippines', *Proceedings* of VIIIth International Congress of Anthropological and Ethnological Sciences, 1968.

ROSALDO, MICHELLE ZIMBALIST. Born 1944, New York City; educated at Radcliffe College, A.B. (1966); Harvard University, Ph.D. (1972).

Lecturer in Linguistics, Stanford University, 1971–72; Assistant Professor in Anthropology, Stanford University, 1972– .

Author of 'Metaphors and Folk Classification', *Southwestern Journal of Anthropology*; 'I have Nothing to Hide: the Language of Ilongot Oratory', *Langue and Society*, 1973; 'It's all uphill: the Creative Metaphors of Ilongot Magical Spells', in *Ritual, Reality, and Creativity in Language*, ed. A. Sanches and B. Blount (in press); co-editor with Louise Lamphere, *Woman, Culture and Society*, 1974.

WILLIS, ROY G. Born 1927, England; studied social anthropology at Oxford University, Diploma, B.Litt., D.Phil., after fifteen years in journalism and industry.

Fieldwork in Ufipa, Tanzania, 1962–64 and 1966.

Research assistant, Department of Anthropology, University College, London, 1965–67; Lecturer, Department of Social Anthropology, University of Edinburgh, 1967– .

Author of *Man and Beast*, 1974, and a number of papers, mainly on Fipa ethnography.

Name Index

Name Index

Subject Index

Abelam (New Guinea), 96n
ambiguity, systematic, 127
animals, *see* Wik-mungkan
anthropological concepts
  debates over, 2
  and native terms, 2, 9, 10
  see also categories, cultural
anthropological investigation, 18–19
anthropologist
  as alien observer, xv
  as uninvited guest, xv
anthropology
  classical world of, damned, xi
  current upsurge of interest in symbolism, xi, xiii
  shift from unitary to dualistic perspective xi
  value-free language of, xi
antonymy, 129n
association, 45, 63, 66–7, 120–2
  coefficient of, 116
asymmetry, 57, 59, 61, 68–70, 72n
  see also symmetry
Atoni (Indonesia), 121
Australian Aborigines, 89, 92, 96n
  see also Wik-mungkan
Azande, 3
Aztecs (Mexico), 43, 102

baby talk, 127
Bakweri (Cameroon), xiii
binariness, principle of, 100
  see also dualism; dyadic set; Na-khi, naming system; opposition; parallelism; structuralism
binary analysis, xiv, 99–100
binary categories, 110, 128
binary opposition, 99, 102, 109, 118
binary relations, 110
binary system, 32
body symbolism, 114–15, 162, 166
  see also Sherpa ritual, *torma*

Bön symbolism, 30, 40
  see also Buddhism; Sherpa, religion; Tibetan (Mahayana) Buddhism
bricoleur, 45
Buang (New Guinea), 130n
Buddhism, xiv, 165–6
  see also Sherpa, religion; Tibetan (Mahayana) Buddhism
burial, live, 70

categories, cultural, 1, 2, 4, 19, 100
  open texture of, 1, 20n
  range of meanings, 2, 18, 20n
  and social structure, 3, 9
  see also anthropological concepts; classification; Ilongot, *be:rtan*; Ilongot, category names; polysemy; symbolism
change, in symbolic system, 120
Chinese Festival Songs, 102
classification, 4, 55, 84, 126
  axis of, 89, 95
  Linnaean, 90
  see also categories, cultural; symbolism
code, 110, 111
coherence, 134
colour symbolism, 28, 140
combination, 118, 124
communication, aspect of behaviour, 2
comparative studies, 19, 121
  see also universals
comparison, formal, 100
complementarity, 55, 57, 59, 68, 128
complementary opposition, 30, 118
  see also opposition
computer, 99, 115
conceptual analysis, 1
concrete, 68
consciousness, 152
contagion, 54
  see also pollution

175